TALES
FROM
DU BOIS

SUNY series in Multiethnic Literatures

Mary Jo Bona, editor

TALES FROM DU BOIS

THE Queer Intimacy of Cross-Caste Romance

ERIKA RENÉE WILLIAMS

Cover image: *The Mulatto and the Sculpturesque White Woman*, Lajos Gulácsy, 1913.

Published by State University of New York Press, Albany

© 2022 State University of New York

All rights reserved

Printed in the United States of America

No part of this book may be used or reproduced in any manner whatsoever without written permission. No part of this book may be stored in a retrieval system or transmitted in any form or by any means including electronic, electrostatic, magnetic tape, mechanical, photocopying, recording, or otherwise without the prior permission in writing of the publisher.

For information, contact State University of New York Press, Albany, NY
www.sunypress.edu

Library of Congress Cataloging-in-Publication Data

Name: Williams, Erika Renée, 1973– author.
Title: Tales from Du Bois : the queer intimacy of cross-caste romance / Erika Renée Williams.
Description: Albany : State University of New York Press, [2022] | Series: SUNY series in multiethnic literatures | Includes bibliographical references and index.
Identifiers: LCCN 2021036173 | ISBN 9781438488196 (hardcover : alk. paper) | ISBN 9781438488202 (ebook) | ISBN 9781438488189 (pbk. : alk paper)
Subjects: LCSH: Du Bois, W. E. B. (William Edward Burghardt), 1868–1963—Criticism and interpretation. | Interracial couples in literature. | Caste in literature. | LCGFT: Literary criticism.
Classification: LCC PS3507.U147 Z93 2022 | DDC 818/.5209—dc23/eng/20211203
LC record available at https://lccn.loc.gov/2021036173

10 9 8 7 6 5 4 3 2 1

*This book is dedicated, in loving appreciation,
to my mother Brenda S. Williams
and in loving remembrance of my (late) father,
Preston T. Williams.*

Contents

ACKNOWLEDGMENTS ix

INTRODUCTION
On Double Consciousness as the Failure of Cross-Caste Romance:
Du Bois's Nationalism Re- and De- formed 1

CHAPTER ONE
A Hymn of Faith Is a Tale of Love: Lohengrin and Platonic Romance
in Du Bois's "Of the Coming of John" 31

CHAPTER TWO
The Queer Gift of Black Folk: Reading Double Consciousness in
Du Bois's Detective Fiction 53

CHAPTER THREE
A Romance of Refusal: Failed Intimacy and Black Fugitivity in
"The Princess of the Hither Isles" 75

CHAPTER FOUR
Crossing Caste and Queering Kinship: Du Bois's Utopian
Afro-Asiatic Romance 97

EPILOGUE
Strange Intimacies: On Exogamy and Endogamy in the
Cross-Caste Romance 121

NOTES	129
WORKS CITED	145
INDEX	153

Acknowledgments

The seeds of this book were germinated circa 1995, in the wake of the reissuance of Du Bois's 1928 novel, *Dark Princess*. This book was a revelation to me. Accompanied by a virtuosic analytical preface by Claudia Tate, the book quickly garnered attention from other renowned scholars including Amy Kaplan and Homi Bhabha. Like many students and scholars, I had been unaware of the rich literary corpus central to Du Bois's legacy as an intellectual, antiracism activist, and artist. I was enthralled with the novel, which I found to be rich, fascinating, complex, and (contrary to popular belief) replete with formalist aplomb and innovation.

After writing about *Dark Princess* and the lone short story from *Souls*, "Of the Coming of John," in my dissertation about the intersection of aesthetics and politics in the Harlem Renaissance, I focused my attention on other writing projects: analyzing a heretofore unknown instance of plagiarism by Nella Larsen and exploring a queer contemporary passing novel by a little-known writer named Linda Villarosa (the beginnings of a longer book-length project probing the function of narratives of queer and transgender transition in contemporary Africana passing narratives). Yet I remained gripped by the prospect of locating the literary Du Bois, taking several trips to his archives at UMass-Amherst, where I discovered his little-known examples of detective and speculative fiction, alongside unpublished versions of his signature essays and fragments of prose. Then in 2009, I embarked upon a pilgrimage to his hometown of Great Barrington, where I visited the Du Bois Center helmed by Randy F. Weinstein; the site of Du Bois's family homestead, now a historical outpost flush with signage yet bereft of any actual edifice (as the home was lost to a fire); and the Mahaiwe Cemetery, where his first wife, Nina Gomer Du Bois, and their children, Burghardt and Yolande, are interred, miles away from Du Bois, whose final resting place is in Accra, Ghana (originally alongside Osu Castle and now in front of his former residence).

Over time, I realized that there was a whole book to be fashioned from exploring and analyzing Du Bois's vast literary output—the various tales that he spun—some in novel form and others in short narratives of various genres. I felt called to build on the work begun by Arnold Rampersad with the publication of his pioneering *The Art and Imagination of W.E.B. Du Bois* in 1976: to develop a framework for interpreting Du Bois's literature, which would not only serve as a vehicle for his political thought but also as an instantiation of the discernible and mature poetics of an author whose imagination and creative practice were shaped by a variety of literary traditions, including European and American romanticisms and Black Modernism. Such work is distinguishable by a penchant for blurring the lines between realism and romance and blending a variety of contrasting generic conventions that sometimes stymied his readers and critics.

When I told various scholars and laypersons that I was writing a book about Du Bois's fictional works, the reactions were mixed: running the gamut from incredulity to sly disapproval. There were murmurs about how, although Du Bois was a genius and *Souls* a prosaic masterpiece, his literary contributions were rather bombastic and "not particularly good." With the publication of *Tales from Du Bois: The Queer Intimacy of Cross-Caste Romance*, I hope to proselytize about Du Bois's accomplishments as a creative writer and to encourage those who may undervalue his literary output to consider his work anew.

A few iconoclasts at the University of Pennsylvania encouraged this project from the beginning: Gerald Prince was the first to suggest to me that I could write an entire monograph centered on Du Bois. Farah Griffin, now of Columbia University, served as my dissertation advisor and introduced me to the importance and excitement of archival work. Herman Beavers, who also helped to shepherd my dissertation, and who is himself an incisive critic of Du Bois's novel *Dark Princess,* offered consistent encouragement and crucial intellectual and professional support, especially as the project drew nearer to manuscript stage.

In addition, Joy Renjilian-Burgy of Wellesley College provided encouragement, mentorship, library access at Wellesley College, and regular gifts of food and shelter when needed. Along the way, Adrian Piper, formerly of Wellesley College, gave generously of her time to sharpen my understanding of Kantian aesthetics and to lend me the vocabulary with which to read race in philosophic terms. And more recently, R. A. Judy, of the University of Pittsburgh, provided a stellar model for how to engage Du Bois's literary imagination and philosophic prowess, as well as counsel about how to frame some aspects of my project. Whitney Battle-Baptiste of UMass-Amherst supported me and this project by choosing me to be among a cohort of W. E. B. Du Bois Visiting Scholars at the Du Bois Center of UMass-Amherst in 2017. There, I relished the opportunity to work amidst the peace, quiet, and beautiful views afforded by the twenty-fifth floor of the Du Bois Library and to make new discoveries in the company of a diverse group of talented and dedicated Du Bois scholars. I also extend thanks to Danielle Kovacs, curator of collections at the Du Bois archives. In addition, I was lucky to be able to share and hone this project via invited lectures and presentations. Francisca Oyogoa of Bard College at Simon's Rock invited me to lead a class in Du Boisian poetics at Bard College of Simon's Rock and to deliver a public lecture in Du Bois's hometown of Great Barrington, Massachusetts, to a keen audience of scholars, students, and avocational connoisseurs of Du Bois. And Mathias Hanses of Penn State and Jackie Murray of the University of Kentucky invited me to join a brilliant and vibrant cohort of Du Bois scholars as part of the W. E. B. Du Bois and the Ancient Mediterranean conference held at Penn State in the spring of 2021.

I extend my appreciation to a number of friends and colleagues at Emerson College. Wendy W. Walters, my teaching partner in the Honors Program for many years and fellow African Americanist at Emerson College, offered friendship, guidance, and writing support as a reader of some chapter drafts. Cara Moyer-Duncan, Kristin Lieb, and Kaysha Corinealdi have been wonderfully supportive colleagues, friends, and comrades-in-arms. Zoë Gadegbeku was a shrewd and meticulous graduate research assistant who worked assiduously to track down sources, organize research, and scan scads of material. Tulasi Srinivas, Nigel Gibson, Claire Andrade Watkins, William Wyatt Oswald, Amy Ansell, Michaele Whelan, Sylvia Spears, and M. Lee Pelton offered collegial, institutional, and other critical forms of support. I also wish to express my appreciation to the students at Emerson College who took my Du Bois seminars from 2012 to 2015. Your hard work, insight, and seamless capacity to read Du Bois's fiction as literary in all the senses of that word delighted and affirmed me.

I also extend my gratitude to Rebecca Colesworthy of SUNY Press, editor and champion extraordinaire, who has responded with alacrity, care, and compassion to the numerous queries of a first-time book author, to the three anonymous readers for my manuscript who offered such sage ideas and insightful critiques, and to the editorial and production staff at

SUNY. In addition, I thank Kathleen Kearns for her expert developmental suggestions and edits. And I thank Matthew J. Phillips for thoughtful and thorough copyediting. My thanks are also due to the journal *Modern Fiction Studies,* which published an earlier version of chapter 1: "A Hymn of Faith Is a Tale of Love: Lohengrin and Platonic Romance in W. E. B. Du Bois's 'Of the Coming of John'" (*Mfs,* 66.4, Winter 2020). I also thank *Studies in American Fiction* for publishing a portion of my second chapter "The Queer Gift of Black Folk" (Volume 48, No. 1, Spring 2021).

Finally, I give thanks to my family, without whose constant support, encouragement, nurturance, and love this book would not have been possible. To my mother, Brenda S. Williams and my (late) father, Preston T. Williams: thank you for loving, encouraging, caretaking, and occasionally scolding me when needed. To my brother Kyle T. Williams: thank you for the hugs, the laughs, and the lunch and movie dates over the years that always help to ground me and bring me joy. I also give thanks to my late grandmother Zenobia Hilda Smith, for her legacy of grit, her ebullient pride in my accomplishments, and her reminders that I am the culmination of my ancestors' wildest dreams. And I thank my great-uncle Samuel Debnam and my (late) great-aunt Maurice Debnam, along with my uncle Alfred J. Smith and cousin Jah Jah Bey for their many offerings of love and support over the years. Finally, last but certainly not least, to my partner in life and literary commiseration, Katerina Gonzalez Seligmann: thank you for being my intellectual interlocutor, political ally, and partner in crime par excellence and for joining me on this crazy journey arcing toward unbounded love and justice.

Introduction

On Double Consciousness as the Failure of Cross-Caste Romance: Du Bois's Nationalism Re- and De-formed

> We wanted national fulfillment as much as we wanted to "be" in love, hardly stopping to worry that the wanting was greater than any possible fulfillment.
>
> —Doris Sommer, *Foundational Fictions*

"Between me and the other world, there is ever an unasked question," opines Du Bois in the opening lines of the opening chapter of his 1903 masterpiece *The Souls of Black Folk*. The inhabitants of this "other world," who, as Du Bois explains, are separated from him by what he perceptively and poetically deems a "veil" demarcating the line between white and Black persons, "approach me in a half-hesitant sort of way, eye me curiously or compassionately, and then, instead of saying directly, How does it feel to be a problem?, they say, I know an excellent colored man in my town; or, I fought at Mechanicsville; or, Do not these Southern outrages make your blood boil?" ([1903] 2007, 7). As my students routinely remark, such statements constitute a series of what we term, in contemporary parlance, "microaggressions." Du Bois's response to such instances of perlocutionary violence was to deploy a variety of strategies designed to mitigate their impact—sometimes by forcing a "smile," sometimes by evincing a modicum of "interest" in their content, and sometimes by "reducing the boiling [of annoyance or even, outrage] to a simmer" (7). Just as Du Bois was not truly seen by those who addressed him, who projected upon him what Claudia Rankine describes in *Citizen: An American Lyric* as the phantasmagoric projections of "white" persons—based more on their fears, desires, and misperceptions than on any experiential notion of reality (see Rankine 2014), so too did the fullness and sincerity of Du Bois's responses to such remain foreclosed. As he professed, to the outrageous intrusion of such missives, he "answer [ed] seldom a word" (7).

Du Bois's adult ruminations about the force and impact of the microaggressions to which he was routinely subjected in the presence of putatively "liberal" white Americans occasioned his recall of a parallel moment of racist oppression from his childhood. Reciting a narrative prelude to the philosophic explanation of his famed theory of double consciousness, which he defines summarily as the "peculiar sensation" of "looking at one's self through the eyes of others," Du Bois recounts in *Souls* a story of having his affections in the form of a "gorgeous" visiting card exchanged between boys and girls during a schoolhouse game, rebuffed by a white female classmate who, apparently outraged by her judgment of his racial difference, refused his gesture of intimacy (Du Bois [1903] 2007, 8):

> I was a little thing, away up in the hills of New England, where the dark Housatonic winds between Hoosac and Taghkanic to the sea. In a wee wooden schoolhouse, something put it into the boys' and girls' heads to buy gorgeous visiting cards—ten cents a package—and exchange. The exchange was merry, till one girl, a tall newcomer, refused my card,—refused it peremptorily, with a glance. Then it dawned upon me with a certain suddenness that I was different from the others; or, like mayhap, in heart and life and longing, but shut out from their world by a vast veil. (7–8)

In this passage, Du Bois suggests that the occasion of having his visiting card, which served as a metonymic marker for himself, rejected by his white peer, marked his very indoctrination into the American system of anti-Black exclusion and thus precipitated the onset of his double consciousness. Indeed, a number of critics have commented upon the centrality of Du Bois's relayed experience of rejection in what I term, in recognition of Du Bois's poetic rendering of his personal experience, "The Tale of the Visiting Card," to the formation of his racial consciousness. Eugene Wolfenstein, for example, employs a Freudian lens to assess Du Bois's reaction to the young white girl's act of anti-Black exclusion as a prolonged defense mechanism, one predicated upon "renouncing . . . the desire to be at home in the world of ordinary human intercourse and sympathy" (22) and more pointedly, the inclination to pursue white companionship (31). (This is a point to which I will return.) George Yancy also interprets the white girl's rejection of Du Bois's visiting card as a "callous" instance of social exclusion (2017, 76) in which a Euro-centered glance leveraged its power to metaphorically "confiscate" a Black body, reducing it, falsely, to "a burden and a curse" (79) and curtailing thereby the expansiveness of a Black soul.

Few critics, however, have substantively plumbed the implications of the fact that this moment of rejection was not just one of failed interracial camaraderie but specifically an instance of failed interracial *romance*, since Du Bois's offering was arguably a token of affection and even unrequited ardor. The perceptibly "gorgeous" quality of the bounty being offered, the fact that the exchange was deliberately facilitated as cross-gendered, and the intensity of Du Bois's hurt feelings upon being so disregarded—a mixture of scorn, anger, and ultimately, as I will detail, a sense of psychic estrangement that would simultaneously be transcended and transmogrified—all compel me to read this moment as exemplary of an anticipated and unrequited romance. As Hazel Carby characterizes Du Bois's offering to his white female classmate as an expression of "courtly, nineteenth-century advances" (2007, 255), her reading of the stakes involved in Du Bois's framing of his youthful memory accords most closely with my own. Yet, while Carby focuses her analysis on Du Bois's revelation of the potential of women to become the instruments "through which the nation-state oppresse [s] black men" (255), I probe the overarching implications of Du Bois's intimation that Black alienation is the result of failed intercultural intimacy, meditating on how attempts to leverage romance to forge political conciliation are inevitably poised both to circumvent and to reanimate the hierarchies of racial caste.

Revisiting the significance of Du Bois's recitation of "The Tale of the Visiting Card" and extending thereby the scope of his theory of double consciousness, *Tales from Du Bois: The Queer Intimacy of Cross-Caste Romance* argues that Du Bois's explicit framing of his theory of double consciousness through a narrative of failed interracial romance emphatically links the emergence of Black subjectivity to the fracturing dispensations of misbegotten intimacy initiated across caste difference. In naming the unsuccessful encounter between Du Bois and his young white classmate a "romance," in particular, I do not rely only upon the traditional definition of romance as a reciprocal exchange of affection or consummated expression of eros but also conceptualize romance as something that need not become patently loving, sexual, or even viable in order to resonate as a significant social relation. I analyze the relation between Du Bois and the white girl whose attention he sought as a foreclosed *romance* because it was still a discernible instance of intimacy, even if a "minor" one in Lauren Berlant's terms, since, as an initiation of cross-racial contact, it was neither sanctioned by nor accommodated within the public spaces of mainstream society (Berlant 1998, 285). As Berlant further explains, while there are some kinds of intimacy that are supported by "normative ideologies" like family, church, or the state, there are other modes of intimacy that remain "discredited" or even "neglected" within the realm of hegemonic institutions. Such intimacies may "emerge from [. . .] mobile [and I would add, unstable,] processes of attachment"; reflect the presence of "contradictory desires"; and transmit subtle affective expressions including "glances, gestures, encounters, collaborations and fantasies" (284–85). Although Du Bois's attempt at romance would yield only an impoverished, hamstrung expression of intimacy, it posed nevertheless a considerable threat to the racial caste system by which Black boys and white girls were neither permitted to freely exchange gifts nor to nourish the interplays of affection betokened therein.

Indeed, my reading of Du Bois's youthful anecdote as a "romance" is emboldened by my analysis of an alternate version of the story that he offers in his 1968 autobiography, through which it becomes clear that this incident occurred not when he was a child but rather when he was a high-school student: more of a young man with adult feelings and intentions than the innocent schoolboy of his literary figuration (1968, 94). As Du Bois explains, tracing the developmental trajectory by which a paradisiacal experience of Great Barrington yielded to a more sobering discernment of the town's casteist politics, by the time he had entered high school "there came some rather puzzling distinctions which I can see now were social and racial [. . .]. I have written elsewhere of the case of our exchanging visiting cards when one girl, a newcomer, did not seem to want mine, to my vast surprise" (94). Although I deem it likely that Du Bois may have exaggerated somewhat the scope of his "surprise," as he no doubt anticipated the sting of racism (even if only subconsciously), the rejection he endured was clearly dispiriting to him, and the circumstances of this rejection were evidently controversial. In effect, the tale that Du Bois told of his childhood rebuff in *Souls* was of the *tall* variety, for it presented readers with a vision of a Black *child* whose friendship was refused by a white one rather than that of a young Black *man* whose romantic—and perhaps even erotic—interest was refused by a young white *woman*. Du Bois's fictive recasting of the story's details, and in particular his reduction of a potentially adult interracial romance to an expression of mere "puppy love," speaks both to the intensity of his encounter and to the entrenchment of the American taboo against miscegenation, which Du Bois strove to deemphasize in his creative retelling of the incident. Indeed, from the audacity of such a romance's reach and from its almost inevitable failure, one gleans not just the blight of interpersonal loss but pointedly the global catastrophe of interracial fracture. For a successful romance between Du Bois and the young woman of his childhood acquaintance would have marked not only the permeability of racial boundaries but also the flouting of a key element of the American racial caste system (and indeed, of caste systems in general): the interdiction against miscegenation and with it, the exigency of racialist and racist separatism.[1]

Before going on to detail the way Du Bois mined his personal narrative of having sustained a misbegotten form of interracial romance in order to produce and proliferate a compelling literary trope, I must note that my use of the term *caste*, often associated with and deemed exclusively germane to South Asian history and geopolitics, is quite deliberate and not a misapplication of terminology. In so doing, I follow a long tradition of scholars and chroniclers of African American history, critical race studies, and caste who have done so including Du Bois himself and more recently, Michelle Alexander, Isabel Wilkerson, Arundhati Roy, Yogita Goyal, and Suraj Yengde. Yengde trenchantly declares that "caste is not a foreign, old, traditional Indian problem; it is as American as white supremacy. The policing of the conduct and biopower of marginalized bodies. A fixated, theoretical, and pervasive system that reproduces for new eras the same channels of oppression upon which this society was developed" (Yengde 2021).[2] As various scholars and writers exploring the structure and legacy of casteism acknowledge, casteism is sustained by an insistence on the superiority of some categories of human beings over others, a preference for endogamous practice (to reify such ontological categorization), a policed and strategic deployment of exogamous practice, and a politics of hereditary apartheid: all principles and practices that resonate within the international history of anti-Black racism both in the United States and beyond. Indeed, in unpacking the cultural history of the visiting (or calling) card, one finds that it was itself a missive specifically intended to navigate and circumvent barriers of class and caste, offering a unique and uniquely aesthetical mechanism for forging sociopolitical intercourse across starkly drawn lines of social and cultural difference.[3] Thus, Du Bois's offering of an attractive calling card to a young white woman cannot simply be read as a benign expression of affection but also as a deliberate and nascent step to deploy assimilation as a method of mitigating racist violence and discrimination—one that becomes most clearly so in the process of being first forestalled and ultimately disavowed.

Upon being rejected, not just as a potential friend but also as a potential suitor, by a young white woman, Du Bois has the epiphany, which only expands as he moves further into adulthood, that although he may resemble (at bottom) his white peers "in heart and life and longing," he is nevertheless excluded from fully participating in the world they would exclusively claim by the imposition of the "vast veil" of racial caste ([1903] 2007, 8). Although Du Bois insists to his readers that it was only those unspecified cadres of "other" Black boys who, in their inability to vanquish their experience of profound racial alienation, opined, "Why did God make me an *outcast and a stranger* in mine own house?," it was arguably the very knowledge that such a seemingly benign instance of interpersonal rejection could render him an outcast in his own country that so troubled, politicized, and even radicalized Du Bois. For as he no doubt gleaned, even in his youth, being barred not simply from fully accessing the various spaces and places of American social and civic engagement but also from expressing the full range of one's affiliations, affections, and desires was both the cause and the consequence of America's racial caste system. Thus, the feeling of being outcast, as provoked by the sociopolitical failure to obtain full citizenship, yet as often experienced as an interpersonal and psychically felt form of loss, may prove by turns productive and alienating.

This book's second central claim is that Du Bois's dramatization of the visiting card incident in the opening chapter of *Souls*, through which he frames double consciousness as the result of a failed interracial romance, is an inaugural instance of his frequent deployment of a trope that I term the "cross-caste romance." An interplay of heightened awareness of and desire for another effected across stark lines of purportedly immutable yet socially constructed difference-rendered-as-status, the cross-caste romance marks the overdetermined yet precarious quality of intimacy between persons whose identities are differentiated by delimited segmentations of culture and status. Such exchanges of awareness, intimacy, and desire, as Eve Sedgwick has noted, may be constituted as much by repulsion or ambivalence as by attraction, and they underscore the power dynamics of racialized, intersubjective relations and place into relief the sociopolitical implications of affect and intimacy. Influenced by Sedgwick's claims about "desire," which she differentiates from the related category of "love" in order to emphasize that "desire" is a structure and not simply an emotion, I claim that the romance proves an "affective or social force, the glue, even when its manifestation is hostility or hatred or something less emotively charged, that shapes an important relationship" (Sedgwick 1985, "Homosocial Desire."). Sedgwick wonders to what degree such a force might become specifically sexual, and I follow suit by suggesting that the force of romance need not be patently sexual or even concretized in order to resonate as a significant social relation.

And yet, as Sharon P. Holland reminds us, intersubjective relations shaped by race, racialism, and racism ineluctably encode the erotic if not the sexual per se. Explaining what she calls "the admittedly tenuous although nonetheless compelling connection between the erotic and racism" (2012, 43), Holland contends that "the psychic life of racism [. . .] ha[s] its erotic, desiring components" (43). Arguably, the young girl's rejection of Du Bois already marks her implicit acknowledgment of the intimate, though not exclusively erotic, possibilities of a taboo, interracial romance between them. Her rejection, effected by a "peremptory glance," marks her awareness of and aversive reaction to Du Bois—however ambivalent—and bespeaks an affective charge that belongs as much to the category of "romance" as do affection and connection.

As I see it, the cross-caste romance, which encodes hegemonic configurations of racial and sexual difference, functions not only as a frame for Du Bois's theory of double consciousness but also as a model for his subsequent and frequent reanimation of such in his more patently literary texts. In deploying the trope of cross-caste romance, Du Bois was riffing on a well-worn discursive and literary tradition by which the nation is often explicitly gendered as female and through which heteronormative romance is positioned as a potential mechanism to bridge the gaps of caste difference (including ethnicity and class) and thereby to ward off the violence ensuing from a national politics based on exclusion. Indeed, the causal link that Du Bois's expository narrative establishes between a failed attempt to forge cross-caste intimacy and the subsequent onset of the ontological alienation that is double consciousness, is exemplary of a transnational continuum of late nineteenth-century "romantic nationalism," well documented by Doris Sommer and Lisa Moore respectively, in which novels or "romances," as they are called, stage intimate affairs between persons separated by differential statuses regarding race, ethnicity, region, and class (all the building blocks of caste) in order to meditate on the possibilities and limitations of pluralist nationalism. Such "romances," which Doris Sommer, in her analysis of early modern Latin American fiction, defines as a genre that is "a cross between our contemporary use of the word as a love story and a nineteenth-century use that distinguished the genre as more boldly allegorical than the novel" (Sommer 1991, Part I), deploy an affective and erotic politics, whether failed or successful, enervating or fulfilling, both to symbolize the fractures threatening the collective unity of the nation-state and to hypothesize their potential resolution.

As I demonstrate throughout this book, the vexed possibility of an affective and variously eroticized and deeroticized nationalist politics that Du Bois stages in his fictionalized account of double consciousness is subsequently posited and contested in numerous examples from his literary corpus, especially those that are judiciously periodized under the capacious term *romanticism*. Literary romanticism is an apt designation, not only for those texts that privilege romantic sentiment, love, or eros but also for those texts that exist in contemporaneous dialogue with or, alternatively, bear the imprint of, the continental philosophies, cultural movements, and literary discourses of the late nineteenth and early twentieth centuries. As I define literary romanticism as part of the "long nineteenth century," extending from the Enlightenment to the beginnings of the twentieth century, I read it as both a harbinger and an iteration of the continuum of modernism that is inclusive of the New Negro and Harlem Renaissance movements. Recognizing Du Bois's participation in and innovation within literary and cultural romanticisms, I have chosen as my focus a diverse yet representative selection of those literary works (some well known and others less so) that Du Bois produced between the early to mid-twentieth century (from 1903 to 1928) that especially embody the poetics and preoccupations of romanticism, including the sole short story from *The Souls of Black Folk*, "Of the Coming of John"; two little-known detective stories from *Horizon* magazine, "The Case" and "The Shaven Lady" (1907); an allegorical folktale from *Darkwater*, "The Princess of the Hither Isles" (1920), and the novel *Dark Princess: A Romance* (1928). In so doing, I suggest that Du Bois's works of literary fiction, the various "tales" that he spun during the first half of the twentieth century, justifiably earn him the title of *neo*-romanticist—one who plied the literary and cultural conventions of romanticism to evoke as well as revoke its idealized, hegemonic constructions of selfhood, love, and national belonging.

By reading Du Bois as an erstwhile romanticist, I concur with a number of scholars who have (implicitly or explicitly) done so including Robert Gooding-Williams, K. Anthony Appiah, Claudia Tate, Alys Weinbaum, and Brent Edwards. Moreover, in foregrounding the romanticist elements of Du Bois's fictional writings, in particular, I am also influenced by Toni

Morrison's groundbreaking work of criticism *Playing in the Dark,* in which she characterizes Euro-American romanticism in particular as "an exploration of anxiety imported from the shadows of European culture" (1992, 36). Morrison proceeds to historicize American romanticist literature as what offered European Americans a vehicle for "the imaginative entertainment of violence, sublime incredibility, and terror—and terror's most significant overweening ingredient: darkness, with all the connotative value it awakened" (36). Morrison concludes that no Euro-American literary romance is free of "the power of blackness" and observes further that the white imagination played upon the Black population to work out its fears and anxieties in prose as well as in life. I submit that this characterization of American romance illuminates both Du Bois's depiction of his white classmate's erotically tinged fear and the subsequent romanticist tales that he penned in the wake of this personal misalliance. In reprising his personal tale of failed interpersonal connection across racial caste, Du Bois reanimated and recast the discursive rhetoric of American romanticism (and undoubtedly, other forms of literary romanticism, as well) that established a lamentable linkage among Blackness, abjection, and aversive desire. He thereby recuperated the power of Blackness to signify delight and pleasure and to remediate the US body politic, effectively inverting American romanticism's abject portrayals of Black America and, accordingly, elucidating the violence, sublimity, and ignominy of Euro-American modes of thought and practice. The connection that Morrison draws between the aesthetics of romanticism and its ideological investment in anti-Blackness provides a useful lens through which to consider Du Bois's innovations within the genre of romance. For I submit that he tendered such romantic tales, in all of their generic variety and stylistic complexity, to equally disaggregate and rebut the misrepresentation of Black persons as objects of derision, placing into sharp relief the vexed process of forging intimacy across cultural difference and caste-based hierarchy.

In the essay "Acts of Union, Sexuality and Nationalism, Romance and Realism in the Irish National Tale," Lisa L. Moore analyzes the trope of cross-caste love as it functions in the nineteenth-century Irish novels of Maria Edgeworth and Sydney Owenson, which were oriented around vexed questions of nationalist belonging. Moore is interested in the way "cross-caste"—or as she also terms it, "star-crossed"—love plays a role in imagining and perhaps even shaping the fabric of a nation, chiefly by signaling what she recognizes as the "transgressive charge" of intimacy, which must first be invoked and ultimately overcome within pluralist projects of "romantic nationalism" (2000, 116).[4] I submit that Du Bois's literary projects are oriented around the same vexed questions of nationalism present in the Anglo-Irish literary romance of the nineteenth century that debated the possibilities of and parameters for reintegrating and revaluing its ethnic others. At stake for Du Bois was nothing less than the establishment of Black American citizenry within an American body politic determined to cast out those whose affective as well as material acts of labor were persistently and violently annexed to establish the nation.

Influenced by Moore's analysis of Owenson and Edgeworth and adopting and extending Moore's romanticist lexicon, I identify the cross-caste romance that structures Du Bois's literary repertoire as his chosen vehicle for considering the limits and possibilities of romantic nationalism and for placing into relief the idea that love for one's country can be rendered by what Moore deems a "passionately personal relationship" that allows a protagonist, whose journey toward citizenship is embattled, to "fall in love with a nation by falling in love with a woman who embodies that nation" and thereby earn the status of "proto-citizen" (Moore 2000, 118).[5] Indeed, with his literary figuration of double consciousness, Du Bois proffers an account of romantic nationalism that is highly contested and undercuts, even as it imagines, the possibility of a nation's seamless and conciliatory integration of its ethnic "others." For if the young white girl's potential acceptance of Du Bois's gesture of affection (and perhaps her return of such a gesture in kind) signaled the possibility of Black integration, and with it the granting of fuller citizenship to the collective of Black Americans for whom Du Bois was synecdochic, then so too did the white girl's refusal of Du Bois signal the failure of the potentially unifying and leveling capabilities of affect, intimacy, and indeed, "romance," to facilitate such nationalist conciliation, thereby stitching together the disparate threads of the nation.

As I will go on to demonstrate, this contested account of romantic nationalism is repeatedly proliferated in Du Bois's literary texts, in which he stages implicit or explicit debates about the efficacy and desirability of romantic nationalism's dependence upon heteronormative forms of exchange and in which he proves loath to resolve states of intersubjective or intranational fragmentation via recourse to the purportedly unifying tenets of romantic intimacy. As Alys Weinbaum has observed, Du Bois's literary configurations of romance are profligate yet also inclined to be "indefinitely attenuated" (2007, 100). For Du Bois recognized that the promises of "love" and intimacy, if premised upon the narrow confines of heteronormative reproduction and subsequently poised to enable the hegemonic absorption of Black persons by certain representatives of white America, would be inadequate and undesirable even if possible. In fact, Du Bois, by illustratively rendering his own failed cross-caste romance and offering it as the framework through which to explicate the theory of double consciousness, illuminated the central paradox that interracial intimacy between Black and white persons was not so much "foreclosed" by the caste system's taboo against miscegenation but paradoxically forbidden and foretold.

Recalling the work of Lauren Berlant, I assess such fraught relations as examples of "minor intimacy" insofar as they are taboo and marginalized. On the other hand, I aver that the misbegotten intimacy between Black and white persons, one presupposed by ardor in the form of overvaluation, was de rigueur within the white supremacist and anti-Black politics of the United States. In fact, Du Bois's decision to offer a token of affection to the teenaged white girl who was his classmate was no doubt already a preemptive attempt at racial reconciliation. It was a gesture undertaken to ward off the imposition of racialized hate with a performance of what I will term compulsory *Europhilia*: a love of whiteness and white persons that, although potentially sincere, was likely, even if on a subterranean level, a defensive reaction to the predominant overvaluation of whiteness in the form of Eurocentrism.

In reflecting further about the ambivalence undergirding Du Bois's illustration of failed interracial intimacy and its implications regarding the vexed possibility of nationalist and pluralist conciliation, it is again instructive to consult *The Autobiography of W.E.B. Du Bois* (1968). For Du Bois muses therein about the scope of his loyalty to the only country he has ever known, framing the question of his nationalist belonging in the specific language of misbegotten love. Recalling his time as a young graduate student observing a German military parade and wondering why such jingoistic jubilation had failed ever to arouse him in his own homeland, Du Bois asks: "How far can love for my oppressed race accord with love for the oppressing country? And when these loyalties diverge, where shall my soul find refuge?" (1968, 169). Although Du Bois described the state of double consciousness as one rooted in clashing loyalties presupposed by divided loves, in retelling the onset of his own split consciousness, he also offered evidence of a mature capacity for a self-love (as Black love) that was both a partial resolution to and a utilization of the state of double consciousness, which would ultimately prove to be both burden and boon. In essence, Du Bois's response to being rejected by the young white woman, to having sustained and expressed his "love" for his oppressive country with a token of affection offered to a synecdochic representation of his country, was not only to despair but also to reject that misplaced love (and thereby, its presumed object). In fact, Du Bois's proposed answer to the failure of a program of romantic nationalism, which was premised upon conscripting an ethnic other into a hegemonic order via affective structures of monolithic and unequal proportions, was not simply to abandon it as something ineluctably out of reach but rather to reject it as something undesirable and even (often) inauspicious.

In other words, in the grip of his alienated state of consciousness, Du Bois was compelled to reorient the trajectory of his desires, and by extension, to proscribe a parallel reorientation on the part of his Black brethren, away from the implicit demand to love (and overvalue) whiteness as a mechanism of assimilation and towards a praxis of Black love via the twin acts of self-regard and cultural reclamation. As I will go on to detail, such acts of self- and cultural love as forms of repossession, which recur with marked consistency and complexity throughout Du Bois's fictional works, constitute queer alternatives to the normative and reactionary dictates of Eurocentrism and US assimilation.

Du Bois, in the wake of expressing hurt, outrage, and indignation at his repudiation by the young white woman, describes in poignant detail the manner in which he began to absent himself altogether from the exigency of her negative desire. Du Bois notes that he had no will then to "tear down" or "break though" the "veil" that was his metonym for the barrier of racial caste but rather to "dwell above" it: "I held all beyond it in common contempt, and lived above it in a region of blue sky and great wandering shadows" ([1903] 2007, 8). Distancing himself from both the imprint of her repudiation and the very spatial confines of his failed initiation of cross-caste romance, Du Bois sought to exist in a world beyond it all, anticipating Fred Moten's adumbration of a Black "fugitivity" that might evade some of the overdeterminations of anti-Black racist politics (2018, 15). In addition, when Du Bois returned to earthly matters, his prior attempt to love and honor whiteness was rather quickly converted into an expression of animus, which even bordered on violence: "That sky was bluest when I could beat my mates at examination-time, or beat them at a foot-race, or even beat their stringy heads" ([1903] 2007, 15). Du Bois's reaction to white repudiation seems to have been designed to recuperate his disparaged masculinity, as Hazel Carby has incisively observed (2007, 253–56). However, such displays of misanthropy might also be attributed to the subtle shifting of his desires vis-à-vis whiteness: from a mode of compulsory adoration as overvaluation to a corrective one of remote disinterest and then disdain, which, as I will go on to detail, signaled the subsequent emergence of his interest in and affection for Blackness. Du Bois thus offered a two-pronged approach for navigating white rejection and the resultant experiences of double consciousness: holding oneself "above" putatively white spaces and places while simultaneously attempting to best white persons at the games to which they would claim exclusive dominion. Although Du Bois depicted himself as existing at a remove from the mainstream, he clearly derived a perverse pleasure from being able "to beat" those white persons who would abnegate him, whether via scholastics, athletics, or even—without euphemism—physical combat. This is not to say that Du Bois was easily comforted by the shifting of his desires or by the insight through which he was disabused of an idealistic belief that white supremacy and its inherent anti-Blackness might be speedily overcome by displays of generosity and affection. In truth, the shifting of his desires, along with his growing epiphany regarding the consequences of racialism and racism, did little to relieve the material realities of his position as an "outcast." Nevertheless, I wish to underscore that with the initiation of Du Bois's feelings of "contempt" for white ways, however much he insisted that such negative feelings must eventually "fade," Du Bois began the process of internally shaking off the urge to love the oppressor. He traded in the compulsory Europhilia, which was paradoxically forbidden and required in the US landscape of the late nineteenth and early twentieth centuries, for a practice of Black reclamation that he implicitly recommended for all his Black compatriots. Indeed, Du Bois ultimately concludes that although he would not wholly Africanize America, neither would he "bleach his soul in a flood of White Americanism, for he knows that Negro blood has a message for the world" (9). In seeking a way to be "both a Negro and an American," without losing material opportunities or benefits but also, importantly, without ceding one's right to the pleasures and protections of self-loyalty and self-love, Du Bois sought a manner to mediate if not resolve the fragmentation that was both psychic and social in quality, as it marked both a paucity of social opportunity and connection for him (and by extension, for all Black Americans) and a potentially diminished capacity to attain personal cohesion and fulfillment—a comfort with and within one's own skin.

In probing further the scope and significance of Du Bois's account of double consciousness and his strategy for mitigating its negative effects, I follow the tradition of many critics who have brought a psychoanalytic approach to Du Bois's characterization of double consciousness including Dickson Bruce, whose research into the source material for Du Bois's theory reveals a framework by which double consciousness might be understood as a kind of subjective fragmentation, akin to or approximating a personality disorder (1999, 241–42), or what Du Bois describes as the phenomenon by which "two souls, two thoughts, two unreconciled strivings; [and] two warring ideals" compete within one person who must struggle to keep from being "torn asunder" ([1903] 2007, 8). I submit that Du Bois's capacity, not only to sustain a psychic and affective division of love and loyalty but also to partially resolve such in a way that proved productive, is fruitfully unpacked by being analogized to another, more routine form of psychological alienation: what Judith Butler terms the "queer melancholy" to which all persons developing under the spell of compulsory heterophily in and as heterosexuality are forced to submit in order to achieve subject-hood. Bearing in mind Butler's analysis, one comes to understand how compulsory heterosexuality marks a process of gendering by which a young subject is ushered into his or her gendered position by submitting to a prohibition that bars his/her own mirror image as an appropriate object of desire, consenting thereby to love, value, and identify chiefly with those persons of the opposing gender and thus in opposition to themselves. Ultimately, the subject preserves the lost or "barred" sexual object as part of their own ego through a process of a presumably "melancholic" identification that proves productive even as it is steeped in loss. For example, the young girl first ceases to identify with the mother whose position most resembles hers, who is then barred as her primary object of love but later, reincorporated through the mechanism of melancholic reidentification. Following this logic, the developing Black subject could be said to be beholden to a compulsory Europhilia that bids them to identify not with themselves and their own but with the white subject whose regard they must seek without any expectation of reciprocity.

Within Butler's schemata, the young person may come to reject such compulsory heterophily, returning to reclaim the heretofore forbidden object of their affection. As Butler explains further, "If one is a girl to the extent that one does not want a girl, then wanting a girl will bring being a girl into question; within this matrix, homosexual desire thus panics gender" (1995, 169). Applying this framework to the experience of young Du Bois, an experience that he attributes to all those of African American descent, I submit that to become "Black" in America is to be importuned, and even required, not to desire, value, or sympathize with Blackness but rather to nurture a forced intimacy in the form of high regard and affection for whiteness—one that is doomed to remain unrequited or otherwise misbegotten. Just as being oriented toward the other sex, thus forcibly enamored of and beholden to your embodied opposite, is the price of becoming gendered as male or female, so too under a white supremacist system is being Black disposed as a matter of loving counter to one's own interest, with one's affections, values, and affiliations forcibly directed outside the bounds of oneself. By extension it follows, as I restate with a difference Judith Butler's phrasing above, that "if one is Black or becomes Black to the extent that one does not want a Black, then wanting a Black will bring being Black into question." Within this matrix, homophilic (as pro-Black) desire thus panics race and racialism and by extension, the abject misapprehension of Blackness).

Extrapolating from Butler, I argue that the pull of compulsory white supremacy is as endemic to the process of becoming a US citizen as compulsory heterosexuality is to the process of becoming gendered (a process that is also imbricated within nationalist and capitalist imperatives for reproduction). Du Bois, by describing how he responded to his rejection by the young white woman—not by wholly despairing but rather by rejecting in turn his former juvenile desires and thus effectively reconfiguring the orientation of his desire and the parameters of his loyalty away from the dominating other and toward his own "kind"—thereby queers his earlier account of romantic nationalism. Du Bois eschews the exigent dictum of Europhilia in favor of a burgeoning self-love and an attendant commitment to honor his beloved Black community via the reclamation of both himself and an undervalued Africanity. Thus, Du Bois's recuperation of Blackness via the history and iconography of Africa is not only homologous to Butler's account of recuperative homophilic melancholy but also an instantiation of it. For, as I will go on to detail, in recovering a concept of Blackness that exists prior to and is thus irreducible to chattel slavery's abject characterization of it, Du Bois essayed to revalue not simply a derogatory sense of Blackness but also a homophilic and homoerotic regard for the Black subject in the guise of the Black man, to whom his narration turns in order to secure a lost African patrimony.[6]

While Du Bois's mitigation of the loss of double consciousness with a program of Black-as-African reclamation might well be said to "panic" heterophily in the form of compulsory Europhilia and white supremacy, such a praxis of Black homophily may also be said to "panic" the compulsory heteronormativity to which, as Mason Stokes instructs us in *The Color of Sex: Whiteness, Heterosexuality, and the Fictions of White Supremacy*, whiteness and the overvaluation of white persons have been historically and philosophically tied (2001, 13).[7] For, as I will now detail, Du Bois's fraught recovery of Africa, from which he and his Black compatriots have all been estranged and whose body politic he can only reclaim through a willful act of imagination, constitutes both a rejection of compulsory white supremacy and a resistance to the compulsory heteronormativity to which it has been historically wedded. In essence, the outgrowth of Du Bois's doubled consciousness was his implicit contestation of two discrete yet interconnected hegemonic structures: racialism—including its outgrowth, racism—and heteronormativity.

African Reclamation as Queer Kinship

Du Bois's response to the general sense of alienation produced by double consciousness and in particular, to the knowledge that he and his Black brethren have been forced to withhold their love from themselves, all the while remaining unrewarded for doing so, was to seek to have Blackness reborn through the cradle of a reconstituted Africa. As Fred Moten contends, much of Du Bois's foundational work reflects his goal to reclaim a narrative of Blackness that exists "before the binary that has been said to define our [its] existence" (2018, 35), a binary that, as I have underscored, is presupposed not only by a cross-caste equation of Black as opposed to white but also by binary, cross-gendered formulations. And yet, Du Bois was significantly challenged to find a firmly delineated source for Blackness, one that would secure for it an indisputable lineage, as well as a discernible ontology that might mitigate the ambivalence of a divided sense of self that proved both alienating and productive. For in Du Bois's attempt to recover a lost Black kinship, he was compelled to grapple with and attempt to transcend the binary between Black and white, to continuously confront the scene of his melancholic estrangement from his Black identity, and to mitigate the loss precipitated by the Middle Passage, which had so viciously ruptured the possibilities of African kinship by, in Fred Moten's estimation, "advancing the black reconstruction [. . .] by way of the black deconstruction of the natal" (35). Observe the following passage from the first chapter of *Souls*, in which Du Bois suggests that the (partial) resolution of double consciousness lies in the formation of a Pan-African and queer alternative to the ineluctably vexed project of interracial romantic nationalism:

> This, then, is the end of ["the Negro's"] striving: to be a coworker in the kingdom of culture, to escape both death and isolation, to husband and use his best powers and his latent genius. These

powers of body and mind have in the past been strangely wasted, dispersed, or forgotten. . . . Throughout history, the powers of single black men flash here and there like falling stars, and die sometimes before the world has rightly gauged their brightness. ([1903] 2007, 9)

Desiring to assert a prideful place at the table of American democracy—"to be a co-worker" and not a handmaiden in the "kingdom of culture," to escape both death and isolation, [and] to husband his best powers and latent genius"—the Black subject of African descent finds that *his* "powers" of both body and mind have been, as a consequence of the violence and chaos of the Middle Passage and, subsequently, the years of racial slavery and casteist oppression, "strangely wasted, dispersed, or forgotten" (or perhaps more accurately, denied) (9). Du Bois's return to Africa appears to center the masculine in its figuration of the prototypical Black subject within a revised account of African history. Yet, in so doing, Du Bois paints a picture of a dissipated and indiscernible Black genius through the metaphoric imagery of spilled semen, a homoerotic conceit conjured by his image of the "powers of single black men" "flashing" and "falling" like stars and evoking, thereby, a continuum of (phallic) tumescence and detumescence. Thus, by recovering Black genius and spirit in his rhetorical and poetic configurations, Du Bois not only privileges the masculine and the male bodied by foregrounding Black men and excluding Black women but also reroutes the pre-American, antebellum origins of Black subjectivity outside the realm of the maternal, excavating a displaced patrimony that one might read, paradoxically, as both a manifestation and a refutation of the Black man's necessary confrontation with what Hortense Spillers has famously described as his internalized female counterpart.

In *Mama's Baby Papa's Maybe: An American Grammar Book*, Hortense Spillers theorizes the historic and metaphysical entanglement between Black identity and the maternal, invoking the antebellum law by which any enslaved person was purportedly to follow the condition of the mother, thereby inculcating the passing on of caste servitude through generations. As Spillers explains, this antebellum legislation, which secured the continued survival of the racial caste system, occasioned a phenomenon by which *all* Black Americans, including men, were compelled to emphatically root their identities in both the literal and figurative bodies of their mothers, coming to understand such female bodies as both the cause and the inextricable fulcrum of their own identities. As Spillers concludes: "It is the heritage of *the mother* that the African-American male must regain as an aspect of his own personhood—the power of 'yes' to the 'female' within" (quoted in Snorton 2017, 146). Yet she also allows that, under the system of enslavement, no Black mother could be said truly to "claim" her own offspring—certainly not in any legal sense (quoted in Snorton 142; see also Spillers 1987, 80).

Bearing in mind Spillers's insights, I reprise with a difference my earlier claim that Du Bois's strategic response to the alienation of double consciousness was to initiate a melancholic reincorporation of the lost mirror image of his own Blackness. For while Du Bois's melancholic recuperation of Blackness-as-Africanity is indeed analogous to that of the young *girl* of Butler's schemata, whose entrance into her female identity is premised not only upon a process of heterophily, loving the other and not the same, but also upon conceding that her gendered position is inferior to that of the male, Du Bois's reclamation is not forged either by seamlessly identifying with any "mother within" nor by wholly accepting the putative derogation of his identity. For, in rejecting the myth of Black inferiority, Du Bois recurs (with some measure of irony) to the putatively superior position of masculinity. As such, Du Bois's melancholic experience accords most directly with that of the young *boy,* for he sought to premise his recovery of an African ancestry that would obviate the "problem" of being Black under the racial caste system of American slavery upon a heretofore foreclosed patrimony, which might be recovered by invoking a noble and rather phallocentric portrait of Africanity. Anticipating in complex ways Spillers's idea of a Black American identity necessarily produced through maternal identification, Du Bois conjures an Africa stitched together from the remains of a thwarted patrimony constituted by a series of Black men whose potential to sire Black generations has flashed and fallen like the stars. This rhetorical move of Du Bois's doubly bespeaks Butler's queer melancholy, for in recovering and redeeming his Blackness, Du Bois expresses a latent love for his lost African father that is not simply homophilic (as pro-Black) but homoerotic (as pro-male). Moreover, as Judith Butler allows, such processes of queer mourning and recuperation may surpass altogether the realm of the individual and become both sociocultural and collective in quality, constituting a "re-articulation of kinship" that might serve both to mitigate and to publicly memorialize the melancholic loss of autoerotic and homophilic love and valuation (1995, 178). As she explains: "The emergence of collective institutions for grieving is thus crucial to [cultural] survival, to the reassembling of community, the re-articulation of kinship, the reweaving of sustaining relations" (178). Recalling Fred Moten's analysis of how reconstructing Black subjectivity depends on deconstructing the natal, one might argue that Du Bois displaces an account of Black maternity under the shadows of slavery and concubinage in favor of an African patrilineage that is queer in its delineation of failed heteronormativity and idealized homophily and, moreover, salvific in its aspirational, intergenerational reach.

Moreover, Du Bois's reconstitution of Black patrimony further unseats the primacy of his symbolic figuration of the young white woman from the "Tale of the Visiting Card," who exemplified the unwelcoming stance of those white Americans whose racism forestalled not just an equitable valuation of Blackness but also a novel and fruitful ethnogenesis for the nation. Effectively, both America in the form of "Lady Liberty" and Africa embodied as a motherland are rendered equally insufficient candidates for the ideal cradle of Black subjectivity. In this sense, Du Bois's reimagined scene of African nativity evokes what Nathaniel Mackey describes as the Africanist phenomenon of "wounded kinship," which Fred Moten underscores as a "thwarted romance of the sexes [implicitly heteronormative in quality]" (quoted in Moten 2003, 15). By displacing the matrilineal in favor of a *queer* account of patrilineage, Du Bois invalidates heteronormative reproduction, not just as a prerequisite for interracial assimilation but also as a foundation for a desired praxis of endogamous, *intracaste* African filiation. Unable to reroute Black subjectivity through a means of reproduction that would prove both inviolable and propitious, Du Bois would recommend for the Black subject a kind of autogenesis, one in which the Black subject (represented as the Black man) would rebirth himself, "turning hither and thither in hesitant and doubtful striving," navigating the seeming "contradiction" of duality, and distilling the "soul-beauty of [the Black] race" that seems to defy translation ([1903] 2007, 9).

While this developmental struggle of the Black subject, whom Du Bois importantly frames as an "artist," may appear to signal the Black subject's "waning strength" ([1903] 2007, 9) and thus, an attenuated account of Black subjectivity, it actually bespeaks the Black subject's capacity to become chiefly by embracing liminality and contradiction. As Nahum Chandler avows: "Having no strictly delimitable scene of origin or presumptively final sense of habitus, the African American subject is quite often 'both/and,' as well as 'neither/nor'" (Chandler 2013, 37). For Du Bois, routing his mediation of the crisis of double consciousness through an incomplete yet regenerative trajectory of African reclamation shows us that Black Americans must acknowledge and navigate their estrangement, not only from white America but also from their own lost African heritage. With Du Bois's figurations of a liminal African space, poised between a sense of loss and a sense of expansion—and only partly accessible to the Black American subject due to the vicissitudes of time, space, and history—he indexes the gaps and asymmetries between opposing states of being and rebuts the historical segmentation of cultures, communities, and identities to which proponents of caste systems (which are paradoxically undergirded and destabilized by binary configurations of race, class, and nation) stubbornly and disingenuously commit. Having marked the interstice between Europe and Africa, the Black subject is, in Du Bois's imaginary, poised to metaphorically travel back to America, endowed with a new sense of self and, with it, a new strategy for accommodating oneself to a hostile nation: one replete with liminality and energized by the praxis of *crossing caste,* understood both as oscillating between ideological positions and as challenging the mythologies of those narrowly delineated ontological categories (e.g., race, gender, and class) presumably affixed to them (Du Bois [1903] 2007, 11).

Thus, double consciousness is not meant to be fully overcome but rather to be mitigated and suspended: mined, thereby, for its productive tension and facilitating what Paget Henry calls the boon of "potentiated second sight" and a newfound perception of one's misrecognition by white persons. It is a novel opportunity to rebut actively one's repudiation by drawing further inward, reclaiming a sense of self, and reassessing the putative limitations of Black being (2006, 37). Riffing on his earlier claim that having double consciousness is to be gifted with superlative vision, Du Bois moves to conclude his mediation on the "souls" of Black persons by proffering an account of Black subjectivity paradoxically derived from the limits of legibility: "In those somber forests of his striving his own soul rose before him, and he saw himself,—darkly as through a veil; and yet he saw in himself some faint revelation of his power, of his mission" (Du Bois [1903] 2007, 11). As I will go on to show, inter- and intrasubjective intimacy, as it functions in Du Bois's fiction, registers not just the possibility of by turns fruitful and fraught instances of what Nancy Yousef describes as the phenomena of "sharing" and "entanglement" on social and political registers but also the potential for the Black subject to practice a form of what Yousef also deems intimacy's tendency to enable acts of protective self-enclosure (Yousef 2013, 1).

Romantic Nationalism Deformed: The Queer Poetics of Crossing Caste

With a profound yet pliable sense of identity, the Black subject as depicted by Du Bois might reenter—or perhaps reassert—their place in the domain of American citizenry to whose margins s/he has been relegated and from whose confines s/he has flown. This reentry—albeit on more agential, judicious, and palatable terms—would reflect an understanding of intimacy as something that might be rendered more reciprocal yet enable the private pleasure of preserving, in Nancy Yousef's phrasing, "an intrinsic psychic inwardness" (2013, 1). After imaginatively crossing back to Africa, rerouting Blackness therein, and attempting thereby to recast a heretofore disparaged form of subjectivity, Du Bois closes the opening chapter of *Souls* by recasting the romantic nationalism he had earlier dismissed and staging a reformed mode of cross-caste romance in which Black Americans would be placed in relations of queer intimacy with white Americans: deeroticized, coeval, resistant, and not premised upon forced labor or concubinage but rather forged through voluntary and circuitously aggressive means of exchange and collaboration. Such a queer mode of cross-caste intimacy would evade the dictates of heteronormative reproduction, the limits of anthropocentric intimacy, and the tenor of xenophobic nationalism alike.

Du Bois concludes the opening chapter of *Souls* by exceeding the romance he earlier staged between a particular Black man and a particular white woman who functioned as allegorical symbols of a failed pluralistic nationalism and refiguring this narrow, interpersonal attempt to forge cross-cultural intimacy as a global, collective romance forged by dialogic exchange between "two world-races [who would] give each to each" their distinctive qualities ([1903] 2007, 13). Although Du Bois characterizes such a romance as a reciprocal relation that might usher in "the ideal of human brotherhood," he also takes care to highlight the unparalleled and perhaps even superior contribution of Black subjects, whom he implicitly renders as constituents of their own Black nation, galvanized under the "unifying ideal of Race" and facilitating a reformed project of cross-cultural exchange that does not concede to the dictates of caste-based prejudice but rather turns such pseudo-logic and ethical outrage on their heads (13). Du Bois then issues a call to Black folk, not simply to resign themselves to the norms and strictures of the American body politic, but rather, to remediate its failings:

> We the darker ones come even now not altogether empty-handed: there are to-day no truer exponents of the pure human spirit of the Declaration of Independence than the American Negroes; there is no true American music but the wild sweet melodies of the Negro slave; the American fairy tales and folk tales are Indian and African; and, all in all, *we black men seem the sole oasis of*

simple faith and reverence in a dusty desert of dollars and smartness. Will America be poorer if she replace her brutal, dyspeptic blundering with light-hearted but determined Negro humility? or her coarse and cruel wit with loving jovial good-humor? or her vulgar music with the soul of the Sorrow Songs? (13–14)[8]

Although Du Bois's language recalls the discourse of betrothal in its proffering of two "incomplete" halves forming a whole and in its intimation of the offering of a dowry in exchange for commitment, in outlining his wish for a revised and redeemed form of interracial exchange, Du Bois nevertheless posits a reformed program of American nationalism that is neither necessarily erotic, conjugal, nor even interpersonal in quality. Such reformed nationalism, perhaps better characterized as *paranationalism* in its refusal to suppress difference and foment conformity, would be defined as a collective enterprise and premised upon the gift of culture rather than the currency of bodies, opposing the historic traditions of compulsory labor and forced or coerced concubinage. Indeed, by the end of the first chapter of *Souls*, Du Bois has moved from marking if not outright bemoaning the failed enterprise of a lone Black American subject intent upon pursuing interpersonal intimacy with a white compatriot (as a means of attaining unity as well as parity) to suggesting that Black Americans might best assert their places in the American body politic by honoring and loving themselves, inculcating their shared experiences and values and, subsequently, offering neither their bodies nor their souls but rather their cultural and metaphysical resources: music, folklore, and even spirit as gifts to be annexed but only upon such conditions as would preserve their distinction and, thereby, the sovereignty and cultural survival of their stewards. Here, then, is the visiting card that a young Du Bois had offered as a ticket of admission into a putatively Eurocentric American body politic considerably transformed, multiplied into a token of Euro-American remediation and a talisman to deflect Euro-American appropriation. Thus, Du Bois deconstructs the very notion of assimilating "the other" that is endemic to the program of romantic nationalism I earlier detailed and that lay beneath the surface of the Black subject's experience of double consciousness—falsely promising a means with which to resolve rather than redeem such alienation. Despite Du Bois's prior contention that "America has [. . .] much to teach the world and Africa" (9), he does not, in the closing sections of the first chapter of *Souls*, posit the Black subject as the primary one in need of guidance and acculturation. Rather, with his image of a collective of Black men serving as beacons of "faith" and reverence (13), Du Bois highlights the paltry soul of a Euro-dominating racist, capitalist, and imperialist America sorely in need of extrication from their historic and ongoing displays of apostasy, irreverence, and cupidity (14). I submit that by proffering the ideal deployment of Black men in the service of ameliorating a broken American body politic, Du Bois subverts the very concept of assimilation and with it the concomitant rendering of African Americans as outcastes relegated to the margins of the nation-state (and by extension, the global stage). Instead, Du Bois's rhetoric articulates what Jose Muñoz has theorized as the praxis of "disidentification," a mode of critical, dialectical engagement that proves *queer* in its capacity to simultaneously identify with and rebut hegemonic formulations from an intimate and insider perspective (quoted in Ferguson 2003, "To Disidentify with Historical Materialism"). If, as Rod Ferguson explains, "queer of color critique decodes cultural fields not from a position outside those fields, but from within them" (2003, "To Disidentify with Historical Materialism") then Du Bois's revised account of romantic paranationalism, as offered in *Souls* and in the literary texts under my purview, indeed anticipates a queer of color methodology.

Finally, by linking his antiassimilationist call for Black America to remediate the American body politic through mutual—albeit less personal—modes of intimacy and exchange to the image of a haven of salvific Black men, Du Bois further articulates a nascent queer epistemology by displacing the familiar, romanticized equation of "one man and one woman" as symbols for the nation's unification, thereby supplanting the heteronormative logic of the couple, which as S. Pearl Brilmyer, Filippo Trentin, and Zairong Xiang have observed, has long functioned as the cornerstone of the hegemonic reproduction of the nation-state (2019, 224). Subverting thusly the conventional proposition of heteronormative reproduction, Du Bois positions a homosocial if not a patently homoerotic collective of Black men redolent of cultural and spiritual edification as improved symbols for a cross-caste romance that could be premised upon a less personal yet considerably more reciprocal mode of intimacy. My reading of Du Bois's configuration of a collective of Black men offering their cultural gifts in a remote or impersonal fashion as "queer" is undergirded and emboldened by queer theory's and queer-of-color critique's capacious understanding of queerness as potentially deontological in quality, as it need not rely strictly upon identitarian formulations of homosexual identity or practice (224). I submit that Du Bois, in moving away from an interpersonal and heterosexual equation of coupledom and toward a homosocial, collective, and aesthetical form of intimacy, gestures toward the limitations of heteronormative reproduction and troubles normative notions of gender, interracial exchange, and intimacy alike, especially for Black persons subjected to the systems of slavery and Jim Crow. Du Bois thus implicitly acknowledges the queer location of the Black subject, whom he places in the position, not of being forcibly conscripted into affective labor, recalling, as one of my anonymous reviewers shrewdly noted, the practice of arranged marriage or concubinage, but rather of willingly entering into a reciprocal relation with a white America sorely in need of remediation.[9] Such a willing act of collaboration on the part of the Black subject is not reactive but rather transformative—and perhaps even subversive—in the context of an American hegemony ineluctably imbricated with normative dispositions of gender and sexuality.[10]

Moreover, by setting up African Americans as ideal remediators of society and harbingers of subversive configurations of gender relations, Du Bois also revises the racial caste system's fallacious account of African Americans as abject, subservient, and thus justifiably relegated to the margins of society. In particular, Du Bois disputes the well-worn narrative of African Americans' historic endurance of conscripted labor and concubinage, especially prevalent during the postbellum and Jim Crow eras, yet continually demanded in their wake as overarchingly submissive in quality. By contrast, Du Bois reconceptualizes such labor and concubinage as having long been aggressively and thereby paradoxically palliative in quality. In the concluding essay of *Souls*, "The Sorrow Songs," Du Bois punctuates the antiassimilationist rhetoric with which he closes "Of Our Spiritual Strivings" by highlighting Black spirituals as powerful retentions of African culture. He reminds his readers that such an aesthetic resource, along with the material resources of labor and the metaphysical resources of "spirit," are the best of the myriad contributions that African Americans have long made to American life: "Here we have brought our three gifts and mingled them with yours: a gift of story and song—soft, stirring melody in an ill-harmonized and unmelodious land; the gift of sweat and brawn to beat back the wilderness, conquer the soil, and lay the foundations of this vast economic empire two hundred years earlier than your weak hands could have done it; the third, a gift of Spirit" ([1903] 2007, 175). With such images of intimate cross-cultural exchange, Du Bois suggests both the comparative weakness and paucity of character within his Euro-American compatriots and, by extension, the latent or hidden strength and fortitude of his Black brethren. Moreover, by offering a vision of Black persons "mingling" with their white compatriots, not only by exchanging metaphysical matter like story and song but also by exchanging those bodily fluids like perspiration and even, by implication, blood, which emanate when one's body is made an instrument of transformation, Du Bois foregrounds the numerous ways in which Black Americans have always engaged in a praxis of miscegenation that surpasses even as it encodes the erotic. In so doing, Du Bois also invokes casteism's obsession with a dialectic of so-called blood purity and pollution (see Subedi 2013, 327; Wilkerson 2020, 115), thereby invalidating the notion that Black blood could be "polluting" and concomitantly adducing the value of such distinctive (if irreducible) physiological matter as some of the richest and most foundational substance of which the United States was formed.[11] Finally, with a move that rebuts the caste system's erroneous conviction regarding the immutable inferiority or superiority of human beings and undercuts the hereditary segmentation of labor by group leveraged to enforce such a belief, Du Bois reminds his readers that although he has heretofore praised the capacity of Black Americans to be obliging and solicitous, they have also always dared to assert themselves—often, aggressively so—into a putatively white-dominated American body politic. For when Du Bois declares that Black Americans have "actively woven ourselves with the very warp and woof of this nation" and furthermore "called all that was best to throttle and subdue all that was worst" ([1903] 2007, 175–76), he posits a relation between Black and white persons in which the Black subject would be poised to exploit their presumed position at the margins of the nation, not just by tempering but also by conquering (when called for) white institutions and, by implication, the white supremacist modes of subjectivity presupposed by them. As Du Bois declares in his 1897 essay "The Conservation of Races," Black Americans are "the first fruits of this new nation, the harbinger of that black tomorrow which is yet destined to soften the whiteness of the Teutonic today" (822). Du Bois further declares that it is the "duty" of Black Americans to preserve their ethos, their voluntary cultural affiliation, and their intragroup (caste) "solidarity," all in the service of "the realization of that broader humanity which freely recognizes differences in men, but sternly deprecates inequality in their opportunities of development" (822). Du Bois thus undermines racial casteism while advocating for the preservation of *voluntary* endogamous affiliation, a precarious rhetorical position to which I return in my readings of *The Princess of the Hither Isles* and *Dark Princess* in chapters three and four respectively.

In a move that we may now acknowledge as having anticipated a queer ontology and rhetoric, Du Bois thus transforms the "bottom position," which, as Kathryn Bond Stockton observes, has been historically allocated to the queer and the racially marginalized subject into one of relative power and potential authority. For in the apparent submission (yet in actuality covert defiance) of the Black American populace, one finds a queer alternative to the conquering predilection of conventional Eurocentric masculinity, one in which a subject curries favor and power by "topping from below."[12] Thus I argue that Du Bois crosses caste by suggesting not only that Black and white persons should both flout the erroneous laws of racial and sexual "purity" but also that they should commit to sharing sociopolitical roles and responsibilities and exchanging power positions, shifting who it is that remains "on top." This move repeats with a marked difference the caste system's investment in separate yet interconnected roles for distinct persons, groups, and paranational cultural communities, while thwarting its recurrence to the fallacious notion of ontological purity and the arbitrarily enforced interdiction against intimate contact among persons across caste positions. Strengthening the talent and constitution of the nation, Du Bois avers, cannot be accomplished by adhering to a caste-based logic dependent upon a false mythos of ethnic purity and the unadvisable a priori ascriptions of power and authority but rather by reinventing—by turns crossing-as-thwarting, crossing-as-traversing, and crossing-as-cross-stitching—systems of social organization and cultural valuation that must remain flexible and dynamic, submitting themselves to transepochal and transnational tests of reason, ethics, and historical progress in order to remain feasible as well as felicitous. Nor can the nation—or perhaps, more accurately, the *denationalist* sociopolitical federation of persons and communities ideally supplanting the confines of the nation-state—flourish if powered not only by rigid hegemonic structures like casteism and racism but also by the unchecked misogyny and compulsory heteronormativity to which such structures are habitually tethered. In commenting on the limits of intersubjective and intercultural intimacy as attempted across the stark lines of caste division, Dalit scholar and writer Suraj Yengde eloquently proclaims in his book *Caste Matters* that "Love within the confines of caste also limits itself to hetero-normative values. It doesn't open up a space for love as an ultimate human virtue that is beyond the constructed identities of gender, sexuality, and caste" (2019, 50).

Reading Du Bois's romanticist poetics and antiracist politics, both as evidenced in *Souls* and as replicated in the various examples from his literary repertoire that I analyze here (particularly through a queer lens), enables me to recognize that the queerness of his rhetoric derives from his tacit resistance to heteronormative and heterocentric structures of affect, kinship, and identity. Such a methodological approach to Du Bois's literature both builds on and deviates from some of the prevailing critical discourse regarding

Du Bois that has emphasized his apparent investment in patriarchal and heteronormative values.[13]

I hasten to add, in this era of the #MeToo movement, which has further opened our eyes to the pervasiveness and perniciousness of the misogynistic abuse and patriarchal nepotism that continue to subjugate women everywhere, that my queer, antipatriarchal reading of Du Bois's rhetoric and poetics may strike some as counterintuitive in the face of the existing and variously credible accounts of his presumed extramarital dalliances and careless mistreatment of some of the young women who worked for and with him. See, for example, David Levering Lewis's biography of Du Bois in which he concludes, "Frequently enough, Du Bois overreached himself, abusing the trust of young women who placed themselves in his hands out of innocent admiration" (2000, 186). Investigating and commenting upon the truth and scope of such extramarital affairs and alleged instances of misconduct are beyond the purview of this book, although that work beckons to be undertaken with rigor and care. For now, I would simply caution against conflating the erroneous politics and/or egregious actions of any artist with the capacious reach and complex registers of their imagination, which often belie not only their entrenched beliefs but even their own interests.

As I go on to demonstrate and expound upon throughout this book, Du Bois's fiction reflects that he was both intrigued by the merits of cross-caste intimacy as a method of achieving Black integration and chastened by its limitations (and by those of romance broadly fashioned and understood). To the exigencies of assimilation, the persistence of caste-based systems of social organization, and the simultaneous lure and limitation of nationalism (both as discourse and practice), Du Bois responded with recurrent yet paradoxical figurations of cross-caste romance that offered by turns visions of nationalist and de-nationalist unification, eroticized and de-eroticized intimacy, and accommodating and resistant modes of Black subjectivity. Indeed, the evolution of Du Bois's poetics, alongside the evolution of his political praxis, reveal his increasing disenchantment with the US body politic and his increasing investment in engaging the politics of endogamy and probing the ethics of romance, which may prove queer in its capacity to uncover resistant, quixotic, and autoerotic modes of intimacy.

Chapter Summaries

In chapter 1, "A Hymn of Faith Is a Tale of Love: *Lohengrin* and Platonic Romance in Du Bois's 'Of the Coming of John,'" I examine the significance of how Du Bois's short story "Of the Coming of John," the thirteenth chapter of *The Souls of Black Folk*, retells the medieval folktale *Lohengrin* (as previously adapted by Wolfram von Eschenbach and Richard Wagner). Itself illustrative of a cross-caste (crossing culture, nation, and species) romance between a German maiden and a divine knight of the Holy Grail, *Lohengrin* was adapted by Du Bois in order to stage both inter- and intraracial iterations of romance that idealized yet scrutinized the capacity of love to facilitate personal and political liberation. Inverting the equation by which white persons would appropriate Blackness, Du Bois stages a figurative romance between John and the European aesthetic culture marked by the music of Wagner for which he has a passionate attachment. In so doing, Du Bois positions John as one who subversively appropriates white culture in the service of Black education and liberation. While *Lohengrin* highlights chiefly the inevitable failure of impossible love, "Of the Coming of John" mitigates love's impossibility by avowing its productivity even when curtailed, extracting it from a patently and narrowly erotic function and suggesting its maximum dissemination. Du Bois's story accomplishes this by revising a Platonic account of love that presents it as what must transcend the narrow configurations of one's beloved, family, or even community, extending, as *Symposium*'s Diotima decrees, across diverse bodies and domains. Subverting the reactionary racialism (read as the hierarchy imposed between "greater" and "lesser" others) challenged yet ultimately upheld by *Lohengrin*, "Of the Coming of John" proffers a syncretic, distributional form of love that would root justice in idealized, deeroticized, and egalitarian exchanges of intimacy across lines of difference.

In chapter 2, "The Queer Gift of Black Folk: Reading Double Consciousness in Du Bois's Detective Fiction," I argue that Du Bois's forgotten detective stories "The Case" and "The Shaven Lady" (both published in 1907 in *Horizon* magazine) deploy the trope of cross-caste romance in ways that queer the Black body by simultaneously eroticizing and deeroticizing it and by extension, deconstructing the way Black masculinity is routinely forced to signify. The stories feature a Black porter, initially cast in a putatively subservient and erotically charged relation to a white passenger, who is subsequently recast into the role of an amateur detective compelled to observe and implicitly critique white romantic intrigues and thus to instantiate himself as the primary viewer and arbiter of mainstream norms. Du Bois thus plies the condition of double consciousness, affectively registered and politically resistant, into an emphatic critique of white, hetero-patriarchal praxis. Yet in so doing, I argue, he does not undo his prior suggestion of the Black man's erotic desirability and vulnerability. Rather, Du Bois plies the homoeroticism he has ambivalently invoked in order to implicitly queer both Black and white subjectivities, deconstructing, in the process, the myths of masculinity, white supremacy, and epistemological certainty.

Chapter 3, "A Romance of Refusal: Failed Intimacy and Black Fugitivity in 'The Princess of the Hither Isles'" examines the intra- and intercultural iterations of cross-caste romance in a critically neglected story from Du Bois's 1920 interdisciplinary collection of memoir, fiction, and polemical essay, *Darkwater*: the allegorical neo-fairy tale "The Princess of the Hither Isles." Here, I analyze how Du Bois deploys the ultimately failed instantiation of cross-cultural exchange between a white-passing Black woman, a princess of her own subaltern isle and both a white, imperialist king who wishes to marry and rule her and a Black male beggar who is likely one of her kin, estranged from her by class and caste-based barriers. Idealizing yet undermining the possibility of interracial or cross-classed intimacy, "The Princess of the Hither Isles" equally troubles exogamy and endogamy as mechanisms for ensuring Black cultural survival, revealing the autoerotic quality of Black fugitivity, one that keeps the princess from entering into affective, erotic, and political relations of exchange. Moreover, the story marks Du Bois's foregrounding of the spatial quality of divisions of race, culture, and nation and in so doing, dramatizes cross-cultural intimacy as a matter of locational convergence and divergence. Considering Du Bois's deployment of the historical alongside the allegorical and folkloric, I explore Du Bois's presentation of the productive and queer implications of fugitivity for the Black subject.

Chapter 4, "Crossing Caste and Queering Kinship: Du Bois's Utopian Afro-Asiatic Romance," examines how cross-caste romance is marshaled in Du Bois's modernist novel *Dark Princess* to proffer a political alliance and historic kinship between persons of African and South Asian descent. I argue that *Dark Princess*, as an amalgam of literary realism and fantastical romanticism, reflects Du Bois's invocation and subversion of caste, which he analogizes to the US system of racialist and racist discrimination. By adapting aspects of Hindu eschatology and alluding to folkloric representations of cross-caste romances including the tales of "Cupid and Psyche" and "Radha and Krishna," Du Bois expands Black politics from a narrowly local to a capacious, global enterprise. I close the chapter by analyzing the way *Dark Princess* projects a version of romance that although seeming to recur to parochial gender politics, gestures nevertheless toward a queer temporality that resists notions of cultural hegemony and linear progress by imagining alternate histories of Afro-Asiatic kinship and decolonial revolution.

Finally, in my epilogue, "Strange Intimacies: On Exogamy and Endogamy in the Cross-Caste Romance," I compare and contrast two folktales that proffer respectively the rewards and risks of exogamous exchange and kinship: the well-known Greco-Roman tale "Cupid and Psyche" and the neglected Liberian tale "Princess Wata." I argue that Du Bois's repertoire of cross-caste romances falls somewhere in the middle of the spectrum of cross-cultural intimacy as bookended by "Cupid and Psyche" and "Princess Wata," ultimately moving from a resigned acceptance of Black assimilation into Euro-centered nations to an idealization of Black resistance to the demands of the racist, imperialist, and capitalist nation-state. I suggest therefore that the progression of Du Bois's literary texts reflects his increasing awareness of the perils of intimacy, especially initiated across lines of cultural distinction and differentials of power. Finally, I close by meditating on Saidiya Hartman's theorizing of love, defined within the context of transatlantic slavery, as a formulation and expression of intimacy inevitably tethered to violence and estrangement.

Chapter One

A Hymn of Faith Is a Tale of Love

Lohengrin *and Platonic Romance in Du Bois's "Of the Coming of John"*

> Du Bois was America's last romantic. And romantic love, in the tradition established by the troubadours, is always an impossible love.
>
> —K. Anthony Appiah, *Lines of Descent* (2014)

In a 1936 essay entitled "Opera and the Negro Problem," W. E. B. Du Bois proclaims that art—and in particular, opera—has a "vital connection" to the everyday struggles of African Americans. Du Bois was especially enamored of Wagner's 1851 opera *Lohengrin*, which he dubbed "a hymn of faith" whose message is that "somewhere in this world, and not beyond it, there is Trust, and somehow Trust leads to Joy." Commenting further about the centrality of trust and joy to the artist's process, Du Bois continues, "It is this theme that a great artist seeks to treat for the thought and enlightenment of mankind. He uses myth, he uses poetry, he uses sound and sight, music and color. . . . The result is beautiful, as in the bride-song" (130). Du Bois's invocation of the power of myth to create beauty highlights the fact that Wagner's opera is a retelling of a medieval folktale and hearkens back to Du Bois's own adaptation of *Lohengrin* over thirty years earlier: the penultimate chapter of *The Souls of Black Folk*, the folktale "Of the Coming of John."[1]

Summarily read as a story of failed "New Negro" development and alienated Black subjectivity, "Of the Coming of John" is fruitfully examined as a retelling of *Lohengrin*. It both reprises the opera's message about the fragile imbrication of faith, pleasure, and love in a world whose material demands seem incommensurate with those of a transcendent realm and alludes explicitly to the opera, as its protagonist John Jones, upon hearing the opera's prelude, has an epiphany about the untenable fact of Black disenfranchisement in a white supremacist society. Yet it is also fruitfully analyzed as a particular provocation to the medieval tale, since it recasts the original's opposition between mortal and immortal love as an opposition between human-centric love and the more abstract love of the beautiful that privileges universal goodness rather than the pleasure or favor of a chosen few. As I will demonstrate, Du Bois accomplishes this by significantly drawing out the aesthetical undertones of *Lohengrin*, imbuing his adaptation of it with his Neoplatonic and neo-Kantian belief in the ethical and epistemological benefits of beauty.

A brief summary of *Lohengrin* is in order. The story begins with the plight of Elsa, a young maiden in the embattled town of Brabant who prays for relief from the political machinations that have dispossessed her father and left her vulnerable to the sexual advances and false accusations of the villainous Count Telramund. As if in answer to her prayers, a knight in a boat steered by a swan appears and agrees to "save" her by marrying her, upon the condition that she never ask his place of origin, name, or ethnicity (*"woher ich kam der Fahrt,/ noch wie mein Nam' und Art?,"* quoted in Berman 1997, 129). Initially Elsa accepts both Lohengrin and his conditions, and she and her townspeople are grateful for their new leader. But Elsa's faith in Lohengrin cannot hold, and ultimately Telramund's wife, Ortrud, urges her to question her husband. She begs Lohengrin to tell her what she has been forbidden to know: his ethnic and national origins. He then reveals that he is a knight of the Holy Grail and now that his interdiction is broken, he must abandon her to return home. Offering some measure of compensation, Elsa's missing brother Gottfried (who had been presumed the victim of foul play) is brought back in a boat steered by a swan, which then carries Lohengrin away.[2]

Within ethno-musicological and Germanic studies *Lohengrin* has traditionally been characterized as a meditation on the impossibility of ideal, romantic love to remain unburdened by law or convention.[3] I submit that only by emphatically bringing the two principal strands of the opera together, the possibilities and limitations of universal love and the ideological pull of cultural identity, might one fully grasp both the complex legacy of *Lohengrin* and the richness of Du Bois's retelling of it. In this vein, it is crucial to acknowledge that Du Bois's engagement with *Lohengrin* proves especially appropriate since both the medieval tale and Du Bois's modernist story share a commitment to the same elements.[4]

It is also crucial to analyze how Du Bois departs from some of the messaging of *Lohengrin*, playing with its formal elements, shifting its political and philosophic contexts, and thereby mediating its presentation of impossible love. In this essay, I argue that Du Bois's "Of the Coming of John" alludes to and adapts *Lohengrin* in order to idealize yet scrutinize love's capacity to engender personal liberation as well as sociopolitical equity. Du Bois accomplishes this by framing the incommensurability of love through an avowal of its aesthetical epistemology, that is, through its capacity to discern value affectively and, often, in contrast to more conventional modes of intimacy. Extracting love from its humancentric and patently erotic dimensions, Du Bois offers instead a Neoplatonic vision of love as the desire to acquire and activate universal, ideal beauty, suggesting its maximally inclusive dissemination and avowing its propensity to engender goodness, despite chasms of cultural difference and errors of prejudice.

To this end, Du Bois also pushes against the very boundaries of caste that serve to undermine intimacy in *Lohengrin*, since the Neoplatonic account of beauty that he offers promotes the perception of a singular instance of beauty as a model with which to better perceive the subsequent, multiple instances of beauty that ensue it its wake, extending its range of regard horizontally until such time as it is maximally distributed and thus rendered universal.[5] Depicting the love of beauty as crossing ontological as well as cultural boundaries, Du Bois underscores the cosmopolitan tenor of Platonic thought and recasts the prototypical formulation of love as insular in favor of a more democratic form of *caritas*.

While *Lohengrin* highlights the inevitable failures of love and justice in the mortal world through the story of a failed marriage between a divine knight and a German maiden who must obey him, "Of the Coming of John" supplants the opera's failed conjugal union by staging two figurative romances. The first is the extracultural affair that a newly educated John has with the music of *Lohengrin*, an instance of European art that wholly transfigures him. The second is the intracultural bond that John shares with the Black community of his hometown, who suffer under the weight of Jim Crow racism. Both these romances not only exceed the parameters of a narrowly conceived love reducible to eros but also cross boundaries of caste difference: those seemingly immutable but actually ideological categories of race, culture, and social status that often dictate the trajectories of pleasure and intimacy. By deploying romance in its cross-caste version, Du Bois, a warrior for social justice with a lifetime commitment to intercultural solidarity and transcultural comparativism, subverts the reactionary traces of Wagner's adaptation of *Lohengrin*, emphatically proffering a diffuse form of love that, oriented toward universal beauty, might offer a persuasive form of social consensus and thus augur a more cosmopolitan world.[6] For, according to the pre- and early modern philosophic discourses of Plato, Kant, and Schiller that so influenced Du Bois, it is the imperative of beauty to transmute pleasure into universal virtue and goodness.[7] Du Bois's adaptation thus complicates the theme of love's impossibility by positing a philosophic account of love as something individual flights of (aesthetic) pleasure may engender while remaining attuned to the demands of communal welfare.

The Making of a "New Negro" Subject and the Boon of Aesthetic Pleasure

From the inaugural passage in "Of the Coming of John," the reader gets a sense of the foreboding that forecasts the story's grim end. The initial setting is Carlisle Street, located in the aptly named Johnstown, and Du Bois describes it as "glow[ing] like a dreamland," a fitting backdrop for the "passing forms of students in dark silhouette against the sky" who move *"like dim warning ghosts"* as they go to and from Wells Institute, a Black college located on a hill above a "white city below" ([1903] 2007, 154; emphasis mine). Then, in the subsequent passage, the story's omniscient voice broadens to include a second-person address as it introduces its embattled hero to potential interlocutors and shifts from a frame tale to an internal *récit*:

> And if you will notice, night after night, there is one dark form that ever hurries last and late toward the twinkling lights of Swain Hall,—for Jones is never on time. A long, straggling fellow he is, brown and hard-haired, who seems to be growing straight out of his clothes, and walks with a half-apologetic roll. He used perpetually to set the quiet dining-room into waves of merriment, as he stole to his place after the bell had tapped for prayers. (154)

In essence, Du Bois begins his story by establishing John Jones not as the hero of a chivalric romance but rather as the protagonist of a folktale, a "legend" in Du Bois's parlance, whose tragic story is recounted at some unspecified point in the future—presumably by a faculty member at John's former college, Wells Institute—to a group of students poised to benefit from its cautionary wisdom.[8]

Settling into the internal tale that relays John's experience from his own perspective, Du Bois depicts John as a struggling student whose initial resistance to education—characterized by his blithe spirit and perpetual tardiness—gives way to an impassioned embrace of intellectualism, as evident in the following passage:

> As the light dawned lingeringly on his new creations, he sat rapt and silent before the vision, or wandered alone over the green campus peering through and beyond the world of men into a world of thought. And the thoughts at times puzzled him sorely; he could not see just why the circle was not square, and carried it out fifty-six decimal places one midnight. . . . He caught terrible colds lying on his back in the meadows of nights, trying to think out the solar system; he had grave doubts as to the ethics of the Fall of Rome, and strongly suspected the Germans of being thieves and rascals, despite his text-books; he pondered long over every new Greek word. . . . So he thought and puzzled along for himself,—pausing perplexed where others skipped merrily. (Du Bois [1903] 2007, 156)

Punctuating his hero's upward mobility and developmental agility, Du Bois describes John's evolution "in body and soul," suggesting a mystical personification of the very wardrobe with which he frames himself: "His clothes seemed to grow and arrange themselves; coat sleeves got longer, cuffs appeared, and collars got less soiled" (156). Thus, the first level of John's cross-caste romance is initiated. As is the case with any romance, which requires a wholehearted embrace of a new person or entity to which one is attracted, John's experience with a Euro-inflected form of transnational education is transfiguring: it literally makes him a new person who requires a new frame.

Such transfiguring glee, however, does not bespeak a wholesale consummation of romance since, as it manifests further, it threatens to destabilize the precarious yet patently racist fabric of the American body politic as represented by John's hometown of Altamaha. Narratively haunted by the admonishment of the white townspeople who insinuate that John will be ruined by his novel acculturation (even as the Black townsfolk dream of the boon that will grace them when he returns), John is implicitly forbidden from acquiring the fullest liberal arts education that he would seek outside the narrow environs of his hometown (Judy 2015, 218). As much as any secret castle or Pandora's box, John's education is the object of an exclusionary prohibition chiefly because of the new status it will likely elicit for him.[9] Thus John's newfound commitment—not simply to a regime of self-transformation but to a process of evolution through which he might circumvent if not altogether eclipse the limitations of his ascribed (caste-based) status—attests to his will to flout the principles, de facto as well as de jure, of American segregation.

The white townspeople's outrage in the face of John's development continues to accrue as he moves from imagined to more material attempts to rend the gates of a Eurocentric society and become "a co-worker in the kingdom of culture," as Du Bois puts it in the opening chapter of *Souls*, "Of Our Spiritual Strivings" ([1903] 2007, 9). As Du Bois makes clear, acquiring virtual access to a wide spectrum of historically relevant and philosophically resonant ideas is one matter but seeking public access to the institutions that house them, especially when they are zealously guarded by such patriarchs of white supremacist nationalism as would presume to claim them, is quite another.

On Beauty and Duty: John's Love Affair with the Music and Magic of *Lohengrin*

John's desire for fuller participation in the echelons of a Euro-American culture that he has been forced to absorb, yet is forbidden to claim, is heightened when he enjoys a brief interlude between completing school and returning home to work on behalf of his community. While traveling as part of a musical quartet, John wanders one day into a theater in which *Lohengrin* is being staged. Upon viewing the grandeur of the space and the well-dressed operagoers around him, John is intrigued. But when he hears the music, he is profoundly moved:

> The delicate *beauty* of the hall, the faint perfume, the moving myriad of men, the rich clothing and low hum of talking seemed all a part of a world so different from his, so strangely more *beautiful* than anything he had known, that he [John] sat in a dreamland, and started when, after a hush, rose high and clear

the music of *Lohengrin*'s swan. The *infinite beauty* of the wail lingered and swept through every muscle of his frame, and put it all a-tune. (Du Bois [1903] 2007, 158; emphasis mine)

Awash in his aestheticized pleasure, intuiting the opera's themes of chivalric love and heroism, John exemplifies the German notion of understanding (*verstehen*), a kind of cognition that—as philosopher K. Anthony Appiah explains—is distinguished in German from the related notion of explanation (*erklären*), since it accounts not for the empirical existence of "nature" but rather for the complexity of "psychological experience" (2014, 78). *Verstehen* thus denotes the affective process by which one may absorb without precisely acquiring objective knowledge of persons or objects, drawing them firmly into one's subjective frame of reference and field of interest. Thus, although John is eventually expelled from the music hall for listening while Black, this does not mean that he leaves before he can apprehend the opera's unfolding messages of love, sacrifice, and failed transformation.[10] For, as Du Bois's depiction of John's aesthetic transport recalls the Enlightenment history of ideas that ascribes to aesthetic experience the capacity to draw out the moral undertones of reason, literal comprehension is rather beside the point.[11] John's grasp of the opera is therefore fuller than one might assume since it is premised upon an intuitive, aesthetical way of knowing that does not depend upon conceptual or narrative frameworks. As I will demonstrate, aesthetical pleasure inspires in John a desire to undertake a greater-than-aesthetic mission, exemplifying Du Bois's Neoplatonic and neo-Kantian commitment to the sociopolitical capability of the aesthetic.

In essence, the capacity of beauty to not only touch but also to transform John in body and soul corresponds to the Platonic link among abstract beauty, passionate sentiment, and ethical aspiration, a philosophic and somewhat mystical triad that Elaine Scarry (1999) records. For John's affective response to the music's "infinite beauty" accords with Scarry's ruminations about the Neoplatonic idea that beauty inspires the practice of "replication"—a process in which an observer of beauty resolves to mirror within what she has perceived without (1999, 9). As Scarry submits, the compulsion to proceed from passionately responding to a singular instance of beauty to enacting an ethic of care (read as love) is part of a Neoplatonic and neo-Kantian tradition that roots universal beneficence in the particularities of aesthetic experience: "Plato's requirement that we move from 'eros,' in which we are seized by the beauty of one person, to 'caritas,' in which our care is extended to all people, has parallels in many early aesthetic treatises" (81). It is a tradition with which Du Bois was familiar and upon which he inventively riffs.[12] Scarry explains further that the heightened perceptions of beauty and subsequent pangs of love that are awakened in human beings help to facilitate social justice by making us more perceptive, compelling us to heed the call of what lies outside ourselves and the familiar environs of our sovereign domains. Extrapolating from Plato's *Phaedrus*, Scarry offers the example of a man shivering with bliss in the presence of a beautiful boy with whom he begins to fall in love and thus about whom he begins to feel solicitous. Yet in her interdisciplinary approach to beauty, Scarry also acknowledges that its multiple modes need not confine themselves to the human form, nor simply elicit a patently romantic or erotic energy. For individual instances of beauty, whether discerned in a boy or a bird and whether pursued on foot or simply sketched in admiration, demand to be matched in kind—reproduced in the spirit and action of the ones under their spells—so that they might reach the level of abstract, ultimate Beauty (imbued with Goodness) to which they gesture.

Thus, by describing John's desire to ascend with the crescendo of musical phrases that enchant him, Du Bois anticipates Scarry's insistence that beauty predisposes us toward justice. He specifically recalls Platonic tradition by invoking Diotima's description in *Symposium* of love as a process by which one "goes upwards for the sake of . . . Beauty, starting out from beautiful things and using them like rising stairs" in order to attain the beauty of "customs" and, ultimately, knowledge of "just what it is to be beautiful" (Plato 1989, 59). Included in Diotima's list of what constitutes the beautiful are the beauty of poems, laws, deeds, and above all the wise and judicious "ordering of cities and households" needed to produce social equilibrium and "justice" (56), which suggests that the joy of aesthetic experience can inspire a sense of duty when it comes to civic organization and caretaking. I will come back to this point.

Returning to Du Bois's description of John's experience of aesthetic transport, I submit that John's feeling of being "all a-tune" is transformed into a deeper, more focused "longing" on his part to echo the beauty he hears, "ris[ing] with" it to reach a brighter, freer space in which he might circumvent the limits Jim Crow imposes. His bodily response to the music deepens, and John resolves further that he would no longer suffer to be "listless and idle" since he "felt with the music the movement of power within him" (Du Bois [1903] 2007, 158). The sounds of music, which John deems a "beautiful thing" in an aesthetic sense, incite him to produce something equally beautiful and correspondingly "good" in return, something that might effectively channel his energies without Euro-American racism undercutting them. In essence, John perceives in the beauty of Wagner's music a pleasurable way to make good on beauty's implicit promise to yield the good and the just (158). Du Bois's depiction of beauty as a catalyst for John's sociopolitical awakening recalls Kant's characterization of aesthetic judgment as what prepares man to bridge his sensory drives to the demands of social equanimity. Moreover, Du Bois's privileging of the aesthetic emphatically evokes the aesthetic philosophy of Friedrich Schiller, who saw in man's appreciation of beauty the possibility of both personal and communal forms of development that would mitigate the conflict between individual freedom and social harmony by offering an affective mode of achieving communal consensus without the political (and likely tyrannical) intervention of the state. As Schiller explained in his *Letters on the Aesthetic Education of Man,* the subject who is attuned to beauty possesses the capacity to "act in accordance with the moral rule and in accordance with [her own] sensuous needs" but without the exigencies of conceptual ratiocination or political coercion (quoted in Hohr 2010, 66).

If one considers John's moment of aesthetic transport in light of the theories of Plato, Schiller, and Scarry, it may appear as if John enjoys his aesthetic interlude at the expense of his homebound duties to his community, since he initially conceives of the choral tour that brings him to New York City as "a breath of air before the plunge" (Du Bois [1903] 2007, 157). In fact, the music inspires him to be of service to his community. Touched by the music that reverberates within his body and soul, John feels the "longing to rise" up and "out of the dirt and dust of that low life that held him prisoned and befouled" and, in echoing beauty's promise, to find "some master-work, some life-service" that would challenge but ennoble and not degrade him (158–59). Moreover, it is in the process of having his heart awakened by the aural beauty of the music he hears that John remembers the plight of the family he has left behind to suffer daily the weight of a system of racist segregation:

> When at last a soft sorrow crept across the violins, there came to [John] the vision of a far-off home,—the great eyes of his sister, and the dark drawn face of his mother. And his heart sank below the waters, even as the sea-sand sinks by the shores of Altamaha, only to be lifted aloft again with that last ethereal wail of the swan that quivered and faded into the sky. (159)

In this passage, "the waters" symbolize both the Georgian coast surrounding John's hometown of Altamaha and the sea into which Lohengrin disappears at the end of the opera, carried back to the land of the Holy Grail in a boat steered by a swan. Du Bois's figuration of these waters exemplifies his multiply figurative poetics, which often involve intercultural and intertextual crossing, as Christopher Powers (2015, 64) points out. Paradoxically registering John's movement away from (yet ultimately back to) Altamaha, the motif of the waters underscores that it is via and not despite the sounds and imaginative presence of *Lohengrin* that John remembers his own people and begins to craft his aspirational mission. John's desire to return to a stultifying environment tarnished by Jim Crow politics is not, then, a retreat from his newfound sense of freedom or pleasure. Rather, it is a burgeoning directive to bring about a world in which pleasure would ineluctably forecast freedom: not just for himself in rare and even stolen moments of interior delight but also for an extended community of others who are likewise in need of aestheticism's power to shift paradigms and instill beneficent energies. Like Lohengrin, John is called to care for something outside himself: his own family, of course, but ultimately, an aggregate of his ethnic compatriots. Emphasizing the comparative proclivity of his own imagination, Du Bois proffers the possibility of an affective connection that might cross if not entirely bridge the gap between different cultures.[13]

Unfortunately, John's rights to revel in aesthetic pleasure and to cull such pleasure to intervene in the world are considerably curtailed. For in the midst of aesthetic transport, his hands "grasping" the chair as if to contain his newfound passion, John Jones unwittingly touches the arm of a white woman seated next to him, thus eliciting the unfavorable attention of his white antagonist, John Henderson. A young man with whom our hero played as a child and now a willing instrument of anti-Black racism, John Henderson hastens to have his former playmate removed from the putatively white space of the theater. John Henderson's objection to the presence of his former playmate John Jones hinges upon the latter's proximity to a white woman who, by the logos of heteropatriarchal, anti-Black racism, is presumed to be the object of a Black man's sexual advances. Priscilla Wald reads John's expulsion from the music hall as his exclusion from a patriarchal economy undergirded by white supremacy—an incisive point that underscores the romantic subtext of this scene (1995, 180).

Yet John Henderson's objection to John Jones's presence and the expulsion of Jones from the theater that ensues from such prejudice are based on a fundamental misinterpretation of the orientation and quality of

John's desire. For what interests and moves him is not the physical body of a white woman but rather, in true Platonic fashion, the textual pleasure derived from the beauty of the opera, with its tender violins, invigorating horns, and intuited call to flout convention on behalf of the oppressed. While John's aesthetic pleasure is initially incited outside the bounds of what is culturally familiar to him, he subsequently mines it to edify the Black brethren whose survival he believes to be part and parcel of a progressive arc toward justice. In essence, Du Bois renders music as muse, underscoring John's desire to participate in an aesthetic economy through which beauty, as embodied in the texture of music, would yield both pleasure and protection. By doing so, Du Bois significantly revises the love story *Lohengrin* proffered, substituting for its conjugal and erotic iteration of romance a more capacious and infinitely dispersed iteration of romance marked by a Neoplatonic figuration of love whose maximally inclusive registers are subtly disposed. Recalling yet modifying Diotima's account of love in *Symposium*, through which one progresses from a visceral attachment to beautiful persons to an idealized attachment to abstract notions of beauty and truth, Du Bois's protagonist moves from discovering a passion for an abstract form of beauty to nursing a messianic love for a particular yet diffuse body of persons: the Black folk of Altamaha whose struggle for equality reflects the clarion call of global justice. "Here is my duty to Altamaha plain before me," declares John. "Perhaps they'll let me help settle the Negro problems there,—perhaps they won't. 'I will go in to the King, which is not according to the law; and if I perish, I perish'" (Du Bois [1903] 2007, 159). Here, Du Bois implicitly compares John to the biblical Queen Esther.[14] In doing so, he invokes another who, like Lohengrin, places conjugal love in the service of social justice, risking her life in the process. As I will later underscore, John's willingness to sacrifice himself evokes a Platonic conception of immortality derived from the memory of a virtue that persists in the wake of death.[15]

John's expulsion from the music hall cannot wholly undo his transformative experience with the music therein. Nor can it break the more impervious, virtual bond between a beauty that neither precedent nor politics presupposes and a love that is supreme yet earth- and duty-bound.[16] Far from a tragically assimilationist subject lured by a misbegotten affection for someone or something that does not honor him, John neither loses his self nor abandons his people in the wake of his aesthetic pleasure. Rather, the selective love John feels for an instance of beauty that derives from a culture outside his own inspires his project of love in the form of Black reclamation, chiefly because it induces in him the Neoplatonic insight that the pleasure of beauty might be catalyzed to promote justice. Thus, John extrapolates from his specific passion for a work of art to craft a love that manifests as solicitous guidance, which he tenders to a collective of Black people whose sociopolitical parity he deems central to the ongoing progression of American democracy. By relishing the opera, John not only crosses the boundaries of the caste position that constrains him but also subverts the very logic undergirding casteism.[17] Moreover, he transcends the material limits of ideal realms of reflection, pleasure, and edification, since he exhibits the same faith in the eventual benefits of his aesthetic education that is demanded in *Lohengrin* (a faith Elsa cannot sustain). Upon being ejected from the opera house, John does not relinquish his fight to access beauty but rather resolves to fight even harder for such beauty for himself and his people in Altamaha. As Du Bois (1936, 130) declares in his synthesis of *Lohengrin*'s moral, "Somewhere in this world, and not beyond it, there is Trust, and somehow Trust leads to Joy." This sentiment recalls his earlier apologia for beauty (Du Bois [1926] 2000, 19), in which he pronounced art as a helpmate in "the great fight" for civil rights and noted that although some may see "eternal and perfect Beauty" as dwelling "above Truth and Right," he believes beauty, truth, and "right" (or justice) to be "unseparated and inseparable" (19). For Du Bois and for his alter ego, John, such trust and the faith that sustains it are rooted in the philosophic understanding that "the apostle of Beauty . . . becomes the apostle of Truth and Right not by choice but by inner and outer compulsion" (22), evidence of a secular mandate the zeitgeist has ordained.

Plato's forms paradigm foregrounds the capacity to progress from a localized passion to a diffuse, broadly distributed regard. As I earlier explained, Diotima's speech describes the movement from loving viscerally to loving ideally the various formations of beauty; it traces a shift from a micro- to a meta-appreciation of Beauty—now capitalized in its highest instantiation as immanent wisdom and perpetual solicitude. Thus, Du Bois's adaptation of Plato's continuum perfectly expresses Diotima's decree that in order to achieve true love, one must begin from a circumscribed iteration of beauty and move outward and upward to embrace the infinite sense of "Beauty" in its most inclusive state.

Yet in another contradictory sense, Du Bois appears to invert the Platonic formula, extending it to more radical conclusions as his hero John moves from appreciating the abstract beauty of a purely aesthetic form to proffering the beauty (and promoting the welfare) of a collective of living beings. Put differently, John does not ascend from a beautiful human form to reach the abstraction of true Beauty; rather, he ascends from his momentary vantage point atop a beautiful object to an even higher state of being from which he can oversee the protection of a number of human forms, the Black folk of Altamaha, whom he views not as a means to "Beauty" but as part and parcel of its ultimate end. Yet, in Plato's estimation, love is not primarily oriented toward any particular form or body. Rather, as Alexander Nehamas incisively observes, "All love—whether we know it or not—is directed at the very nature of Beauty (Plato 1989, xxii). Nehamas also explains, extrapolating from Gregory Vlastos, that "Plato considers the love of individuals inferior to the love of abstract programs or theories and their love, in turn, inferior to the love of beauty itself" (2007, 2). Vlastos reminds us that although persons with beautiful bodies may indeed inspire love, so too might "impersonal objects," including "literary compositions," "social or political programs," and even "the Idea of Beauty itself"; such objects, Vlastos insists, "are not only as good as persons, but distinctly better" (quoted in Nehamas 2007, 2). Synthesizing Nehamas and Vlastos, I submit that Du Bois's positioning of John on a higher step of the ladder of love, one already beyond the limitations of the human form, actually extends what is implicit in Plato's philosophy to its more emphatic conclusions. Du Bois thus reprises and revises Diotima's equation by which the pleasure of beauty yields beneficence without requiring that the particular instance of beauty from which caritas emerges ever be embodied in human form.

Although John is moved by an instance of beauty that proves irreducible to the particular dimensions of the human body, he deduces nonetheless that the universal beneficence to which all individual instances of beauty (such as music) are oriented would be aptly met by furnishing equality to Black people, special exemplars of humanity. Eric King Watts has observed that Du Bois explicitly politicized the Platonic notion of beauty. He argues that Du Bois's 1926 essay "Criteria of Negro Art" "appropriates Platonic idealism and constitutes a pious trinity made up of the life struggles of black folk (Truth), artistic expression (Beauty), and social justice (Goodness)" (Watts 2001, 196). This trinity registers a philosophic characterization of beauty as truth and in turn, of truth as ultimately redeemed by goodness that is Platonic, neo-Kantian, post-Enlightenment and otherwise resonant within a long, Western (although not exclusively so) history of ideas regarding the connections among beauty, truth, and virtue. By this logic, the trials of Black folk everywhere would constitute not simply a regrettable truth but more profoundly, insofar as they result from racist discrimination, the sign of a tear in the very fabric of goodness that true beauty embodies. Clearly,

Du Bois had begun his practice of politicizing beauty and art with the publication of *Souls* over a decade before his 1936 article addressing opera.

And yet, the particular way that John offers his Black community love seems to challenge the very parameters by which his brethren understand themselves as an ethnically distinct community. His love aims at helping them acquire social parity—it manifests chiefly as a practice of socioethical leadership, not political governance per se. In this way, John signals Du Bois's understanding that embedded within Plato's account of beauty is the notion that beauty's goal of forging universal solicitude is best manifested not by interacting chiefly with those entities or persons with whom one is closely affiliated but rather by drawing out love's propensity to be maximally inclusive. Thus, in riffing on Plato, Du Bois carries his ideas to their more emphatic conclusions, privileging an overarching form of love that need neither begin nor end in discrete attachments to beautiful persons. For John will endeavor to care for his community not in a manner that depends upon his prior or cultural relation to them but rather in a manner befitting a global, Levinasian duty to the other.[18]

Because John has been separated from the Black folk of Altamaha by differences of education, regional experience, and implicitly class (all aspects of caste), he has become to them what Farah Griffin (1995, 8) would term an "ancestor stranger," familiar to them on the basis of their shared history yet foreign to them in the guise of his current persona and views.[19] His efforts to love his people across chasms that divide and alienate them from one another affirm love as a transformation and not just an extension of self. They also underscore the potential for Platonic love to be distributional and to bespeak not just a vertical movement up to a transcendent realm of ideal Beauty but also a horizontal movement across discrete bodies, entities, and even moments in time that exist beyond the habitual or proximate range of any individual's frame of reference or existence. As Diotima advises in *Symposium*, a judicious lover "should love one body and beget beautiful ideas there; then he should realize that the beauty of any one body is brother to the beauty of any other and that if he is to pursue beauty of form, he'd be very foolish not to think that the beauty of all bodies is one and the same." As I have argued previously, Du Bois's instantiation of Platonic thought implies that such an egalitarian framework of love might be so fully expanded as to include not only loving bodies as bodies per se (that is, through eros) but also loving human souls or even humanistic endeavors—thus bypassing humancentric love altogether (Plato 1989, 57–58).

Politically oppressed by the racist apparatus of Jim Crow ideology, vulnerable, and in need of the capacious arm of justice, the Black folk of Altamaha compel John to cross back over to them, for he no longer shares their caste affiliation due to his absence and ensuing novel experiences of education and travel. As Plato intimates and Du Bois emphatically affirms, love is inevitably a crossing from self to other, and learning to appreciate an example of beauty (implicitly, an indicator of value) outside one's own culture may indeed help prepare one for the multiple crossings—from here to there, inside to outside, familiar to unknown—necessary to ensure inclusive solicitude and global justice. This transversal love, if taken to its emphatic conclusions, might project a sentimental affect sustainable even among those who differ in background, temperament, or ideological viewpoint. It would thus "ratchet down" the complex requirements for political consensus that Martha Nussbaum (2013, 382) imagines a pluralistic democracy to impose. In essence, as Du Bois's story suggests, loving and caring widely across putative barriers of difference are necessary to ensure well-being for all who dwell in a pluralist society.

The Return of the Prodigal Son and the Aesthetic Alternative to Conventional Intimacy

However, this Neoplatonic form of love, provoked by pathos, grounded in ethos, and oriented toward a munificent end that surpasses the quotidian interests of those persons to whom it is tendered, can be rather abstruse in quality and thus difficult to receive. Although the members of John's community have eagerly awaited his return, when he finally appears, they do not recognize the carefree youth they once knew in the somber man they now perceive: "The people were distinctly bewildered. This silent, cold man,—was this John? Where was his smile and hearty hand-grasp? 'Peared kind o' down in the mouf,' said the Methodist preacher thoughtfully. 'Seemed monstus stuck up,' complained a Baptist sister" (Du Bois [1903] 2007, 160). The gap between John and his community only widens at the welcome party they throw for him, where "[r]ain spoil[s] the barbecue, and thunder turn[s] the milk in the ice-cream," foreshadowing a more profound failure to come: John's alienation of the very community he has come to assist (160). Initially, John's people are alienated from him due to his purportedly strange mien. Then such alienation heightens when John speaks out against religious factionalism, calling instead for a secular form of political idealism that might accord with the insights of a more modern world—"with broader ideas of human brotherhood and destiny." "What difference does it make," opines John, "whether a man be baptized in a river or wash-bowl, or not at all? Let's leave all that littleness, and look higher." At these words, which bear traces of divine value yet seem to disparage the particular rituals of religious experience, John's community grows silent and further bewildered: "Little had they understood of what he said, for he spoke an unknown tongue" (161). The phraseology of this passage suggests that problems of communication and interpretation have curtailed John's attempt to lead his community, as critics have noted.[20] For the community is loath to endorse a program of liberation seemingly at odds with the semantic and ideological structuring of their lives.[21] Yet, I submit that, as a reflection of his drive to help shepherd a universal justice, John's critical style of leadership is not so much a commentary on the people he would assist as it is on the boundaries of the unequal society to which they have seemingly resigned themselves. Oriented toward a higher realm of being that recalls John's watershed desire to ascend with the rising music above the limits of a racist society, John's admonishment of religious division and parallel call to embolden such ideals as "human brotherhood and destiny," gesture toward a measure of value that exceeds what could be contained within any specific brand of religion and indeed within any particular, essentialist cultural practice (161).

Nevertheless, John's message also flies in the face of accommodation to the political hegemony of Jim Crow rule. In this vein, it is important to note that John's leadership praxis is not simply negative but additive, as it offers his community viable alternatives to their habitual ways of living, some that are germane to the rhetoric of African American politics in the postbellum era. After speaking more broadly of "brotherhood and destiny," John offers compelling ideas with which to shift the ethos of his community including "the rise of charity and popular education" and "the spread of wealth and work" (Du Bois [1903] 2007, 161). Although admittedly drawn "in vague outline" (161), John's advice constitutes a practical program of industrial education, community organization, and fiduciary conservation that—with the Booker T. Washingtonian echoes that Robert Gooding-Williams (2009, 119) also perceives—recalls and expands much of the community's earlier wishes for what John's return might bring them: "Then what parties were to be, and what speakings in the churches; what new furniture in the front room . . . and there would be a new schoolhouse with John as teacher; and then perhaps a big wedding; all this and more—when John comes" (Du Bois [1903] 2007, 154). In fact, even though John's speech criticizes the community's investment in the hierarchies of organized religion and champions a universal humanism that, in its loftiness, may puzzle them, it also incorporates some key traditions and social structures that John's community values.[22] Nevertheless, even though John's leadership rhetoric evokes equally the familiar principles of personal development (evocative of yet not limited to "uplift") and collective work, his dreams exceed those his community voices, not just in the audacity of their reach but also in the remoteness of their offering. For, as the community's speculations about John during his absence reveal, they had hoped not simply for a capable leader but also for an intimate bedfellow with whom they might renew former bonds of kinship (those lost in the course of John's educational sojourn in the north) and forge new and improved bonds of material and social prosperity. To the Black community of Altamaha, the proper objects of love are not abstract thoughts or lofty ideals but rather the concrete scaffolding of community and family.[23] Had John positioned himself as a brother, he might have appealed to his community's sense of filial loyalty and solidarity, recurring to a common judgment and parlance. Alternatively, had John offered himself as a conjugal lover, akin to his implicit alter ego Lohengrin, he might have appealed to at least one community member's romantic desires, or even, less desirably, relied on the authoritarian command of patriarchal submission (both to the heteronormative conjugal unit and to the attendant call of procreation). By foregrounding the Black community's desire for a grand wedding, Du Bois not only underscores their rather parochial vision of successful postbellum participation in the American body politic but also intimates that had John followed Lohengrin's precise path, he might have been able to reach his community of proto-strangers by taking one of their own as his wife and, accordingly, by persuading her of his honor through the mechanisms of passionate love and/or conjugal devotion.[24]

Yet "Of the Coming of John" significantly revises *Lohengrin,* as it problematizes the potential for erotic, conjugal, or even filial love to be liberating if tied to a rigid structure like marriage or traditional kinship. Refusing to position John as either a brother or a lover, Du Bois rather presents him as a Neoplatonic philosopher whose love is an undifferentiated paean to beauty and justice and thus is offered not just to a select one or few but to an overarching humankind poised to benefit from it. Exempt from the parochial expectations of fraternity and the narrowly erotic and potentially autocratic imposition of conjugal intimacy, John is thereby freed from adopting an identity politics too easily rendered essentialist, insular, or antiprogressive in quality. Yet he is hard-pressed to find a mode of persuasion that, in substituting for conventional or familiar forms of intimacy, would mediate nevertheless the differences that threaten to estrange him from those on whose behalf he labors. While John was sufficiently persuaded by the beauty of the music he heard and the unexpected joy it evoked within him, the community is not afforded a more sensual means with which to place their faith in John. As such, the nexus of joy and faith that Sieglinde Lemke (2008, 39) identifies as the central site of tension in *Lohengrin* is strained to the point of dissolution.[25]

In sum, I contend that Du Bois's retelling of *Lohengrin*, and in particular, his theoretical framework of liberating, globally distributional love are both deliberately unhinged from the erotic (or erotic-as-conjugal) imperative, since Du Bois recasts the Platonic account of love into one even more diffusely aimed at global solicitude. For the erotic—whether by its exigent intensity (in hetero- or homoerotic configurations) or its utility, as a means to the end of procreation—risks being too insular to be maximally disseminated.[26] In the absence of the parochial familiarity of fraternity, the conventional appeal of marriage, or the evolutionary pull of procreation, how best to bequeath one's legacy of converting the fuel of eros's pleasurable delirium into the bounty of *caritas*? Put differently, how might John have effectively persuaded others to join him in resisting the status quo? This was a tall order given the entrenched nature of social institutions and the community's justifiable fear of racist recrimination.

Certainly, John might have found another way to communicate with his people, perhaps one that drew on the translatable yet antidiscursive capability of aesthetic transport, the mode that had so inspired his own growth and action. He could have deployed music, an artistic form well rooted in African American history, which he, as a member of a vocal quartet, could even have performed himself.[27] Alternately, he might have mirrored Du Bois's own declarations about art and beauty in "Criteria of Negro Art," in which he advised that it was the "bounden duty of black America to begin this great work of the creation of Beauty, of the preservation of Beauty, of the realization of Beauty" ([1926] 2000, 22). Yet in this story, the answer to the question of how best to tender one's righteous love lies in the peculiar capabilities of pedagogy, an instrument for begetting beauty in Plato's philosophy and a method of personal and sociopolitical edification in Schiller's theory of aesthetic education. And in many of Du Bois's nonfictional and fictional works pedagogy is a mode of intersubjective leadership through which one guides others toward ideal practices of being and doing, prodding them to make intellectual and not simply spiritual leaps of faith. The benefits of pedagogy are well disposed in Plato's discourses about love, where they are broached through the tradition of pederasty, a homoerotic relation involving parties of unequal status through which erotic love and knowledge are simultaneously exchanged. I pointed out earlier the deficits of autocratic love. Pederasty is at once centralized and problematized in *Phaedrus* (Plato 1995, xvi, 7–8) and (implicitly) subtly idealized by Diotima in *Symposium* (Plato 1989, 56–57) as one example of how a soul replete with latent beauty and wisdom might seek out another with whom to reproduce "beautiful deeds." Evoking the complex, controversial practice of pederasty historic to Platonic thought yet disentangling it from his favored praxis of pedagogy, Du Bois depicts John's pedagogical approach as maximally inclusive in scope, as it moves beyond binary or otherwise narrow limits of erotic or patently romantic intimacy to encompass a true humanism that is, nevertheless, politicized in its expression.

Having heightened the stakes while limiting the reach of John's Neoplatonic project of salvific love, Du Bois offers some measure of compensation for his hero's seemingly forestalled leadership, as he casts John not as some elitist philosopher-king but rather as a philosopher-teacher whose discourse, which is full of virtue and wisdom in the Diotimean sense, is put to the politically resonant task of forging a pro-Black resistance movement (a prerequisite for global, transcultural, democratic pluralism). Nowhere is this more evident than in John's decision to flout the submissive imperative of Jim Crow rule by instructing his students about the merits of the French Revolution, a historic event meant to point the way toward an alternative, radical political program for the Black people of Altamaha (Du Bois [1903] 2007, 163).[28] While the elder community's appreciation of John is uneven, since in the narrative voice's assessment they are "rent into factions for and against him," many of his students work admirably if ploddingly to learn from their teacher-leader, who takes pleasure and pride in "the little comforting progress" they make (164). Having learned to love beauty in the particular form of music and having fallen appropriately under the spell of a love that presupposes the possibility of universal justice, John now seeks to amplify the beauty within his Black students, casting them collectively as his platonic beloveds and attempting to create with them a type of figurative creation that, distinct from biological reproduction, would engender symbolic if not actual immortality, not simply for himself or even for them but for future generations of Black people writ large.[29]

The possibility of an immortality that might ameliorate the experience of Black life as well as forestall (even if only symbolically) the threat of death to which Black folk are especially vulnerable under the rule of white supremacy comes to its climax when John is abruptly fired from his position for teaching his students the merits of the French Revolution and thus for being presumed "a dangerous nigger" (Du Bois [1903] 2007, 163). Although John is chastened and hamstrung by the lack of support from some of his compatriots, it is worth remarking that the emphatic tragedy of his story is caused not by any ambivalence about his particular method of leadership but by the annihilative violence of the white supremacists who police Altamaha. His civic mission thwarted, walking pensively along the sea, John comes suddenly upon his sister Jennie being assaulted by his white namesake, John Henderson. After killing the attacker in a protective and sacrificial gesture, John resigns himself to his impending murder by a charging lynch mob. As he waits to die, John is haunted by the aural memory of *Lohengrin*: "With an effort he roused himself, bent forward, and looked steadily down the pathway, softly humming the 'Song of the Bride'" (165–66). This moment underscores the limitations of cross-caste love even while it reanimates its implicit promise to break down metaphysical as well as geopolitical borders.[30]

Yet the story does not entirely end at this moment—nor does it culminate wholly in loss. For, when John is murdered, he becomes most recognizable as a symbol for the cause of Black liberation. This is illustrated by John's speculation about the impact his story, or "legend" as it is called, will have on those readers (or listeners) who will later learn of his fate: his former teachers and in particular, their students, who will constitute the next generation of Black life.[31]

The indefatigable presence of John is also underscored by the fact that his self-referential allusion to his life's narration seems to have been borne out by the second passage of Du Bois's story, which inaugurates the frame tale through which John's story unfolds. As I earlier outlined, the frame tale's narrative voice recounts a story that has taken place in the past, one that the reader now understands to be the instructive illustration of John's tragic fall. Yet, just before the narrator begins the story, which s/he relates in the past tense ("He came to us from Altamaha, away down there beneath the gnarled oaks of Southeastern Georgia"), s/he curiously refers to John in the present tense ("And if you will notice, night after night, there is one dark form that ever hurries last and late toward the twinkling lights of Swain Hall,—for Jones is never on time" (Du Bois [1903] 2007,

154). After this present-tense allusion to John, the entire story, even those scenes whose specific details would likely have remained unknown by the narrator, is told in the past tense. The question arises as to what this tense shift signifies. Is the storyteller simply being evocative, trying to bring John vividly back to life? A clue to the puzzle of the shifting tense may be found in the story's opening passage, described earlier. The "dim warning ghosts" the narrator mentions suggest the social death of those who have little interaction with "the white city" from which they are mostly excluded (153). Surely, it is not too great a move from imagining a group of ghostly students to imagining a former student who may be an actual ghost, one who continues to haunt the place where he had truly begun to evolve, "ever hurry[ing]," "straggling," bursting out of his garments, and moving always out of time (154). Here, Du Bois plies the conventions of what is now identified as Afro-futurism, casting John as a ghostly presence whose death need not mean his expulsion from the future.[32] In the final analysis, John has lost neither his mission nor his life in vain, for his story "linger[s]" on (as perhaps he also does, if only in chimerical form) (155). John's circular movement back to the community of Black scholars and teachers who once nurtured him and who continue to nurture those who may benefit from the instructive speculation inherent to his story meets equally the didactic and sentimental imperatives of the folktale. A thing of beauty himself, John is now the object of posthumous, redemptive recognition. In death, he joins legions of those annihilated through racist acts of violence and is thereby forever wed to an ancestral line of Black folk, including even those who would misunderstand or doubt him. He is theirs now, and they—whether descended from Johnstown, Altamaha, or as yet untold geopolitical locales—may claim him in story and song.

Chapter Two

The Queer Gift of Black Folk

*Reading Double Consciousness in
Du Bois's Detective Fiction*

As I argue in my introduction, the foreclosure of the potential cross-caste romance between Du Bois and the young white girl of his memory plays a key role in the account of double consciousness that Du Bois offers in *Souls* as well as in his implicit program for multicultural nationalist reform. Recall my explication of how the failed cross-caste romance between Du Bois and his young white classmate both precipitates the instantiation of his doubled consciousness and provides a model by which the Black subject might mine such division to fashion a viable—albeit contested—form of assimilation into the American body politic. As I have detailed, Du Bois countermands the failure of the literal, interracial romance between himself and his young white classmate by projecting a second, figurative version of romance in its wake: the auspicious union of the American nation with the collective of its Black inhabitants, who are, in Du Bois's estimation, poised to redress the sins of Euro-American hegemony (e.g., capitalism, imperialism, and other forms of cruelty and injustice). Speaking in idealistic terms that proffer the merits of equal exchange and evoke implicitly the rhetoric of conjugal partnership, Du Bois sketches in *Souls* a scenario by which Black men in particular might make gifts of their culture to a putatively white America, edifying it with their spirituality, morality, and bountiful humanity ([1903] 2007, 13–14). In so doing, as I have argued, Du Bois displaces a heterosexual mode of romantic nationalism with a queer iteration of romantic nationalism, which might be consummated, not through idealizing the cross-raced couple but through foregrounding America's collective, national praxis of annexing its Black male inhabitants, whom it had formerly consigned to the margins of the nation. This queer iteration of romantic, cross-cultural (and cross-caste) intimacy is reprised in Du Bois's detective fiction from *Horizon* magazine (the precursor to *The Crisis*), as I will go on to analyze.

From Du Bois's romantic configuration in *Souls* of an ideal postbellum relation between white persons and Black persons in which the latter would edify and remediate the former—largely via appropriation—a complex account of Black subjectivity emerges. On the one hand, Du Bois carves out a singular space for Black persons, who must somehow accommodate themselves to Euro-American culture by paradoxically retaining (yet still sharing) their distinct cultural legacies. On the other hand, Du Bois allots to Black persons and Black folkways a subordinate function in which they might consent to being appropriated rather than disregarded, nullified as sources of value, and excluded from shaping or otherwise contributing to the fabric of public life. Thus, Du Bois proffers Black desirability alongside Black agency, paradoxically offering Blacks a method of assimilating into a putatively Euro-American-dominated nation that is nevertheless presupposed by navigating vexing modes of subordination and appropriation—a fact about which Du Bois's narrative evinces marked ambivalence. However, an apparent capitulation to white dominance may constitute, as Darieck Scott persuasively argues, a passively aggressive and indeed "queer" form of agency, which he describes as converting the offal of abjection into additive fuel and which thereby "endow[s]" the Black subject with a form of "counter intuitive power" (2010, 7–9). As I go on to argue, Du Bois's poetics of intercultural relations, which paradoxically advocate both assimilation and antiassimilation—and thus both dialogic exchange and autonomous resistance—are *queer*, both as they underscore (partly, to circumvent) the historically eroticized underpinnings of miscegenation and as they upend normative and hegemonic constructions of culture, nation, and subjectivity writ large.[1]

In "The Case" and "The Shaven Lady," both published in *Horizon* magazine in 1907 and both largely forgotten and neglected by critics, Du Bois reprises and extends his account of double consciousness as resulting from and reenacting a vexed form of intercultural romance.[2] I argue that the *queer* terms by which Du Bois offers a program of nonderogatory Black assimilation in *Souls*, those enabled by a mode of interracial cooperation in which the gifts of Black men are absorbed by an American body politic, are reanimated and contested in "The Case" and "The Shaven Lady." Thus, recovering and analyzing these neglected stories prove valuable exercises, not only in and of themselves but also for what they reveal regarding the queer nodes of intimacy that undergird Du Bois's poetic account of double consciousness. For, through the lens of Du Bois's fiction, his most important theoretical concept may be fruitfully interpreted to novel ends.

I thus analyze how the queer mode of Black assimilation (as antiassimilation) into white society that Du Bois animates yet contests in *Souls* is reprised and further rebutted in "The Case" and "The Shaven Lady," in which he restages the cross-caste romance between himself and a young white girl in the form of a homoerotic, homosocial exchange between a Black porter and a white passenger who desires both intimacy and information. As Du Bois does in "Of Our Spiritual Strivings," in both "The Case" and "The Shaven Lady," he frames the drama of double consciousness in terms that highlight the Black man's disputed value and rebut white projections of disparaged Black subjectivity. Again, he suggests that while Black men are sufficiently skilled to be equal participants in society, they—and by extension, all Black persons—are also sufficiently desirable and valuable to be embraced as correctives to Eurocentric values.

I argue that with his forays into detective fiction, Du Bois explicitly expands the framework of romance to include not simply the heteronormative relation between a Black man and a white woman that he seems to idealize in his anecdote of childhood rejection but also the homoerotic and homosocial relation that might occur between Black and white men. Thus, Du Bois even more emphatically adumbrates the queer nodes of interracial, nationalist exchange that he began to broach in "Of Our Spiritual Strivings." Deploying an explicitly homoerotic economy in "The Case" and "The Shaven Lady," Du Bois suggests both that white dominance may be undermined by white male expressions of desire for Black men and that Black masculinity may be incited, attenuated, or otherwise transmuted, insofar as Black subjectivity proves a desirable object of white consumption. Yet Du Bois's detective stories also undermine the practice of consuming Black subjectivity as a basis for reforming the nation by offering a Black porter and amateur detective who refuses the desires of a white passenger and chooses instead to enact what Fred Moten describes as the phenomenon by which a person rendered a commodity "speaks back" (Moten 2003, "Resistance of the Object: Aunt Hester's Scream") signaling a "fugitive" form of Black subjectivity that is unproductive, "disruptive," and resistant to wholesale assimilation (Moten 2018, 34).

As I outlined in my introductory chapter, Du Bois's declaration of the important contribution of the "submissive man" (as opposed to the "strong" one) anticipates his later characterization in *The Souls of Black Folk* of the Black man as uniquely poised to redeem the health of the American body politic (broken by its sins of slavery and capitalism). For in the notion of submission one finds both an effeminate and a queer alternative to the conquering predilection of conventional Eurocentric masculinity. For Du Bois, then, the feminization of the Black man is not just a historical necessity, as acknowledged by Spillers in her theory of the "mother within" all Black subjects who are wedded to their status as Black persons through their mother's position as an enslaved woman but also an ethical posture to be adapted—yet not without ambivalence.[3] By suggesting an alternative cross-caste romance to the heterosexual, interpersonal romance betokened by the failed interracial courtship of his youth, substituting for the image of a lone, desiring Black man one of a desirable body of "faithful" and "reverent" Black men, Du Bois queers the Black man and by extension, the Black subject, whom he places in the homoerotic position of being betrothed to a white America in need of the remediating influences of good "faith" and goodwill. As such, I contend that Du Bois shifts, not only from an interpersonal to a polymorphous iteration of cross-caste romance but also, in so doing, from a heteronormative to a queer method of interracial collaboration. In "The Shaven Lady," in particular, Du Bois also queers his account of white masculinity. For Black men, a queer posture seems a necessary form of survival and accommodation, but for white men, it may paradoxically mark either a dishonorable form of aggression or, alternately, a viable method of deconstructing hegemonic trajectories of power.

Yet, as I will go on to show, Du Bois's detective fiction is especially attuned to the limitations of Black assimilation-as-submission that are broached in *Souls*. For as he intimates in "The Case" and "The Shaven Lady," such subversive and putatively progressive interracial exchange is haunted nevertheless by the perpetual specters of white malfeasance and Black resistance. Thus, while the detective stories showcase the desirability and value of the Black (male) subject, they also question the wisdom of fostering such use value or exchange value by wielding the fugitive resistance of a Black porter who prefers to remain remote from white folk and their machinations rather than to be conscripted into their unequal economies of desire and exchange.

Quashing the Cross-Caste Romance: "The Case" as Itinerant Black Resistance

As critics have largely neglected "The Case," a brief summary of it is in order. It begins as a frame tale in which an unnamed white passenger relays how he once persuaded an unnamed Black porter to beguile him with a story about a train wreck involving a beautiful, sad, and mysterious young woman. After evoking the porter's sympathy and soliciting his aid in safeguarding an equally mysterious briefcase, the young woman is killed when the train derails, leaving the Black porter and the white passenger (and narrator of the external tale) uninformed about the details and significance of her story ([1907a] 1995, 109–13). In "The Case," Du Bois reanimates his prior queer figuration of the Black man as one who is faithfully betrothed to white America in *Souls* by emphatically depicting Black desirability in an explicitly homoerotic exchange—ultimately foreclosed—between a Black porter and a white passenger. Here, the cross-caste romance established in the narrative of the visiting card recurs but with a marked difference. In contrast to the young white girl who rejects Du Bois as a romantic partner, the white male passenger takes an active homoerotic interest in the Black porter, which the porter subsequently rejects. Du Bois thus redresses his own prior repudiation, by which not only Black male agency (manifest as subjectivity) but also Black desirability (manifest as objecthood) were denied, by deploying narrative strategies that complicate romance, both as a method with which to redeem dishonored subjectivity and as an opportunity to restage racist patterns of interracial desire.

The figure of the white girl from Du Bois's story of the visiting card is retained in the figure of a young white woman who, as the potential subject of a criminal act, enacts the detective story's famed role of the femme fatale. Her "minor" relationship to the porter is ultimately deeroticized in favor of a tenuous alliance that depends upon the woman's enlisting the porter as a consort and confidant.[4] Through this triangular configuration of the Black porter, the white male passenger, and the white female femme fatale, Du Bois asserts the indisputable desirability of Black men. However, Du Bois also evades both the taboo and the risks of interracial romance and sex by depicting the porter's refusal of white interest and intimacy. The porter's refusal of white intimacy and his concomitant critique of "the ways of white folk" suggest that being desired by the very white persons who may bar one from full citizenship, whether a genial, bourgeois white man whose interest might augur successful assimilation or a vulnerable young white woman who may prove either victim or vamp, is nevertheless haunted by the specters of white deviance and even violence.

I turn now to analyze the significance of Du Bois's reprise of "The Tale of the Visiting Card" in "The Case" and in particular, to examine how "The Case" evokes double consciousness in order to counter the myth that the Black man is neither suitably masculine nor sufficiently desirable. By placing his protagonist in the role of an amateur detective, Du Bois sets up the Black man as the primary viewer and arbiter of white folk, even while he positions him as an object of desire—this time not to the lost white woman of his youth but rather to a white man whose claim to unchecked power is thereby mitigated by his own taboo desire.[5] I submit that Du Bois's neglected detective tale reprises the trope of cross-caste romance in order to simultaneously eroticize and deeroticize the Black body, which is configured as romantically desirable in the queerest of terms, marking a desire that transcends the putative borders of masculinity, highlights the homoerotic economy of Eurocentric hetero-patriarchy, and refuses the boundaries of heteronormative, interracial reproduction. Du Bois thus queers his account of white masculinity as well, showing it to be premised upon a sexual and social economy that is neither heteronormative nor undergirded by racial purity. He thereby extends the theory of double consciousness into a critique of white, hetero-patriarchal practice.

In a 1926 issue of *The Crisis*, dedicated to exploring and improving African American representation in literature, Charles Chesnutt declared: "A Pullman porter who performs wonderful feats in the detection of crime has great possibilities" (1996, 52). Stephen Soitos suggests that Chesnutt was likely alluding to a working-class detective persona that had already been utilized by early exemplars of African American detective fiction such as Pauline Hopkins and J. E. Bruce (244). Yet I submit that Chesnutt was more specifically referring to his friend and colleague Du Bois, who had by that time published not only two detective stories in *Horizon* in 1907 but also a story in a 1920 issue of *The Crisis*, "Murder on Ninth Avenue," in which a porter was explicitly named as an amateur detective. Why the choice of a Pullman porter for a detective? How might the role of a Pullman porter have been particularly commensurate with Du Bois's interest in exploring the detective genre in particular? Excavating some of the history of Pullman porters and considering some key conventions of American detective fiction prove equally instructive.

Not too many years before Du Bois wrote and published his detective stories, a number of events highlighted the struggle of the Black worker in general and the Pullman porter—nearly an exclusively Black occupation—in particular. In 1894, a national strike protesting the mistreatment of Pullman porters occurred throughout the Midwest, and by 1925, Asa Philip Randolph, founder of the Brotherhood of Sleeping Car Porters, had composed a letter to Du Bois thanking him for his public support of porters in *Crisis* editorials that predated the detective stories.[6] A firm advocate for the working class, Du Bois was a vociferous critic of discriminatory labor policies that forbade Black porters from joining or forming unions—a policy ultimately changed by Randolph. While Du Bois had lamented in a commencement address he delivered at Fisk University in 1898 that too many educated African Americans were working as porters, he did recognize their prideful place within the Black community and their contribution to the postbellum process of "uplift."[7] Overall, Du Bois saw the Pullman porter as an integral part of the Black community's progression toward economic parity, even as he lamented that so few occupations outside of this purportedly "unskilled" one were available to Black workers.

Moreover, the interdisciplinary demands placed upon the porter make him a particularly good subject to investigate a mystery and thus to serve as Du Bois's instrument for the adjudication of white norms and actions. As David D. Perata observes, the porter had to simultaneously function as a domestic servant, amateur psychologist, and travel expert (1996, xxi).[8] It may also be argued that a job involving serving, sewing, and cooking is a domestic and thus a feminized one. And yet such a job ineluctably placed the porter in the worldly position of one who must subtly command an interracial, mobile space marked by porous borders, a unique segmentation of social roles, and a chronotropic liminality sustaining a "doubly consciousness" gaze that might circumnavigate the putatively white space around it.[9]

With respect to the generic tradition of detective fiction, Du Bois establishes the porter as a storyteller in "The Case," gesturing toward what Stephen Soitos acknowledges as the shared roots of the detective story and the folktale (1996, 14). "The Case" begins with a frame story in which an unnamed white narrator, a passenger riding on a train called the "Southern," persuades the unnamed Black porter who is the story's hero to recount a story about a train wreck ([1907a] 1995, 109).[10] By crafting a story narrated at the outset by a white railway passenger but chiefly (through the internal story) by a Black porter-as-investigator, Du Bois manipulates the detective story, employing the frame tale and the generic device in which the detective's story is narrated by a close associate, to establish the porter as the main conveyor of information and the white passenger as a passive recipient of a Black man's storehouse of knowledge.[11] As I will go on to discuss, this parasitic relationship is specifically homoerotic since the white passenger depends upon the Black man he considers a servant for pleasure as well as information (and indeed, for the pleasure of information). And yet the quality of the information exchanged between porter and passenger is mitigated by its ultimate rendering as elusive, since the porter never learns the significance of the briefcase and is therefore unable either to solve any "mystery" or to impart any pointed "wisdom" or moral therein, either to the passenger or the reader. As the Black porter warns his white interlocutor, due to the transient nature of life on the railroad, any story he tells will inevitably be incomplete: after all, a porter may only have "glimpses" into the lives of the people he meets. (Ironically, the porter avoids any mention of the material barriers of racial and class hierarchies that inevitably estrange African Americans from their Euro-American compatriots.) While the porter appears chiefly to oblige his passenger's desire for a good yarn, in relaying his story and thus exhibiting all the inductive aplomb of an archetypal detective, he intuits much about the hidden lives of those white persons under his purview. Moreover, in the process of asserting his cognitive skill and distinctive identity, the porter interrupts his passenger's appraisal of him, thereby disrupting the white man's exclusive claims, both to epistemological authority and heteropatriarchal masculinity. For, as I go on to show, the porter both indulges—to a point—the passenger's homoerotic interest in him and seeks to assert himself—albeit with caveats—into a heteronormative sexual economy in which he and the passenger might both commiserate about the white woman at the center of the recounted intrigue. Indeed, the primary motive of "The Case" is not to stage the dialectical suspension and resolution of a mystery. Rather, "The Case" affords Du Bois an opportunity to restage and revise the figuration of cross-caste romance as he offered it in *Souls*—as both a cause and a symptom of double consciousness and, moreover, as a matter of queer intimacy.

Before the porter's story progresses, Du Bois details the desiring, homoerotic gaze of the white passenger who characterizes his "associate," the porter, as a "finely made fellow—tall, strong, with velvet dark brown skin and pleasant, smiling eyes." Then, the white passenger undermines his own honorific glance, reminding himself that his status is above that of the porter: "If he had been white—but he wasn't" the passenger thinks, trailing off, ostensibly to imagine what greater opportunities the porter might have been afforded if not for his "unfortunately raced" existence. Yet the passenger does not truly allow himself to conceptualize how things might be different if not for the subaltern status of the porter. He fails to draw out the benevolent trajectory of his admiring gaze, and he effectively puts the porter in his place: first by complaining about the tardiness of the train and then by demanding that the porter entertain him. Perhaps in the passenger's seemingly contradictory responses to the porter one finds a sublimation of more taboo desires for how the porter might serve as a source of pleasure to an idle man bored by an uneventful train ride on a "dull, gray day," which offers little more than a circumscribed view of a landscape devoid of "company" and "color" ([1907a] 1995, 109). [12]

In spite of routinely having his consciousness infringed upon by the intrusive actions of various white passengers, Du Bois's porter—in true detective fashion—bypasses somewhat the barrier of racism and intuits much about the hidden lives of those white persons under his purview. To the white passenger's entreaty to be told a story about a wreck, the porter responds with a warning that such a story would inevitably be incomplete. The passenger responds by noting that the porter must "have to guess at the rest"—a prescient remark that underscores the gaps in shared knowledge that estrange African Americans from their Euro-American counterparts. While the porter seems to oblige his passenger's desire for a good yarn, in relaying his story the porter asserts his independent motives and identity and, moreover, disrupts both the white male passenger's appraisal of him and any uncontested claims to epistemological authority routinely assumed by white persons. Importantly, the porter also challenges the white passenger's presumably exclusive claim to masculine authority, as I will go on to detail, since the porter dares to assert himself into a homosocial yet heteronormative sexual economy in which he and the passenger might equally commiserate about the white female subject at the center of the recounted "mystery."

Before discussing the homosocial commiseration between the porter and passenger, I must rest a bit longer on the homoerotic nature of the passenger's interest in the porter and thus draw out the implications of such for considering how this story reprises Du Bois's racialized and gendered account of double consciousness. To what end did Du Bois, a self-proclaimed stranger to homosexual trajectories of desire, insert markedly homoerotic subtext into the cross-caste relation of the porter and passenger?[13] As I suggested previously, Du Bois's move illustrates the now common understanding of the continuum upon which the homoerotic and the homosocial are located and the importance of both as bases for patriarchal exchanges—in Eve Sedgwick's parlance—"between" men. Yet there is more to be gleaned from Du Bois's characterization of white male desire for a Black man, especially when one recalls the tale of the visiting card with which I began this book, in which Du Bois rebuts the myth that Black persons are undesirable and, by extension, unworthy. While Du Bois's queering of the white passenger arguably undermines his self-proclaimed authority and besmirches the prowess of his whiteness (which seems to presuppose an equally hegemonic sexuality), it also redresses the rejection of Black persons as objects of desire and participants in romantic economies of exchange. By acknowledging the allure, intelligence, and charm of a Black porter, the white passenger reprises the specter of the white girl featured in the opening chapter of *Souls*, countering the myth that the expected or typical response of a white person to a Black one is derision. Rather, the homoerotic expression of desire for the porter proffers Black persons as worthy to be enjoyed and relied upon as sources of entertainment and, even more subversively, information.

On the one hand, Du Bois seems to shore up Black masculinity by presenting an inadequate, "perverse" iteration of white masculinity. By presenting a white man with obvious homoerotic interest in a Black subordinate, Du Bois counters an imperialist discourse that characterizes Black sexuality as inherently aberrant. Such discourse is truly an example of Euro-American projection since, as Aliyyah Abdur-Rahman points out, white men sexually abused enslaved persons of African descent (both male and female) throughout the slavery and Jim Crow eras—largely with impunity.[14] Yet on the other hand, Du Bois eroticizes and feminizes the Black man, who becomes vulnerable to the desiring gaze of the white man. This subverts that very same masculinity and acknowledges that Black assimilation may require a measure of feminization for Black men who, unable to engage in taboo relations with white women, must nevertheless garner the interest of white men—albeit in a deeroticized, homosocial (as opposed to homoerotic) fashion. Ultimately, Du Bois asserts the desirability of Black men (and Black subjects overall), yet he also undercuts the unchecked desires of white men, since the porter refuses his passenger both intimacy and knowledge.

This white passenger's gaze is first stripped of authority when the porter recounts how he had cast his own gaze upon a white female passenger: a gorgeous femme fatale with a mysterious air who reprises the lost white woman of Du Bois's adolescence yet with a marked difference. For in "The Case," the white woman is the one being gazed upon and judged in kind by a Black man presumed to be below her in station (i.e., caste status): "I tell you she was a stunning-looking woman, not so very tall yet with an appearance of tallness, brunette with dark hair and the most wonderful misty eyes you ever looked at. [. . .] She had an air, too—wasn't exactly a lady." With this last statement, which seems to cast aspersions on the so-called purity (if not the character) of the woman being described, the white passenger's hackles are raised: "'What do you mean by that?' [he] growled." At this, the porter assures him that he only means to comment on the woman's class status, to say that she had not always been accustomed to "money and good society," and he reassures the passenger that "she had the making of a lady in her" ([1907a] 1995, 110). With this exchange, the passenger appears to recognize that the porter has just mirrored his own stance, both as he desires to objectify him (offering a seemingly honorific yet qualified judgment of his appearance), and as he casts a judgment against him, lamenting his less than elevated because racially subaltern status. In a move that boldly claims the Black man's right to judge the seemingly sacred ideal of white womanhood and also ascribes to Black judgment a weight equal (if not superior) to that of any white person, Du Bois's porter effectively speaks back to power, undermining the seamless authority of the white male subject and displacing the homoerotic bond between himself and the white passenger in favor of a more acceptable homosocial bond through which they might both, in Gayle Rubin's terms, "traffic" in women: one that is central to the heteronormative, patriarchal order the porter seeks to access and also to the ideology of whiteness it purportedly ensures.[15]

Presumably, this redeems the porter's masculinity, substituting the figure of the white woman as the object of desire and leaving his own body intact and above regard or reproach. Such a narrative move recalls and rebuts the vulnerability of Du Bois's young Black body as figured in the visiting card story. With the porter's turn toward the white woman of his memory and away from the desiring glance of the white man, Du Bois appears to affirm Black masculinity as sufficiently virile in quality and heteronormative in orientation. Yet Du Bois does not undo his prior suggestion of the porter's erotic desirability—and to more than just female persons. Nor does he render the porter's interest in the white woman particularly substantive (or romantic), as the porter evinces no real amorous interest in her. (I will return to unpack the quality of interest that he *does* evince in her.) Accordingly, I submit that Du Bois recuperates Black masculinity, not by rigidly reinforcing its heteronormative borders but rather by differentiating the possession of homoerotic desirability from the active expression of homoerotic desire. The message is clear: Black men are not the perpetrators of taboo sexual acts (with either white women or white men) but rather the recipients of sexual (and other forms of) interest by white persons. As such, Black male sexuality is paradoxically wrested from the particular taboo marked by interracial (and homoerotic) sex and invested with an erotic desirability that exceeds the parameters of heteronormative masculinity and sexuality. In this sense, Du Bois's story might be said to simultaneously harbor homophobic traces and manifest homocentrist and antipatriarchal commitments. For "The Case" critiques a white man's expression of homoerotic desire for Black bodies while rendering auspicious a Black man's homoerotic allure.

As the porter continues to relay his story—and the sparsely plotted mystery therein—he continues to upend the conventions of white supremacist heteropatriarchy by revealing the extent of his perceptive powers, as he presumes to possess knowledge about the white passengers in his story. Moreover, he asserts himself as someone who can judge a white woman's character as mysterious and even notorious and yet still forge a somewhat intimate alliance with her. In his story, the porter recounts that he noticed a "lonely" young clergyman who shared his interest in the young woman. The clergyman struck up a conversation with the "femme fatale," and another romance was thereby signaled. Yet the porter perceived in the scene something more intense and potentially sinister to be unearthed. The key to the impending trouble seemed to be located in the appearance and presence of the woman, recalled by the porter as "beautiful" yet possessed of "a certain indefinable grace and innocence and vigor" that vexed him. "There was something not quite right about her," he recounts to the passenger and then reflects further about her state of mind: "Beneath all her enthusiasm and interest there were little furtile [*sic*] gleams almost of terror that came into her otherwise beautiful eyes [. . .]. Now and then a far away look of passionate pleading struggled across the very mirth of her laughter" ([1907a] 1995, 112).

By crafting a "minor" romance, to recall Lauren Berlant's formulation, between the porter and the mysterious white woman, one based not on their brief interactions but primarily on his imagined empathy for her, Du Bois suggests the possibility of an affective, platonic alliance between the porter and the woman and thereby revises the ghostly, failed cross-caste romance of his youth. Such an alliance seems to derive from a shared sense of fear, for the porter recognizes the woman's fear insofar as he, a fellow subaltern subject to the gazes and whims of white men, shares it—an insight strengthened by his description of the white woman as "veiled" and also by her perceived terror in the presence of the police.[16] As the porter tells it, when police suddenly entered the train searching for an unnamed someone or something, the young woman picked up a large leather case and foisted it upon the porter, "commanding" that he hide it. Another authoritative figure entered the train—perhaps a private detective—and recognized the clergyman, whom he pressed for information about the young woman. "Rising to the occasion," Du Bois writes, the mystery woman compels the clergyman to cover for her and falsely introduces herself as his wife. Although the clergyman subsequently begs the woman to be his wife, telling her that he "knows all" about her presumably illicit deeds, she pushes him aside and again, presses the porter into service by having him dispatch a telegram to an acquaintance. In recounting this story, the porter insists to his interlocutor that this had been "no evil woman." Yet the narrative would seem to intimate otherwise, for as the porter explains, the woman was seemingly punished for unknown sins—killed in a train wreck that caused an iron bar to "crush her down in all her splendid young beauty and grind her between the seats while the car jolted and screamed." As the porter looked away from the horrific sight of the woman's dead body, the briefcase (which he had somehow retrieved) was stolen from his hands by a "stranger" whom the porter had seen talking to the young woman when she first boarded the train. Thus, to the passenger's query about the case's contents and the woman's true story, the porter can reveal nothing of substance. Both the briefcase and the case of the woman's identity are out of bounds—opaque and thus resistant to conventional or legible ways of knowing ([1907a] 1995, 113).

Echoing the porter's loss of the literal case that belongs to the mysterious femme fatale, Du Bois abandons the figurative case for which the material case is emblematic (as an unsolved mystery), thereby subverting the key impetus of detective fiction to resolve a crime. This is a fitting example of what Stephen Soitos calls the Black detective writer's "retardation" of plot or climax, which I extend in my interpretation of Du Bois's story as a perpetual deferral of the detective plot (1996, 49). Yet the porter's lack of access to the case—in dual senses of the term—serves chiefly to curtail the desires of the white passenger (and by extension, those of the reader) and points to the limits of knowing—not just for the subaltern subject positioned outside the systems of power that construct knowledge but also for the white subject who desires to claim a place at the center of those systems of power that paradoxically elude him. Moreover, Du Bois undermines the mystery's paradigm by which questions are answered and truths revealed. Du Bois uses the mystery both to advance the possibility of Black persons evaluating white persons and to undermine the ideal of white womanhood. Du Bois's underscoring of the limits of knowing not only makes a political point about how racialized power does not necessarily yield knowledge but also unsettles the parameters of the detective genre and the reader's expectations for the epistemological certainty betokened by the mystery's resolution. The lack of closure regarding the mystery also frustrates the white passenger's homoerotic and homosocial conscription of the porter, who pushes back against the white passenger's attempt to extract pleasure as well as information from him.

Clearly, what matters in "The Case" is neither the resolution of the plot nor its dénouement but rather the porter's exercise of perception and judgment: his insertion into the lives of "white folk" and his right to wield interpretive authority about them—an authority that, as Du Bois suggests, both in *Souls* and in his essay "The Souls of White Folk" (published in *Darkwater*), is derived from the "peculiar" vantage point of the subaltern toward the dominating subject.[17] Du Bois thus subverts the conventions of the detective genre by eschewing any revelation of an actual crime. Yet if one looks at some lesser-known mysteries from the period of American romanticism, such as, for example, Edgar Allan Poe's 1840 short story "The Man of the Crowd," one finds a model for the kind of perceptive curiosity of a detective that need not depend upon an actual mystery or crime in order to be unleashed. In Poe's story, a detective sits reading newspapers in a café when he suddenly notices an older man whose "countenance" "arrest[s] and absorb[s]" his attention:

> As I endeavored, during the brief minute of my original survey, to form some analysis of the meaning conveyed, there arose confusedly and paradoxically within my mind, the ideas of vast mental power, of caution, of penuriousness, of avarice, of coolness, of malice, of blood-thirstiness, of triumph, of merriment, of excessive terror, of intense—of supreme despair. . . . Then came a craving desire to keep the man in my view—to know more of him.[18] (258–59)

This passage is eerily reminiscent of the porter's description of the mysterious young woman who ultimately eludes him. Significantly, it also recalls

Du Bois's statements in "The Souls of White Folk" about his own clairvoyance with regard to white "souls" and behaviors, which simultaneously "intrigue"—whether by fascinating or repelling—him ([1920] 1999, 17). In the Poe story, the detective judges the mystery man to be guilty, yet he neither observes nor solves any crime involving him. He concludes that following him would be futile for "I shall learn no more of him, nor of his deeds" ([1840] 1993, 262). The lesson seems to be that one need not have full access to reality in order to make judgments about it—an insight gleaned from Du Bois's theory of double consciousness, which recognizes knowledge as liminal. While Du Bois's porter-as-detective has no proof that the young white woman is guilty of any crime, he nonetheless perceives her as a societal outsider and holds the key (insofar as there is one) to interpreting her story for the listening passenger despite its opacity.

Double consciousness thus proceeds, not simply via affirmation of Black lives and Black values but also by negation of white ones. For whiteness is deconstructed to undermine the authority of hegemony, even if little is revealed about its contents. Du Bois thus implies in his fictional tale what he declares outright in "The Souls of White Folk": whiteness is empty—simply a "phantasy" (Du Bois [1920] 1999, 19).

Perhaps Du Bois penned such an anticlimactic mystery in order to place coyly under a microscope the nexus of racial and gendered relations as exemplified in the exchanges between the Black porter and the white passengers whom he does not truly know yet in whose presence he feels at turns incited or estranged. By reversing the foreclosed romance between his younger self and the young white girl of his boyhood, Du Bois reframes the lost romance as homoerotic and homosocial, and only subsequently offers a potential heteronormative alliance—deeroticized yet still romanticized—between a Pullman porter detective and a white woman who is likely embroiled in some sort of illicit or criminal activity. As the porter characterizes the young woman as beautiful and sympathetic, he invokes a typically masculine authority to assess the physical (and by extension, moral) value of women. Yet by underscoring her fear, longing, and pleading, both the porter and his creator Du Bois suggest some shared points of commonality between white women and Black men who, in their subservient positions, are both subjected to the whims of the various white men upon whom they often depend. In the lines, "There lay love and bewilderment, honor and yearning, [and] beneath it trouble and fear" with which the porter seems to read into the soul of the mysterious woman, one might also read his own description of himself and other Black American souls: all of whom go similarly unperceived by their white peers ([1907a] 1995, 112). Like the souls of Black folk, the young femme fatale's soul is opaque—at least to all but the porter.

Du Bois's treatment of the young woman seems progressive, despite the fact that her death revives the Victorian tradition of women's bodies being subject to punishment or annihilation, especially as furthered via the trope of the "femme fatale." Perhaps Du Bois revives the young woman who scorned him in childhood only to punish her for the "sin" of misrecognition. Yet given the sympathetic nature of the porter's gaze upon the mysterious woman, both her violent death at the narrative's end and that death's subsequent foreclosure of intimacy and knowledge also underscore the arbitrary nature of violence as it routinely impacts the Black subject. Perhaps Du Bois's moral is that to be desired by white men is to be vulnerable to destruction. Du Bois may endeavor to recover the Black male body from its abusive history at the hands of white men by imagining the debasement of the white female body, but once that body is struck down, it offers concrete evidence of the destructive propensity of white male sexuality, thereby excavating what had seemed to be the concealed association of whiteness with criminality.

In contrast to the prototypical mystery, Du Bois's story does not offer satisfaction via resolution. Rather, "The Case" stages a number of desires only to foreclose them and thus to foreclose various opportunities to achieve erotic as well as epistemological fulfillment (for both characters and readers). The death of the white woman, for example, frustrates the resolution of the mystery: for who was she, and what (if any) misdeeds might she have committed after all? In addition, the young woman's death also frustrates any lasting alliance she may have forged with the porter. Finally, the porter's refusal to resolve the story of the mysterious woman (not entirely at his disposal) also frustrates the white passenger's desire for knowledge, not only of Black lives but also of any and all lives. Thus, in having his porter decline, both to pursue further intimacy with a white woman and gratify the homoerotic wishes of a passenger, Du Bois refuses the primacy of white desire. The problem and puzzle of white desire and the range of possible Black responses to such are reprised in Du Bois's second *Horizon* detective story, "The Shaven Lady."

Appearing in *Horizon* in August of 1907, "The Shaven Lady" adapts the detective genre to broach the criminalization of the Black man, oft subjected to a white gaze that is not just disapproving but mercenary in orientation. The story relates how a Black porter moves from being a suspected criminal to becoming an amateur detective, as he struggles to clear his own name after being falsely accused of theft and, ultimately, stumbling onto a rather pedestrian case of white interpersonal intrigue involving a case of mistaken identity.[19] The story opens with the white passenger-as-narrator fuming about the loss of his watch and intimating that the porter may have stolen it. In response to this implicit accusation, this porter, markedly different from the porter depicted in "The Case," casts his "sharp unsmiling eyes" upon the white passenger. When the watch is located in the white passenger's coat pocket—an instance of foreshadowing, as will be revealed later—the porter then calms down and tells a story of another time when he was unfairly accused of a crime. The relationship between the two men purportedly smoothed over, the white man is now free to indulge his desire for the Black man: "After a time, [the porter] came in, stretched himself easily on the couch and lighted a delicate cigarette. I noticed his long, thin, brown hand; beautiful fingers he had, then that voice of his—I'd give anything to hear him talk" (1907b, 1). Note that Du Bois expands the scope of the homoerotic desire of the white passenger for the Black porter, as presented in "The Case," and emphatically shows the range of white responses to Black persons; the white passenger moves from suspecting and implicitly denigrating the porter to admiring and desiring him, both for his physical body and for his affective, artistic appeal. This desire is quickly undercut by Du Bois, as he has the porter again turn his gaze on a white woman—this time, a young ingénue who is engaged in an emotional discussion (about which the reader soon discovers more details) with her father. Two distinctive iterations of white womanhood also appear in this story: a "prim fussy old lady" and a "tall, rather large woman," who is, in an evocation of the primacy of vision and perception, both "spectacled" and "veiled" and who greets the young woman with a kiss. The porter's investigative insight is again awakened as he sees "immediately that there was going to be an interesting exchange of confidences" between the young ingénue and the tall, veiled woman (1907b, 3). Once again, the porter is conscripted into some white intrigue: the large, veiled woman gives him a note and asks him to deliver it to a clergyman on the train. Yet before this particular mystery can unfold, the porter is abruptly accused of stealing the fussy old woman's purse. In the act of defending his honor, casting off the aura of criminality foisted upon him, the porter is drawn further into the act of detecting. He follows the tall, veiled woman into a dressing room, where he discovers that she is shaving and thus immediately tags her as the likely thief, in part because she is apparently guilty of another putative crime: the duplicity of having been a male presenting himself as female. Pointing to her purportedly "mannish shoulders and suspiciously abundant hair," the porter declares that she is not a woman but rather, a cross-dressing man (1907b, 4). At once a mystery is unveiled: the tall young woman is actually the male suitor of the young girl and has been deemed an inappropriate prospective husband by the girl's father due to his lower caste (as working-class) status. In order to be able to secretly marry her (which he does shortly after the porter's discovery), the young male suitor has had to engage in subterfuge and masking, cross-dressing, and presenting as a woman. He thus underscores the queer undertones with which Du Bois begins the story. Only one mystery remains: since our porter is innocent, who has stolen the fussy old woman's purse? As it turns out, it is none other than the porter himself! In gathering the bedding to be washed, he had inadvertently taken the "pocket book" (5), which he now finds in his own pocket. Upon learning that he is in fact the thief, the porter "crumples" and wears a sickly smile on his face, fearing that he will be condemned although innocent of malfeasance. In this moment, Du Bois's story anticipates the fiction of Richard Wright, whose embattled characters, often fighting criminal charges, exemplify the notion of a circular prophecy: that the Black man might become what white society presupposes for him.[20] Fortunately, the porter's white boss believes that he is of the "respectable" variety of African American men, so he lifts the purse from the porter, tucks it into the pocket of the young fiancé who has been masquerading as a woman, and effectively frames the young fiancé for the crime (although this is never explicitly acknowledged in the story) (1907b, 6).

What *is* the place of the cross-dressing masquerade plot? Aside from adding to the mystery and exemplifying the "red herring" trope inherent in classic detective fiction, this plot allows Du Bois to do two somewhat contradictory things: the first is to cast the white man as the criminal, with the crime being that of subterfuge and dissimulation. Again, the Black man remains heroic and noble, subject both to the untoward advances of white men and to their criminal machinations. But Du Bois also suggests an analogical relationship that might be drawn between the porter and the young white man, whose only way to squire and eventually to become betrothed to a woman above his station is via subterfuge and masquerade. The fact that this man, dressed as a woman, is "veiled" offers a subtle clue that Du Bois sees some lines of commonality between the Black porter and the white fiancé. Recall that in *Souls,* Du Bois describes the Black subject as disconnected from white society by a "veil," which has both racial and gendered overtones. The young white man's commandeering of a veil, then, suggests both his intent to disguise himself as feminine, in order to gain power by "topping from below" (recalling Kathryn Bond Stockton's deployment of this queer phrase and practice) and Du Bois's subtle instruction that he and the Black subject share a comparable if not identical position vis-à-vis the dominating (white, upper-class) culture. Both are subject to the ungenerous and dismissive gazes of the white upper class, and both are allotted only limited access to the heteropatriarchy. In this sense, Du Bois renders them both emasculated and thus, in one sense, queered, via the societal curtailment of their sexual agency.

Nevertheless, the suggestion that a man dressing as a woman is somehow untoward and even criminal remains, and given such, one is perhaps justified in suspecting Du Bois of trafficking if not harboring homophobic and perhaps even transphobic biases. Although, as Mason Stokes has pointed out, Du Bois claimed to be ignorant of the phenomenon and prevalence of homosexuality (see Stokes 2001, 289–316), it is quite likely that during his time as a graduate student in Germany, Du Bois became aware of cutting-edge theory about queer sexuality—specifically, about the figure of the so-called invert—as advanced by scientists including Richard von Krafft-Ebing and Havelock Ellis, both of whom published tracts about sexual "inversion" before the publication of these detective stories. As Siobhan Somerville reminds us, the texts of Krafft-Ebing and Ellis drew on eugenicist discourse to mark out the sexual "abnormalities" of "the other," and their foundational iterations of sexology often compared the "invert" to the Black person, since both were characterized by their purported pathological sexuality (2000, 17–18). For the white man, engaging in homoerotic or even homosocial praxes would constitute a crack in the veneer of his claims to "normalcy" and power, as Stokes has also observed (13). Yet for the Black man, currying homoerotic desire to gain favor from a member of the dominating class or relying upon homosocial intimacy with those white men upon whom he might depend for his livelihood (e.g., the conductor) were often necessary acts of survival and assimilation. Indeed, as C. Riley Snorton theorizes, drawing out the insights of Hortense Spillers regarding the "gender indefiniteness" of the slave under a system whose mandate of perpetual labor did not necessarily sanction any gendered division of such, the experience of Black Americans in the aftermath of slavery often required an embrace of what he terms a praxis of "gender fungibility" (Snorton 2017, 73). Snorton offers the infamous example of Ellen and William Craft, a husband-and-wife team who escaped from slavery disguised—and in Ellen's case, cross-dressed—as a white male "master" and her Black manservant (94). As Snorton points out, "the difference in color between William and Ellen" "produced a rationale for her cross-gendered escape," since her appearance as a white-looking woman traveling with a dark-complexioned Black man would have drawn a level of "scrutiny and surveillance" that would have endangered them both and thus thwarted their plan for freedom (95). Paradigmatically speaking, the story of Ellen and William Craft is an example of how subalterns are often compelled to "speak" by resorting to subterfuge in order to beat a system stacked against them. While Du Bois drew on a historic tradition of gender fungibility as enacted by Black Americans during and after slavery, in "The Shaven Lady," he transposed such history onto the experience of a young white man, who, in spite of his whiteness, does not have access to the upper echelons of the white supremacist caste because he does not (yet) have the requisite class status required for acceptance. Thus, Du Bois's depiction of a *white* man who "cross-dresses," performing a gender identity that is fungible and, in some sense, "trans," in order to circumvent a system that would bar his access to the fullness of humanity manifested as power and agency recalls yet reprises the history of *Black* men and women who have cross-dressed, not in order to thrive but rather to survive. Indeed, as Snorton submits, to "feel black in the diaspora, then, might be a trans experience" (23).

Du Bois's figuration of a white male masquerading as a female may recall and perhaps even reproduce a homophobic discourse in which those supposed "inverts" whose identities or actions were thought to undermine strict gender differentiation were deemed "pathological" and even criminal. However, within such a figuration one may also see reprised a history of Black persons either forced to embody or strategically adopt a posture of sexual transgression and flexibility; this suggests that one might interpret more favorably Du Bois's queer politics. For in ascribing to a white man at the lower rungs of his own ethnic community a passively aggressive practice historically enacted by Black subalterns, Du Bois suggests the possibility of a resemblance and perhaps even an alliance between Black and white men of the working class or underclass (caste). I hasten to add that a white man masquerading as a woman might also recall a very different history: that of white men engaging in minstrel performance, who, as Eric Lott relates, often engaged in what he terms "blackface transvestism" (2013, 159). As Lott explains, "The blackface 'wench' character was just a more extravagant form in which to achieve" the misogyny endemic to much minstrelsy (159). The echoes of this history in Du Bois's cross-dressing young white man are in line with my argument that he marshaled homoeroticism and transgenderism to cast aspersions on the character of white men. And yet this reading does not displace my parallel claim that Du Bois also outlined a similarity between Black men who "wear the mask," as Paul Laurence Dunbar proclaimed and white men who engage in masquerade. Just as Du Bois suggests in "The Case" a shared experience and potential alliance between the Black man and the white woman, both subject to the whims and machinations of white men in power, so too does he gesture in "The Shaven Lady" toward a shared praxis of compulsory masquerade for the Black man and the white man "outcast" from the upper echelons of a capitalist American society. Indeed, Du Bois's illustration of the potential for alliances to be forged between Black and white men reprises with a difference his portrait of Black and white men joined together in homoerotic and homosocial union in the opening chapter of *Souls*. For his detective stories subtly warn against the dangers of misrecognition and misalliance between whites (especially poor or disadvantaged ones) and Blacks in America, prefiguring his socialist and eventually Communist commitments and anticipating his repeated advocacy of such in works like his biography of John Brown (1909) and his 1950s satires of American capitalism and anti-Communism, embodied, for example, in stories like "The Countess's Sables," which he tried and failed to publish under the pseudonym "Bud Weisob" after being blacklisted for his Communist affiliations (see David Levering Lewis, *W.E.B. Du Bois: The Fight for Equality and the American Century, 1919–1963*).

Yet perhaps one of the most profound legacies of Du Bois's forgotten detective fiction is their implicit reappraisal of "criminality" and their more pointed rebuttal of the myth that criminal behavior is endemic to Black identity and experience. While "The Case" offers a Black porter-as-detective attuned to and critical of the misalliances and miscreant behavior of white folks, "The Shaven Lady" offers a more pointed antithesis to the mythology of the Black man as a likely criminal, for the porter in this story is not only innocent (in the spirit of truth) of any criminal behavior but also responsible for the discovery of the "real" criminal. And yet, as Du Bois draws a line between the Black subject's strategy of survival by subterfuge and the strategic masquerade of the story's young white fiancé, unable to win his beloved except by "hook or by crook," he also undercuts the moralism at the basis of imputations of "criminality" to those who must outsmart a system that refuses to accommodate them. In the subtext of "The Shaven Lady," then, one finds evidence of what Fred Moten deems Du Bois's antiphonal tonality, which Moten variously terms a "whistle," a "dissonant echo," and "the overdub of or accompaniment to [his] normative ideals" (2007, 327–29), such as Black uplift and Victorian morality. Moten continues, riffing on Henry Louis Gates Jr., by noting that the "doubleness" of Du Bois's normative ideals marks their "repetition" yet with a marked "difference"—one that deploys a nuanced notion of "the criminal [. . .] [as what] animates [black] radicalism" (329). Moten astutely notes that Du Bois's *The Philadelphia Negro* is the repository for some of his most troubling iterations of Black respectability politics (and implicitly, his reproductions of American myths of social equity and meritocracy). And yet, as Moten avers, even in that work there are the beginnings of Du Bois's recasting of criminality as radical anticapitalism (327–28). Submits Moten: "Just as the commodity's (exchange) value is understood by Marx to have been conferred from outside, so is deviance or criminality understood by labeling theorists [including Du Bois] as a function of nomination—'a consequence of the application by others of rules and sanctions'—and not as a quality of the act or the person that is called deviant or criminal" (328). Criminality, then, through Du Bois's figuration of it, may be rethought, as Moten instructs, "not as a violation of the criminal law (however illegitimate one thinks such law to be) but rather as a capacity or propensity to transgress the law as such, to challenge its mystical authority with a kind of improvisational rupture" (344). Whether enacted by subtly consenting to court the desires of a powerful other or by just as subtly refusing to fulfill such desires and masquerading in order to fulfill one's own forbidden desires—thus defying the orders of law or convention—such acts of "improvisational rupture" constitute the overarching conceit of Du Bois's mysteries—romantic in their evocation of affect and desire yet antiromantic in their privileging of (Black) fugitivity.

Chapter Three

A Romance of Refusal

Failed Intimacy and Black Fugitivity in "The Princess of the Hither Isles"

> The will of the world is a whistling wind, sweeping a cloud-swept sky, / And not from the East and not from the West knelled that soul-waking cry, /But out of the South,—the sad, black South—it screamed from the top of the sky, / Crying, "Awake, O ancient race!" Wailing, "O woman, arise!" / And crying and sighing and crying again as a voice in the midnight cries, — / But the burden of white men bore her back and the white world stifled her sighs.
>
> —W. E. B. Du Bois, "The Riddle of the Sphinx" (1920)

> The problem of the twentieth century is the problem of the color-line,—the relation of the darker to the lighter races of men in Asia and Africa, in America and the islands of the sea.
>
> —W. E. B. Du Bois, "Of the Dawn of Freedom" (1903)

In this chapter, I examine one of Du Bois's underanalyzed stories "The Princess of the Hither Isles," from his 1920 interdisciplinary collection of memoir, essay, poetry, and short fiction *Darkwater*. The allegorical fairy tale relates the tragic fate of a beautiful young princess confined to the swampy "Hither Isles" and courted by a powerful and cruel white king whose affections she does not return but whose colonial empire offers the promise of "flying" above her inauspicious environs and circumstances. Gazing upward at the sun, she eventually sees a Black beggar in whose face she senses "unfathomed understanding" and perhaps also a more glorious past than his tattered clothes and bedraggled retinue suggest. Burning with her desire to be with him, she rips out her heart, is subsequently attacked by the king, who cuts off her hand, and ultimately, leaps to her death—perhaps to be united with the "Empire of the Sun," whose whispered voice urges her on (Du Bois [1920] 1999, 46). The few scholars who have addressed this story seem to agree that it depicts an interracial, anti-imperial romance between a white princess and the Black beggar for whom she feels an affection based on her anti-imperial "solidarity," encapsulated in her presumed desire to relinquish her own tenuous link to colonial power (see Weinbaum 2007 and Joo 2019). Yet I challenge this prevailing reading by countering that Du Bois's story is more plausibly and productively read as the story of two failed iterations of cross-caste romance: the first is between a young princess, likely a white-passing Black or mixed-race woman, consigned to a protocolonial space within an archetypal colonialist regime and a white imperialist king who aggressively courts her; the second is between that same princess and a Black beggar, a more pronounced victim of imperialism for whom she feels an affinity but with whom she shares only a remote form of unreciprocated intimacy. The juxtaposition of these two failed cross-caste romances, one interracial and one intraethnic, I argue, reflects Du Bois's deployment of the drama of cross-caste romance, not as a mechanism of building anti-imperial solidarity, indexing what I characterized in my introduction as a possibly "conciliatory" form of nationalist assimilation, but rather as the very means of imperial conquest and cultural annihilation (see Sommer 1991 and Moore 2000). Moving from a relatively auspicious figuration of cross-caste romance in the first chapter of *Souls* to increasingly more vexed instantiations of such in "Of the Coming of John" and the *Horizon* detective fiction, Du Bois presents his allegorical fairytale to assiduously demonstrate not only how insufficient romance and intimacy might be in forging political coalitions and overcoming political errors but also how romance and intimacy might be deployed, in contradistinction, as the very vehicles of racist colonial violence and expropriation. "The Princess of the Hither Isles" thus marks a significant shift in the political and poetic trajectory of Du Bois's literary works. The death of the princess, then, is emblematic of the tragedy, not just of failed political alliance but also of the ancestral and personal losses wrought by colonialism.

I anchor my unorthodox interpretation of the "The Princess of the Hither Isles" by employing a methodological approach attentive to the story's historical contexts, intertextual echoes, and ideological discourses of anticolonialism and anticapitalism. Attuned to the allegorical nature of Du Bois's fantastic fairytale that is set neither in any particular time nor any particular space but rather evokes at once several temporal and spatial settings, I plumb the historical allusions and intertextual resemblances within and without his own literary repertoire, which he uses to further the themes of the story and, when taken together, offer key clues that challenge the common reading of the princess as a white woman.

Chief among these historical contexts is the fact that "The Princess of the Hither Isles" is appended as a kind of postscript to the anticolonial, antiracist, and pro-Black liberation tract that appears just before it: "The Hands of Ethiopia" (Du Bois [1920] 1999, 32–42). In this paean to anticolonial justice and pro-Black liberation and sovereignty, Du Bois argues explicitly for an independent postcolonial Pan-African (and Pan-Asian) liberation against white imperial violence, and he augurs a future in which Black nations will have cast off Eurocentric rule. Why, I found myself asking, would Du Bois center a story that punctuates his call for pro-Black liberation on a *white* princess? Moreover, upon what bases could the princess be reasonably interpreted as being solely or chiefly of European descent? Is the evidence for such a reading based purely on color descriptors, or alternately, on reader assumptions about the politics of race? Moreover, to what extent might Du Bois offer other clues that characterize racial identity, not on the basis of physical appearance or visual semiotics but on the basis of geospatial location, moral action, and proximity to power? On what basis would a protagonist who, consigned to a desolate, dreary, swampy place and resistant to capitalist exchange and sexual commerce, be deemed a colonizer and not a member of the colonized class? Indeed, if one recognizes the various ways in which the story suggests that the princess is a person of color, then the interpretation and implications of the story change considerably. Chiefly, to interpret the princess as nonwhite and likely of African descent is to debunk the notion that Du Bois's anti-imperialist allegory is a romanticized portrait of interracial romance. If one acknowledges the princess as a woman of color whose destiny is imperiled by the hegemony of imperialism and not just a sympathetic bystander opposed to imperialism on disinterested moral principles, then Du Bois's anti-imperialist critique appears even stronger, and his portrait of interracial and even cross-caste and intraracial romance seems even more skeptical.

A Remote Princess: Not a Colonialist Maiden but Rather a Colonized Damsel in Distress

Before delving into the historical context of Du Bois's essay "The Hands of Ethiopia," which I recognize as intimately connected to the "Princess of the Hither Isles," I begin in close-reading mode by noting the salient yet often overlooked fact that Du Bois's narration recounts that the princess lives in and presumably rules over a swamp that is "flat," "cold," and covered in "drear-drab" light and all manner of slimy, creeping things, and "piles of dirt and clouds of flying dust" (Du Bois [1920] 1999, 43).[1] We readers find no evidence of royal subjects or servants at the princess's beck and call, and she shrinks from the sounds of "sordid scraping and feeding and noise" (43), bespeaking her placement within a community that must labor in order to survive. In addition to being a dreary, barren place that hardly recalls royal splendor or imperialist wealth, the "Hither Isles" recall Du Bois's statement in "The Hands of Ethiopia" about the practice by which imperialists expropriate lands from the Indigenous and Black inhabitants of the regions they conquer. As Du Bois explains it, through a law reuniting South Africa that is evidently the Native Land Act of 1913, white colonists took the choicest of the native lands for themselves and consigned the Black inhabitants to undesirable lands, specifically, "thirty-six million acres of swamp and marsh for four and a half-million blacks" (33).[2] By this act of so-called nationalist reunification, as Du Bois astutely notes, native African people were dispossessed of their lands and forced onto reservations that amounted to only 7 percent of the available land, largely of the unfertile variety.

I do not mean to suggest that "The Princess of the Hither Isles" is solely reducible to a literary replica of the historic displacement of Indigenous Africans in South Africa. Nor do I believe that Du Bois intended to hone in on any one historical or cultural context to the exclusion of other contexts of Afrodiasporic and other global instances of displacement and dispossession across nation and epoch, since he also mentions several other Pan-African and Pan-Asian contexts in which such expropriation of land and displacement of people occurred (e.g., Ethiopia, Latin America, India, etc.). Rather, I argue that Du Bois offers the dispossession and displacement of colonized persons of color, not as an isolated incident but rather as an indication of the archetypal experience of inhabitants of Africa, Asia, the Caribbean, and Latin America, for he delineates several transnational and transepochal instances in which such expropriation and reallocation of lands have been marshaled as protocolonial maneuvers to dispossess Black people, in which, as he puts it: "Negroes of ability have been carefully gotten rid of, deposed from authority, kept out of positions of influence, and discredited in their people's eyes, while a *caste* of white overseers and governing officials has appeared everywhere" (Du Bois [1920] 1999, 33; emphasis mine). Nor am I insensible to the fact that Du Bois chose the genres of allegory and fairytale precisely to merge diverse historical contexts, trace out various patterns therein, and suggest imagined alternatives to the material horrors of colonialism, racism, and caste disenfranchisement. However, I do wish to call attention to the fact that Du Bois's choice to set his story in the context of white colonialist dispossession of African peoples offers poignant evidence with which to counter the reigning critical assumption that his story is one of a vulnerable, sympathetic, and downwardly mobile white princess. Instead, I submit that Du Bois's allusion to actual historical instances of colonialism adds to his subtle characterization of the princess, not as someone who wishes to abdicate an uneasily held privilege but rather as a subject of colonialist and patriarchal intrigue who is "lonely," vulnerable, and, by virtue of her status as a white-passing Black or multiracial, Afro-descended woman, confined to an isolated, paltry domain reflecting a precarious existence that she abhors and wishes to transcend.

Although the land is characterized as rather mystical and pan-geographical, as if it could be found anywhere, Du Bois's descriptions of the Hither Isles as "dusty," "dreary," "cold," "swampy," and punctuated by the sounds of "sordid scarping and feeding and noise" render it a territory that has plausibly been besieged by war and colonialist ravages. In keeping with this vision of the "Hither Isles" as a land informed by the vicissitudes of colonization and expropriation, the princess, Du Bois intimates, can barely keep the sordid scraping and slime of her environs at bay. Only her "soul" exists somewhere beyond it all, resting "silver-throned," "veiled in humility and fear," and always looking westward to the sun and beyond a hill that Du Bois later describes as having formerly been glorious but ultimately rendered dismal and barren: as "once [. . .] golden, but now [. . .] green and slimy dross" (Du Bois [1920] 1999, 46).[3]

All in all, Du Bois presents a composite picture of a princess who is isolated, disenfranchised, forced to labor amidst ruins, and possessed of the self-same double consciousness attributed to the archetypal Black American subject: with her laboring body torn asunder from her beautiful and "veiled" soul (Du Bois [1920] 1999, 43; see also Du Bois [1903] 2007, 8). The princess, as I will go on to elaborate, symbolizes the liminality of the Black subject caught between Black and white worlds and between states of sovereignty and dispossession—whether in the Caribbean, Latin America, various parts of Africa, or the United States.

Although the Hither Isles seem to be geospatially sovereign or autonomous territories, the islands are also considerably under-resourced, and they lie outside the center of archetypal colonial structures of power. The Hither Isles are certainly wanting when compared either to "Yonder Kingdom" whose setting is "the mountainside where the sun shone warm" and whose "golden-crowned" and "white, thin-lipped" king continues to lay claim to stores of stolen gold (Du Bois [1920] 1999, 43) or to the "Empire of the Sun" from which both the princess and a Black beggar she will soon encounter are barred. Distinct from the golden kingdom and the "silver-hued" swampy isles stands the Empire of the Sun, which Du Bois locates in contiguity to Heaven, in which the sun is itself the sovereign, bedecked in Heaven's blue robes and wearing a crown of its own reflection (44). It is into this space that Du Bois inserts the "beggar man" who seems to be a lost child of the Empire of the Sun and has somehow been confined to the lower reaches of the isles (44). I submit that Du Bois's depiction of a swampy, resource-deprived island, juxtaposed both with a flourishing man-made kingdom of plundered riches and with the natural dominion of the sun recalls the caste division and attendant polarization of white colonial and capitalist enterprise that is thoroughly addressed by Du Bois in "The Hands of Ethiopia," elsewhere in *Darkwater* (in essays like "The Souls of White Folk"), and even in *The Souls of Black Folk*. Indeed, Du Bois's "beggar man," whom he describes as "little and bald and black" and wearing rough, dirty clothes, is flanked by a "squalid, sordid, parti-colored band of vacant, dull-faced" comrades. Together, they function as metonyms for the Empire of the Sun, a colonial site of dispossession (44). The princess, whose natural setting is neither flush with riches nor wholly devoid of resources, is not only geospatially liminal but, I argue, racially and culturally liminal as well.[4]

Indeed, Du Bois's allegorical division of geographic and geopolitical space is what signifies the parallel divisions of racial and caste status—not biology or its seemingly corresponding morphological and visibly legible features. At the top of the geographical pyramid sits "Yonder Kingdom," with its expansiveness and infrastructure fomented by plunder. In the middle between "This and Now" rests the flat, swampy land of the "Hither Isles," flanked by greener hills, high mountains, and the sun. And at the bottom of the scheme sits the beggar who belongs to the purportedly lesser class of the swamp-dwellers and so is doomed to crawl across the swamp and exist in proximity to "a cavalcade of Death and Pain" (Du Bois [1920] 1999,

45). Du Bois's underscoring of the range of geopolitical divisions of caste and his invocation of an island space in particular recall his prior analysis of race in "Conservation of Races" as a matter not so much of biology or morphology but of geographic divisions and distinctions (see Du Bois [1898] 1989). As Paul Taylor avers, race is patently a matter of "social location" (see Taylor 2009).

Thus, while previous readings of the princess as a European colonizer seem reasonably to follow from Du Bois's physical description of her as having a face constituted by "white and blue and pale-gold" (Du Bois [1920] 1999, 43), I nevertheless assert, in addition to the evidence previously gathered, that Du Bois's descriptions are never assigned the specificity or authority of ethnic designations: for he does not call the princess "white," and he does not assign her any specific racial, ethnic, or cultural identity. Rather, Du Bois describes the princess, neither as white nor patently Black but rather as having a face that consists of an abstracted "white and blue and pale-gold" (43). Even the king is described as "tawny" in addition to "white," which undermines the visual clarity and purported "purity" of his whiteness, which is betokened mostly by his unbridled arrogance and power (43). And while the beggar is called "black" in appearance, the existence of his "parti-colored" retinue and the king's dismissal of him and his peers as "niggers and dagoes" suggests that his racial identity may also be more complex than a simple matter of Black or white, as it suggests a multiracial group of people joined in poverty and subjection and not necessarily united in appearance or corresponding racial designation.[5] Indeed, Du Bois's racial cues are deliberately left ambiguous, unmoored as they are from the authority of empirical logic and confined to the level of abstract, imagistic description. These are mere physical descriptions, visual markers that nevertheless cannot be assumed to carry the authority of racial designations. While Du Bois's description of the princess could mean, as perhaps may be assumed by some readers, that she has a white face, blue eyes, and hair of "pale-gold," it might equally be the case that she has white hair, blue eyes, and skin of pale gold—perhaps suggesting a mixed-race woman of Caribbean, Latin American, or another multiethnic descent.

Moreover, it must be acknowledged that, as Du Bois well knew, persons of African descent cannot be divined as such merely by recourse to their physical descriptions. In the 1913 issue of *The Crisis*, in which "Princess of the Hither Isles" first appears, the story (called an "editorial") is flanked by photographs of African American children and families, many of whom are white-appearing, especially when juxtaposed to their darker-complexioned siblings. These photos hearken back to Du Bois's own curated photographic show at the Paris Exposition in 1900. In an essay on Du Bois's visual representations of Black life, cultural historian Shawn Michelle Smith points out how the Georgia Negro Exhibit that Du Bois sent to the Paris Exposition "dismantled" the idea of a "negro type," or more pointedly, the visual logic of racialism whereby racial identity was said to correspond to skin color and hair texture: "Indeed, the albums represent a diverse array of individuals who are not bound by physical appearance, by the 'hair and bone and color' that Du Bois rejects as singular signs of racial belonging in his essay of 1897 'The Conservation of Races'" (Smith 2007, 357). Du Bois's album shows blond and pale examples of Black people, which as Smith allows, "challenge [. . .] the color line as a marker of racial difference and the body itself as sign of racial meaning" (357). In particular, the portraits of "white-looking African Americans in the Georgia Negro albums contest a white supremacist racial taxonomy of identifiable (because visible) otherness" (359). The photographs provide "evidence" of the fallibility of racial taxonomy and racial legibility via scopophilic measures of empiricism. Of the white-looking women in particular, Smith says that white supremacists often "posed the light-skinned woman of color as both the object and instigator of interracial mixing, as both the sign and cause of racial degeneration" (361). Du Bois's photographs, as Smith submits, "reclaim [. . .] the image of the pale African American woman so highly fetishized in racial hierarchies, re-presenting her as a woman of grace, elegance, and refinement" (361). I suggest that in literary works like "Princess of the Hither Isles," Du Bois shows a light-skinned and even white-appearing Black woman as a most emphatically unwilling victim of white interest and intrigue. By rejecting white interest, intrigue, and identification, the princess becomes a potential symbol of a Pan-African nation or even of a Pan-African alternative to the nation-state. She represents the audacity of a Black woman who wishes to be with her own people "in the sun" and not to claim the white privilege perhaps falsely ascribed to or accommodated by her pale skin.

The Hither Isles as Maroon Territory

Admittedly, the notion of a "princess" with her own territory, autonomous yet under-resourced and under siege, is somewhat paradoxical. The princess and her setting of the Hither Isles may indeed symbolize the geopolitical vulnerability of colonization, yet they may also symbolize the precarious geospatial sovereignty that persons of African descent often carve out within and despite imperial political structures. In fact, I submit that in the princess's geopolitical setting, as sketched by Du Bois, one may fruitfully read an intimation of a resistant, fugitive territory actively resistant to colonial rule and expropriation, such as that represented by the various borderlands and hinterlands of Pan-African maroon communities within the Caribbean and the United States. With his invocation of the "swampy" quality of the "Hither Isles" (Du Bois [1920] 1999, 43), Du Bois may well have been alluding to what was termed "the Great Dismal Swamp," a maroon community on the border of Virginia and South Carolina, shunned by the leaders of the US southern slaveocracy and commandeered as a refuge for African American and newly arrived African slaves seeking to escape or avoid slavery. Such maroon communities are described by Sylviane A. Diouf as "dynamic site[s] of empowerment, migrations, encounters, communication, exchange, solidarity, resistance, and entangled stories" as well as a "contested terrain" sought after by slaveholders and other members of the Euro-American or European power structure (2014, 10). The "Great Dismal Swamp" was initially inhabited by Native Americans and by the eighteenth century, and up until the end of the Civil War, it became a refuge for persons of African descent. Captured in literary discourses by Harriet Beecher Stowe, Harriet Jacobs, Martin Delaney, and Henry Wadsworth Longfellow, whose poem, "The Slave in the Dismal Swamp," centers the great dismal swamp (located on the border of Virginia and North Carolina), these Afro-maroon communities, which maintained some degree of sovereignty, even as they were unable to fully extricate themselves, either from slave or indentured labor, were also addressed by Du Bois's friend and literary executor, Herbert Aptheker, in his work *American Negro Slave Revolts* (see Aptheker 1937). As Diouf explains: "The arrival of large numbers of Africans, their propensity to run away, the lure of the mountains, European colonial jousting for territory, and events in Jamaica all coalesced to shift the colonists' focus to the eventuality of established maroon communities" (2014, 37). Some maroon territories had more fluid borders than others, standing, as Diouf notes, "at the intersection of three worlds. One was their refuge, another the white-controlled territory of the fields, the Big House outbuildings, and sometimes the Big House itself. The third was the physical and social terrain carved out by the enslaved community, from the quarters to the neighboring plantations and farms" (8). This corresponds roughly to the three spaces outlined by Du Bois in the story: the Hither Isles; the "Big House," as emblematized by Yonder Kingdom; and the slave plantations, symbolized by the beggar and his retinue. Moreover, as Daniel Sayers points out, outside of the context of the plantation, some borderland maroons also worked in European-run capitalist projects, such as building canals (Sayers 2014, 115). The hinterland maroons, or what Sayers calls those who dwelled in "the scission" (114), were more remote from and somewhat autonomous with regard to the imperial strictures of the body of the Americas.

Although there were accounts from colonial statesmen of maroons who appeared to be "mulattoes" (Sayers 2014, 88), indeed, there were also likely some maroon communities made up nearly entirely of Africans, where they built their own houses and, according to amateur historian T. E. Campbell, "set up a tribal government under a chief, who had been a prince among his own people before slave traders brought him across the Atlantic" (quoted in Diouf 2014, 60). Such an account corresponds to folktales about maroon communities that included descriptions of "tribes of negroes with descendants of African kings" (Diouf 2014, 225). Although there is no literal royalty mentioned in such accounts, and indeed, most historians of maroon communities point out that women were few among the numbers of refugees, Du Bois's figure of the princess may certainly have meant to evoke the mythological possibility of African royalty on American soil and with it the promise of an anti (and ante) colonial and antislavery form of African liberation. Imagining the princess and her "isles" may have been Du Bois's way of indexing a Pan-African environ in which African royalty or their descendants could rule over their own lands. Nevertheless, it is useful to recall that although marronage marks the possibility of Black autonomy, most maroons had to maintain some labor relations with those outside their sovereign territory, as Herbert Aptheker maintained (Sayers 2014, 88) and as Sayers underscores in his assessment of labor practices in the maroon communities. This is a key point because it explains both how the princess could be a site of exchange, with her island poised for expropriation, and how the beggar could be both a maroon *and* an indentured or otherwise vulnerable laborer. On the one hand, the princess holds a position elevated above that of a beggar or laborer. Yet on the other hand, her elevated position—whether political, social, or cultural (if indeed she is of a "mulatto" or mestizo class), renders her peculiarly vulnerable to European encroachment and sexual violation.

The "Real" Princess of the Hither Isles: Historical Allusion or Imagined, Revisionist History?

My claim that Du Bois's allegorical fairy tale showcases and honors the resistance of a white-appearing or white-passing Black woman is punctuated in suggestive ways by the recent work of historian and creative memoirist Adele Logan Alexander, whose book about her grandmother, Adella Hunt Logan, a white-passing Black woman and antiracism activist, foregrounds the possibility of racial passing as an act of subterfuge. Adella Hunt Logan was the wife of one of Booker T. Washington's closest associates at Tuskegee and an acquaintance of Du Bois who sometimes contributed pieces on women's suffrage to *The Crisis*. Possessed of a pale face and a progressive spirit opposed both to women's oppression and Black accommodation (the kind recommended by her husband's employer and friend Booker T. Washington), Adella Hunt Logan suffered for her racial liminality, even as she exploited it for progressive purposes. Extraordinarily, Logan Alexander actually titles the partly fictionalized and partly biographical account of her grandmother *The Princess of the Hither Isles* because she believes that Du Bois may have had Adella in mind when he created his story (Logan Alexander 2019, 159, 353). Logan Alexander bases her speculation partly on a secondhand story of her grandmother's meeting with Du Bois, as related to her by African American scholar Charles H. Wesley (343), an acquaintance of her grandmother. Logan Alexander speculates not only that the princess may have been based on her grandmother (also an isolated, sometimes sad white-passing Black woman) but also that the "Hither Isles" may have been inspired by Tuskegee, as it was also a "remote and secluded realm" (159, 259) and its founder and leader, Booker T. Washington, an authoritative man who enjoyed smoking, as does the ruler of Yonder Kingdom. Writes Logan Alexander: "W. E. B. Du Bois never disclosed his story's derivation or the inspirations for his dramatis personae, but recognizing his vitriol toward Mr. Washington, [it was possible] that [Du Bois's] gold-hungry King was a fictionalized portrait of the Wizard of Tuskegee or even of her husband as the institute's treasurer" (260). Aside from the reference to Charles Wesley, Logan Alexander offers no evidence for her premise about the sources of Du Bois's story. Indeed, her reading of Booker T. Washington as the King of Yonder Kingdom seems somewhat improbable. Washington was not, after all, an imperialist (if perhaps he sometimes played the role of tyrant). Nevertheless, Logan Alexander does offer us a portrait of a white-passing Black woman and an isolated and barely Black-governed Tuskegee. Her reading of her family's princess as a Black woman, simultaneously hemmed in and protected by her seclusion, hews so closely to my own reading of the "Princess of the Hither Isles" as a lonely, ambivalent white-passing Black or mixed-race woman that I find it auspicious to offer it here.[6]

Moreover, Adele Logan Alexander's reading of Du Bois's allegorical tale as reflecting a domestic scene of African American experience is also interesting to me because it countermands the common critical interpretation of the story as exclusively reflecting Du Bois's anti-imperial and international interests. While the story is clearly symbolic of colonialist tropes including those of a secluded island setting and a geopolitically divided power, it also offers cues about Du Bois's critique of an American landscape as a protocolonial region, one torn apart by racial injustice and ready to be met with Black resistance. For example, the princess decidedly recalls Du Bois's characterization of Black Americans (and by extension, other members of the diaspora removed from Africa) in the opening chapter of *Souls*, as marked by the presence of a veil that symbolizes the Black American's removal from some of the basic rights, resources, and luxuries often commandeered by those inhabitants of the white or Euro-dominating world. Like Du Bois's prototypical Black American subject, endowed with a double consciousness that leaves her suspended between two disparate heritages and social locations (marked respectively by Africa and Euro-America), the princess has a "soul" that is veiled—hidden, as it were, by the shadow of racial caste prejudice. The princess thus recalls Du Bois's previous depictions of the Afrodiasporic subject trapped in a liminal space of limited mobility and mitigated privilege. In articulating her desire to "fly" above the dust and dreariness of her existence (Du Bois [1920] 1999, 43), the Princess of the Hither Isles reprises both Du Bois as he presents himself in the opening chapter of *Souls*, trapped as an "outcast" in the only home he knows, and his protagonist John Jones from the penultimate chapter of *Souls*, who also wishes to "rise" above his circumstances and merge with the setting sun ([1903] 2007, 8, 158). Moreover, as the princess experiences a frustrated form of intimacy with the white king of Yonder Kingdom, she might also be said to recall Du Bois's story of the visiting card that I highlight in my introductory chapter, in which a Black subject tries and fails to forge intimacy with a white one. This time, in a reversal of the moment in *Souls*, it is the princess who repudiates the king, as she finds him altogether too "icy" to inspire within her any embers of affection (Du Bois [1920] 1999, 43).

Moreover, the fact that the princess keeps her soul "veiled" in "humility and fear" suggests not only her subaltern status (certainly not befitting a royal) and her vulnerability to powerful forces out of her control but also her fear of sexual violence in particular. This fact places her in the long line of Black women that Du Bois describes elsewhere in *Darkwater* as particularly vulnerable to white male violation (e.g., in the poem "The Riddle of the Sphinx") in which he bemoans the Black woman "crying and sighing and crying again as a voice in the midnight cries," while "the burden of white men bore her back and the white world stifled her sighs" ([1920] 1999, 30). The princess's feelings for the king are ambivalent at best and at worst border on repugnance, as she concedes to his advances chiefly to escape her impoverished locale and vulnerable position. Yet she does not love him and cannot relate to him, as she finds him made of "singularly sodden clay" (43). Ultimately, the princess is indignant in the face of the king's avarice, and she meets his suggestion of "finding" more gold with a rebuke: "Hell seize your gold!" She adds further that any gold in the king's store belongs not to him but to those dwellers of the Empire of the Sun (44).

In addition, the princess's humility and anticapitalist spirit, which Du Bois frequently attributed to persons of African descent, as for example, in his essay "Jefferson Davis" (which I refer to in my opening chapter) in *Souls,* and in works like *The Gift of Black Folk* (1896), is sharply contrasted with the arrogance, stinginess, and rapaciousness of the colonialist king. The princess palpably embodies Du Bois's repeated portraits of persons of African descent as antiracist and anticapitalist, since she is repulsed by an America (or perhaps by a region of the Americas) that she conceptualizes, as does Du Bois in *Souls,* as a "dusty desert of dollars" (Du Bois [1903] 2007, 14). Thus, she is ambivalent about if not wholly successful in her resistance to the appropriation of herself and her brethren.

Unimpressed, disturbed, and even fearful of what seems to be her only way out of the drabness of the island, the princess is nevertheless uninterested in the form of salvation offered her by the king. She is resolutely unwilling to raise her status via recourse to plundered riches or other sources of capitalist exploitation or via any sexual commerce with the king (a point to which I will return). By contrast, she is easily lured by the sun above her, whose "own face is blackness" and in whose visage she "senses" "unfathomed understanding" ([1920] 1999, 44). Allegorically speaking, the sun symbolizes Blackness (ontologically and historically, insofar as it indexes a lost African empire), patently contrasted with the icy, cool, damp, and morose qualities of both the king and his kingdom, and with the princess's own damp and dusty domicile that seems to be simultaneously out of time and out of place. Drawing out his theme of misbegotten romance, Du Bois places in the princess's path the beggar man who is "creeping across the swamp" (44) as an extension of the sun's warmth and brilliance. Although the princess exits at the zenith of the Hither Isles, enthroned in a place of pride, the beggar must crawl, even "writhe" (44) across his environs. This suggests that although the princess and beggar may belong to the same territory or nation, they occupy markedly different stations within it. The king is quick to dismiss the beggar and his crew as a bunch of beggars who are also "niggers and dagoes"—which suggests not just anti-Black but also anti-Brown racism (along with classism) and also, again, points to the fact that the allegorical setting for Du Bois's story is a plausible composite of some colony in the Caribbean or the Americas, of African territories that share a history of expropriation, and that of the settler colony that is the United States as well.

Yet the princess is undeterred and finds herself gazing yearningly at the beggar who returns her gaze with a look "full and slow" and who elicits in her not only sympathy but a sense of "understanding" and familiarity that underscores the fact that they may not be so much strangers as estranged kin: "He looked upon her full and slow and suddenly she saw within that formless black and burning face the same soft, glad gleam of utter understanding, seen so many times before. She saw the suffering of endless years and endless love that softened it" ([1920] 1999, 45).[7] The princess turns toward and away from the beggar in an oscillating display of desire and terror (45). Reading the princess and the beggar not as racial opposites coming together against the odds but instead as estranged racial kin drawn together in an intuitive but fraught and inchoate iteration of intimacy, I argue that the relationship between the princess and the beggar is not the interracial romance that Alys Weinbaum and others describe as the symbol of anticolonial exchange. Rather, it is an intracultural yet cross-caste romance, one ultimately redolent of failed intimacy, which symbolizes the drama of the Middle Passage and of forced Afrodiasporic dispossession at the hands of Euro-American imperialists.

As the princess regards the beggar as a remote yet familiar subject, of whom she may have some dim memory and for whom she feels a mystical form of connection ([1920] 1999, 45), she is emblematic of the tenuous relation that Nancy Yousef has identified among intimacy, knowledge, and sympathy, which she attributes to transcontinental romanticism belonging to the "long nineteenth-century" and beyond and finds reflected in the works of thinkers and writers ranging from Rousseau to Wordsworth to Jane Austen. Yousef meditates on the long-standing philosophic conundrum about whether intimacy and sympathy depend upon knowledge (2013, 202), and Du Bois seems to suggest that both intimacy and sympathy might be of the nonreciprocal and intuitive variety. Like the "passing stranger" found in the imaginary of Walt Whitman, an American romantic poet with whom Du Bois would certainly have been familiar, the princess regards the beggar with equal parts longing and familiarity, a sense of mystery flanked by the intimation of a distant memory and an expression of solicitude bordering on duty. It is as if she, like the narrator of Whitman's poem, believes of the beggar that she has "somewhere surely lived a life of joy with [him]" ([1900] 1998). Like Whitman's stranger, the beggar gives the princess the "pleasure" of his "eyes, face, and flesh." And like Whitman's narrator, the princess does not speak to the beggar but nevertheless becomes determined "not to lose [him]" ([1900] 1998).

The juxtaposition of the familiar and the strange in the princess's limited engagement with the beggar also recalls Du Bois's neo-romanticist and Pan-Africanist figurations in *The Souls of Black Folk* and beyond of the Black American and/or Afrodiasporic subject, whose link to Africa has been severed yet who nevertheless feels a strong affinity for that nation and its inhabitants and by-products. This is exemplified in Du Bois's description of the Black artist who senses the "soul-beauty" of a race from which he has been forcibly estranged and who must nurture and translate that beauty for his Black and white American compatriots ([1903] 2007, 9). And it echoes firmly in this passage from his essay on Black spirituals, or "sorrow songs," as Du Bois terms them, in which he describes how one might "know" the offspring of one's cultural heritage without actually knowing them in a rational or empirical sense. Of his ancestors and their cultural gifts, Du Bois insists, "They came out of the South unknown to me, one by one, and yet at once I knew them as of me and mine" (167). And of the gamut of African folk songs, he insists, "I know little of music and can say nothing in technical phrase, but I know something of men, and knowing them, I know that these songs are the articulate message of the slave to the world" (169). The intimacy and intuited knowledge of ancestral kin and the offshoots of their cultural legacy that Du Bois imputes to the exiled Black American resonate in his description of the princess's intuitive yet strained understanding of the beggar. She knows him without knowing him, intuits his value, and sees in him a half-formed message and, importantly, a faintly perceived call to action. Arguably, this form of knowing without knowing is what K. Anthony Appiah has described as *verstehen*, an intuitive form of apprehension not dependent upon empirical or rational knowledge (2014, 78–79). This is itself a type of double consciousness, as it functions as a kind of "second sight," an intuitive form of *ante*-knowledge that is based in a dialectical epistemology, one that reveals truth as an amalgam of divided thoughts, "warring ideals," and "unreconciled strivings" (Du Bois [1903] 2007, 8).

Drawn to the beggar and all that he represents, the princess nevertheless appears to concede to the king's request for her hand. To his request that she see his gold "when they marry," the princess seems to verbally consent, uttering the phrase "I come" ([1920] 1999, 45). Yet astute readers of Du Bois will recognize in that phrase an echo of John's statement in "Of the Coming of John" just after he hears the strains of Wagner's opera while sojourning in a New York City opera house, far from his home. Initially, John's "coming" refers to his intention to return home to his own Black folk. And when repeated, it signals his willingness to commit suicide (after having committed murder on his sister's behalf) rather than to be killed or to see his kin hampered by shackles or shame ([1903] 2007, 154, 159). Emphasizing again the intertextual echoes between the "Princess of the Hither Isles" and *Souls*, I submit that Du Bois draws a line between John and the princess, suggesting that she, like him (and also like the dispossessed beggar), is a Black subject lost to the vagaries of assimilation and poised to return to her rightful homeland.[8] This archetypal and apocalyptic search for one's homeland is captured by Du Bois in this, one of the story's most abstract passages:

> And so they marched and struggled on and up through endless years and spaces and ever the black beggar looked back past death and pain toward the maid and ever the maid strove forward with lovelit eyes, but ever the great and silken shoulders of the king of Yonder Kingdom arose between the princess and the sun like a cloud of storms. ([1920] 1999, 45)

Indeed, this story of a lost Black subject marching on through time and space in search of the homeland from which s/he has been estranged and hindered in her search by the ruthlessness machinations of Eurocentric political schemes is paradigmatic of the Afrodiasporic experience. Just as the Black beggar represents the pain and suffering of the Middle Passage, of slavery, and of colonial servitude, so too does the princess represent the partially assimilated Black subject of the Americas saved from the fate of literal death but fated to suffer a social death (in the form of isolation or captivity) from which she seeks release. Similarly, the white or colonialist-caste king stands between the Black subject seeking her past and her kinfolk. Indeed, the "spaces" (45) that Du Bois repeatedly describes as marking the distance between beggar and princess and princess and king serve as reminders of what repeatedly happens in instances of colonial displacement. The romances here are both inter- and intraracial or cultural, and their failures—or "impossibilities," as Hee-Jung Serenity Joo astutely terms them (2019)—

mark Du Bois's revision of his trope of cross-caste romance: not as a site of conjugal or other intersubjective union between two people but more so as a site of autoerotic resistance that refuses sexual commerce between those estranged by caste and class difference and perhaps even sexual exchange writ large.

In fact, Du Bois's depiction of the "romance" between the princess and the king, although always frustrated, takes on an even more inauspicious tone as the story concludes. For Du Bois positions the king not as a means to the princess's ascension to a higher-class status but rather as a threat to the princess's development and even her very existence. Du Bois writes that the king's "silken shoulders [. . .] arose between the princess and the sun like a cloud of storms" ([1920] 1999, 45), suggesting that he is in the way of her destiny, which is anchored in the lost African kingdom symbolized by the empire of the "rising, blazing sun" (45). In yet another allusion to the loss wrought by the Middle Passage and the nostalgic dream of African retention, Du Bois writes that the beggar, under the loving gaze of the princess, takes on the look of ancient royalty as he becomes "enhaloed and transfigured," stretching out his arms like Ethiopia herself (45; Psalms 68:31). The princess's ultimate decision to offer her heart, whether to the Black beggar or to the sun that he represents, constitutes her decision to refuse romantic or sexual commerce with the king and thus to refuse to enter into assimilationist and colonialist relations of exchange. Regardless of whether the princess is a white-passing Black woman or a mestiza woman, the "romance" in the story is embodied not simply in the foreclosed one between the princess and the beggar but also in the failed one—and violently so—between the princess and the white king, who, upon being rejected by her, dismembers her. The king not only insists that the princess have no intercourse with the beggar—and indeed no commerce with the Empire of the Sun—but he violently commandeers the princess's body, punishing her gesture of love for the beggar and the sun (for she has ripped out her heart for them) by cutting off her hand until it drifts "disembodied" through the air (46). The extreme violence of the king recalls Du Bois's frequent descriptions of white imperial violence against Black women.[9] The profound and overarching implications of the king's violent response to the princess's benevolent gesture are that the very earth is "rent" (46). And then comes Du Bois's emphatic reminder that the violation of the princess is emblematic of the violation of a colonized land deprived of its former glory but nevertheless haunted by the ongoing glory of its ancestral domain, the Empire of the Sun:

> On yonder distant shore blazed the Empire of the Sun in warm and blissful radiance, while on this side, in shadows cold and dark, gloomed the Hither Isles and the hill that once was golden, but now was green and slimy dross; all below was the sad and moaning sea, while between the Here and There flew the severed hand and dripped the bleeding heart. (46)

This moment of tragic violence is punctuated by the cry of the princess, which recalls the cry that comes out of "that sad black South" with which I began this essay (30). It is a cry, Du Bois instructs, that emanates from the princess's "soul," and it betokens a sound of the kind of despair that only "babe-raped mothers" and "murdered loves" experience (30). Palpably, this cry recalls those uttered from the Global South—in its various regions—as embodied in the figure of a Black woman violated and disenfranchised by a white man who "b [ears] her back" and a white world who "stifle [s] her sighs" (30). Indeed, the princess leaping to her death can be read both as an act of murder and one of suicide, which renders her both a victim and a renegade who refuses and thereby protests the narrow terms of her existence. In "The Souls of White Folk," also found in *Darkwater*, Du Bois emphatically defines whiteness, not as skin color or biological lineage, but as what is facilitated through an expression of "the ownership of the earth forever and ever, Amen!" (18). As "The Princess of the Hither Isles" instructs, such ownership of the earth includes the territory of women's bodies, especially those of women of color.

On Failure and the Possibility of Black Fugitivity

As the princess chooses her own death over a relationship with the imperialist king, the ending of her story indicates the failure of Black assimilation into the Euro-dominated Americas. As Claudia Tate indicates, the end of "The Princess of the Hither Isles" suggests the failure of Black culture to resolve its physical, psychic, and geographic fragmentation (1995, xviii) whether by capitulating to the white world (as the princess refuses to marry the king) or by reuniting with the Black one (as the princess is unable to find true intimacy with the beggar). This marks the story's dystopia, echoing the failure of "The Tale of the Visiting Card" from the opening chapter of *Souls* and bemoaning the impossibility either of Afro-accommodation into European- or American-dominated body politics or of African retention and reclamation. For the story also seems to negate the possibility of Black reunification, symbolized by the princess's misbegotten and foreclosed intimacy with the beggar. Indeed, the failure of the princess to concretize her feelings for the beggar symbolizes the foreclosed utopian possibilities of what Du Bois advocates in "The Hands of Ethiopia": the synthesis of people of color for the cause of pro-Black liberation. Moreover, one could read her disembodied hand as belonging to Ethiopia itself, perhaps blurring the line between being "cut off" and "outstretched" ([1920] 1999, 42; Psalms 68:31).

With this story, then, Du Bois takes his favored trope of the cross-caste romance, often presented as a vehicle for interracial and intercaste conciliation and turns it on its head. For he now shows us not only how insufficient romance and intimacy might be in forging political coalitions and overcoming political errors but also how romance and intimacy might be deployed as the very vehicles of racist and colonial violence and expropriation. "The Princess of the Hither Isles" thus marks a significant turn in the political trajectory of Du Bois's literary works, from a more resigned attitude toward assimilation and interracial cooperation to a pointedly negative assessment of its drawbacks. As I earlier argued, the strength and poignancy of Du Bois's anticolonial and antiassimilationist critique are fruitfully discerned if one recognizes the princess not as a white woman who objects to a colonial enterprise but as an Afro-descended woman of color directly impacted by and emphatically resistant to it. The intersection of eros and politics, then, is less a matter of nationalist "conciliation," akin to what Doris Sommer and Lisa Moore describe in their respective studies of nineteenth-century Irish and Latin American literary romances, than a matter of transnational, interracial, and cross-caste violence.[10]

Finally, in thinking further about the historical echoes of Du Bois's configuration of romance as the very site of violence and African cultural annihilation, I reflect upon the history of medieval and classical literary romances in which romance, as Stacey Triplette argues, proves a phenomenon in which "marriage substitutes for warfare, and colonial relationships become predicated on marital ties" (2010, 23, 34). Such unequal cross-caste instances of expropriation also occurred in the Amadis de Gaula medieval romances in which Christian knights would conspire to marry and "convert" their pagan brides and thus, to "assume leadership over their new wives' inherited territories" (23), including, of course, the domains of their bodies. An infamous example of such appropriative exchange is found in Cervantes's famed medieval romance, *Don Quixote,* which features Micomicona, an Ethiopian princess who wishes to marry a European knight who promises to defend her from a giant but who in actuality conspires to sell and exploit her. It is important to note that said princess has a "snow-white complexion and golden tresses" (45), underscoring the fact that the presence of African ancestry need not manifest in the visual details of the body. Moreover, such a plot in which a European man with colonialist aspirations is interested, not only in consorting with but in marrying a fair-skinned woman of Africanist ancestry draws attention to the practice by which European men have historically transgressed racial boundaries, not in order to defy the logics of racialism and racism but rather to further reinforce and exploit them. Here, I recall the complex workings of intimacy, as Nancy Yousef, Lauren Berlant, and Darieck Scott have all described them, which may just as easily accommodate antipathy, abuse, and inequity as they do affection, solicitude, and reciprocity.

The failures and limitations of intimacy would seem to apply equally to the princess's feelings for the beggar, which do not amount to any change in political structure or to any program of justice, even when she makes the dramatic gesture of ripping out her heart. Nevertheless, the futility of her gesture of love and the continued estrangement of the princess, both from the beggar and from the domicile of the sun that he embodies, may be mitigated if one considers, not the telos of reciprocal justice (clearly something Du Bois was gesturing toward) but rather, the potential of what Jose Muñoz describes as "queer failure." As Muñoz elaborates, queer failure is "aligned" with "a certain mode of virtuosity that helps [one] to exit from the stale and static lifeworld dominated by the alienation, exploitation, and drudgery associated with capitalism" (2009, 173). Extrapolating from Muñoz, I submit that one may read the conclusion of "The Princess of the Hither Isles" as bespeaking a form of "queer failure" that constitutes a "radical negativity," virtuosic in its rebuttal of the untenable realities of the unjust sociopolitical structures that dominate and demarcate the present. As such, radical negativity ". . . becomes the resource for a certain mode of queer utopianism" (12). Such "radical negativity" also corresponds to the quality and scope of Black resistance, in particular, which Fred Moten theorizes as the capacity to evade commodification or subjection by "speaking back" from the perspective and position of the commodity and thereby exerting a "dispossessive force" (2003, loc. 80 of 5, 898). Moten further conceives of Black resistance as a form of "fugitivity," which he defines as "a performative against all performances of freedom and unfreedom dependent on the historical dilemma of a lack of meaningful distinction between freedom and slavery" (2018, 247).[11] I believe that this notion of fugitivity, which transcends even the differentiation between freedom and captivity and relies upon a paradoxically nonperformative mode of performance, is perfectly encapsulated in the princess's death, especially when read as suicide, and thus as her refusal to enter into sexual or any kind of commerce, either with a proponent of white colonial power or even with the forces of life itself. For in tearing out her heart, she does not allow it to be placed into any but symbolic service. As the princess refuses to be a colonial or a sexual commodity, dismembering herself and flouting the very exigency of living in favor of extricating herself from the pain of social death, she speaks back through the affective language of gesture, undercutting at once the "logics" of white supremacy, imperialist plunder, and sexual or reproductive exchange.

Chapter Four

Crossing Caste and Queering Kinship
Du Bois's Utopian Afro-Asian Romance

In Du Bois's 1935 essay "India," he cites the ineluctable correlations between African and Indian histories and thereby asserts the shared political destinies of the African and Asian diasporas (quoted in Mullen 2005, loc. 330 of 2535). As Bill Mullen has argued in *Afro-Orientalism*, Du Bois nurtured "a vision of an alternative modernity rooted in and routed through the African and Asian worlds" (2004, 7). Du Bois's belief in the correspondence between ancient Africa and ancient India was likely informed by his belief in the controversial and disputed "two-race" theory of India as a culture constituted by a clash of Aryan and Dravidian (Indigenous) peoples.[1] As Yogita Goyal submits, Du Bois's account of the formation of India is, in his words, one of the "fierce struggles between these whites [Aryans] and blacks [original inhabitants] for . . . mastery" (quoted in Goyal 2019, 57). Yet Du Bois need not have relied on any ethnological or anthropological discourse to affirm his belief in India as a nation "of color," for as always, he tended to theorize racialization more as a matter of geopolitical position than biological or metaphysical character. In his characterization of India, Du Bois declared: "She has long wished to regard herself as 'Aryan' rather than 'colored' and to think of herself as much nearer physically and spiritually to Germany and England than to Africa, China or the South Seas. And yet the history of the modern world shows the futility of this thought. European exploitation desires the Black slave, the Chinese coolie and the Indian laborer for the same ends and the same purposes, and calls them all 'niggers'" (quoted in Mullen 2005, loc. 338 of 2535). Du Bois's desire to assert a historical kinship with India and to analogize its caste system to the caste logic undergirding the American slaveocracy (see Mullen 2005 and Goyal 2010, 2019) was buttressed by his political affiliation and personal camaraderie with Indian nationalists including Lala Lajpat Rai, one of the founders of the Hindu reform movement Arya Samaj and a proponent of Indian Home Rule. And it was developed artistically in his 1928 allegorical novel *Dark Princess*.[2]

The story of two persons of color both undergoing European exile to escape racist and imperialist oppression, Matthew Towns, a Black American medical student barred from ascending the ladder of his profession and Princess Kautilya, a young Indian princess fighting for the political independence of her country, *Dark Princess* stages the cross-caste romance of the embattled pair as the catalysts for an international mission to forge global solidarity among distinct communities of people of color, proffering a revolutionary, queer form of kinship by which Africa and Asia would be reunited as lost branches of an Afro-Asiatic family estranged by European colonialism. After working together on their anti-imperialist mission, being separated and undergoing parallel periods of renunciation, Matthew and Princess Kautilya reunite for the birth of their child, the "mixed-race" embodiment of "reproductive messianism," in Madhumita Lahiri's terms. The child functions, then, as the "political solution" to the twin problems of racism and empire and cements a new genealogy of Afro-Asiatic royalty that simultaneously invokes and inverts the caste logic undergirding both Indian nationalism and US racism (Lahiri 2010).

In this chapter, I analyze Du Bois's investment in a form of Afro-Asian solidarity and kinship that relies on his analogizing of the Indian caste system to American racial apartheid, plumbing his uses of romance, allegory, and folkloric allusion to index a revisionary history and utopian, transnational politics that together aim to rebut the nation-state's participation in racist isolationism and the Western European tradition of capitalist imperialism. Such revisionist history and progressive politics also proffer new forms of Black subjectivity and transnational "colored" communities, which mark Du Bois's transition from Afro-nationalist politics to global decolonial politics and also help to illuminate his repertoire of cross-caste romances as increasingly resistant to the drawbacks of assimilation. By exploring Du Bois's most direct and extensive deployment of the discourse of caste, I analyze the way he analogizes caste and race in order to posit a connection between Africa and India that is, as Homi Bhabha allows, both "archaic and avant-garde," signaling a precolonial logic that values the

Indigenous claims and folkways of ancient civilizations while simultaneously embodying a postcolonial praxis committed to dismantling imperialism (2004, 146). Du Bois uses the analogy between caste and racism to posit an alternative geopolitical location for African Americans in India, both to invert the caste system that misrecognizes Black persons as less human than Europeans and to build a modern, anti-imperial alliance between persons of African and South Asian descent in which, as Bill Mullen remarks, India might become "the significant other" to Black America (Mullen 2003, 235). While I acknowledge that Du Bois's address of Indian history and politics in *Dark Princess* was undertaken, chiefly to dramatize and internationalize the cause of Black liberation, and was therefore, somewhat appropriative of South Asian history and politics, I nevertheless find his stand against global imperialism to have been a significant display of solidarity for the cause of Indian independence.

In my previous examinations of Du Bois's *Souls* in the introduction and first chapter of this book, I theorize how Du Bois uses the cross-caste romance to mark the possibility of conciliatory assimilation or productive exchange between white and Black persons as a trope for nationalist reunification (albeit of the pluralist variety), and in my analysis of "The Princess of the Hither Isles" in chapter 3, I analyze how cross-caste romance, when fraught, failed, or otherwise undermined, functions as a trope for antinationalist, decolonial praxis. With my analysis of *Dark Princess*, I explore how an idealized configuration of a cross-caste romance, unfixed from European cultural or political hegemony, might be proffered as an instrument of decolonial reclamation. In this formulation, the binaristic logics of racialism, capitalism, and imperialism are equally undermined, proffering forms of revolution and kinship that, as I will go on to outline, are decidedly queer. I argue that Du Bois, by deploying the discourse of caste in *Dark Princess*, crosses and romances it, simultaneously reanimating and subverting its laws, selectively adapting its values, and positing alternative trajectories for its development, or better put, its devolution. As I acknowledged in my introduction, numerous critics, including Claudia Tate, Michele Elam, Paul Taylor, Alys Weinbaum, Brent Edwards, R. A. Judy, and Herman Beavers have commented on Du Bois's fictionalized investments in eros and/or love as vehicles of political and anti-imperial protest, especially as demonstrated in his novel *Dark Princess*, which he claimed to be his "favorite" work, one published in the midst of the Harlem Renaissance: a period in which artistic and erotic energies were routinely marshaled in the service of Black liberation. Michele Elam and Paul Taylor, in particular, in their collaborative essay "Du Bois's Erotics" recognize that *Dark Princess*'s advocacy for the political currency of romance and eros is reflected in the various intellectual movements coterminous with the publication of Du Bois's novel, including Victorian "erotomania" and Nietzschean perfectionism, which ascribe to erotic and sexual energy an intellectual and political capability (Elam and Taylor 2007, 220).

In her analyses of *Dark Princess*, Yogita Goyal also insists upon the pointedly political trajectory of the novel's interest in the power of intimacy, since the novel reflects Du Bois's commitment to the political qualities of romance, a literary genre and mode of discourse that Goyal associates with internationalist narratives of diaspora and that she also views as marking Du Bois's particular investment in positing India as an important site of Black reclamation and anticolonial politics.[3] Drawing on key analyses of *Dark Princess*, and in particular, on the insights of Mullen and Goyal, who examines in particular Du Bois's frequent analogizing of race in the United States and caste in India, Madhumita Lahiri, and Homi Bhabha—all of whom foreground *Dark Princess* as reflective of Du Bois's commitment to Afro-Asian solidarity—I argue that Du Bois's novel derives its political significance as a paean to decolonization, chiefly from its invocation and somewhat subversive treatment of caste. Analogizing caste to the US system of anti-Black racism, Du Bois ironically undermines caste by inverting its logic so as to place Black and Brown persons (of African and Indian descent, respectively) at the top of a transhistorical and transnational cultural and political hierarchy. By staging a cross-caste romance between Matthew Towns, a thwarted African American medical student, who sutures the wounds of racism with a temporary exile in Berlin and Princess Kautilya, an Indian member of royalty working with an international group of subalterns aiming to extricate themselves and their nations from imperialist political systems, Du Bois flouts the proscribed rules, both of caste and of US racism (most explicitly, in their shared taboo against miscegenation between persons of different "racial" groups), even as he uses the logic of caste hierarchy to realign the parameters of Black subjectivity, which he proffers as equally possessed of ancient, precolonial cultural value and modern, revolutionary political valor.

An Unexpected Romance: Cross-Caste Intimacy in Exile

Du Bois establishes the novel's interest in deploying—and subverting—the logic of caste early on in the novel, when Matthew, a medical student aspiring to be an obstetrician, is forbidden from treating white female patients and subsequently, chooses to exile himself in Berlin. Echoing a signal line from the opening chapter of *The Souls of Black Folk*, in which Du Bois recounts his rejection by the young white girl to whom he has extended a token of affection, Matthew wonders at the illogical nature of "a man outcast in his own native land!" (Du Bois [1928] 1995, 7; see also [1903] 2007, 8). Although he feels some relief in Europe, where he is treated more or less as a human being, Matthew speculates about what would happen if he tried to breach the logic of caste, still practiced in Europe and, in fact, worldwide. "What would they [white Europeans] say if he asked for work? Or a chance for his brains? Or a daughter in marriage?" ([1928] 1995, 7). Evoking the specific protocols of caste as practiced in its South Asian context: the taboos against freedom of choice in labor, intercaste marriage, and equal access to education, Matthew, serving as a kind of alter-ego for Du Bois, laments the narrow limitations of his social existence even within the seemingly more progressive oasis of Europe. And yet, he also harbors a longing for "black America"—represented for him in the possibilities of "clasp [ing] a dark hand," "hear[ing] a soft Southern roll of speech," and "kiss[ing] a brown cheek." Just when he is considering the joys of "see [ing] warm, brown, crinkly hair and laughing eyes," he spies the princess, who represents to him, initially and chiefly, a profusion of color: "a glow of golden brown skin" that is "darker than sunlight" and seems "a living, glowing crimson, veiled beneath brown flesh" (7–8). Matthew finds her to be beautiful as well as "faultlessly" attired and comported, and he intuits that she is of royal ancestry even before he is told so (8). Although the verisimilitude of the princess's persona is key, reflecting both Du Bois's interest in historical accuracy (in spite of the allegorical and fantastical overtones of the novel), it is also important to note that Du Bois devised the princess as an overarching, undifferentiated "woman of color" in today's parlance, one whose symbolic trajectory from assimilation to antiassimilation could be reasonably analogized to the historic experience of Black Americans.[4]

After rescuing the princess from the untoward advances of a white American man who accosts her in the café, Matthew comes to recount his tale of woe to her, and she shows interest right away in "American Negroes" ([1928] 1995, 11). His story of having suffered the anti-Black discrimination experienced by all Black Americans is recounted—again in ways that highlight anti-Black racism as a system of caste prejudice. Because of the way those of his "race" are judged by the gatekeepers of a white supremacist American body politic, Matthew is forbidden to complete his education and assume the kind of labor endeavor (as profession) for which he has trained. The refusal of the white administrators of the medical school to let Matthew attend to pregnant white women is a perfect example of the antimiscegenation, pro-purity, and antipollution laws of caste systems at work, as the interdiction against Matthew treating white female patients is an implicit suggestion that his touch would "pollute" them.[5] To the princess's suggestion that Matthew has "run away" and that he might still have pursued a career in medicine while exclusively attending to African American patients, he counters that to have done so would have been to "surrender a principle" (16). Clearly Du Bois, through the mouthpiece of Matthew, not only addresses the particular subjugation of Black Americans but also emphatically outlines a theory of antiracist and anticaste revolution.

Despite the arguably casteist undertones of the princess's intimation that Matthew perhaps should have surrendered the principle of equality in order to work at his profession in a limited yet still productive way, the princess does engage in her own attempt to undermine race and caste-based hierarchy on a global plane. Explaining her plan for the "vast emancipation of the world," the princess brings Matthew to a party to meet some of her comrades, a multinational group of men and women committed to eradicating imperialism who hail from Egypt, Japan, China, and India. Du Bois uses this party scene to comment on the existence of intercaste discrimination within groups of subaltern folks "of color." Some seemingly benign banter about whether or not the princess is "a Negro" ensues. Her Indian compatriot insists that she is not, but the princess, functioning in this moment as Du Bois's mouthpiece, notes that she is "essentially" of African descent and furthermore, posits a history of Afro-Asiatic solidarity that views the fates of Africa and India as intertwined ([1928] 1995, 19–20). Nevertheless, the unjust racist and procaste politics of the group persist, and it is clear that most in the group believe that although they belong to putatively "superior" races unjustly subject to European rule, Matthew and his fellow members of the Black American "nation" do not. To the Egyptian group member's rhetorical question as to "What art ever came out of the Canaille?," Matthew responds by singing the "Negro spiritual" "Go Down Moses," recalling the tradition of enslavement and freedom that informs the crux of African American experience. His efforts are met with "a chorus of approval" and, most importantly, he wins the interest and the affection of the princess (26, 221). Convinced after Matthew's performance that "the mass of the workers of the world can rule as well as be ruled," Princess Kautilya decides to enlist Matthew's services in her anti-imperialist group and to learn for herself if and how "slaves can become men in a generation" and "if it is true that wallowing masses often conceal submerged kings" (34).

Princess Kautilya's expression of her anticaste ideation, as Madhumita Lahiri incisively observes, opens up yet another intertextual source for the princess, as it marks her evocation of the famed Indian nationalist and anticolonial peacemaker, Mahatma Gandhi. As Lahiri explains, "Du Bois's transfiguration of Indian anti-colonialism in *Dark Princess* perhaps most explicitly responds to Gandhi. Gandhi's trajectory is echoed in odd and surprising ways through Kautilya, starting with their common youth and education in England, which is marked in both cases by admiration and Anglicization, followed by disillusionment" (Lahiri 2010, 543). Yet, as Yogita Goyal observes, to the degree that Du Bois invoked Gandhi, he no doubt did so with an awareness of the controversial complexity of Gandhi's attitude toward caste. For Gandhi, perhaps surreptitiously exemplifying the traces of his now critically acknowledged racism (not to mention his initial reluctance to abolish the caste system altogether), once noted that the condition of Black Americans under slaveocracy and subsequently Jim Crow was demonstrably worse than that of the Dalit people (Goyal 2019, 63).[6]

Nevertheless, as I will go on to demonstrate, Du Bois's novel was committed to subverting if not wholly undoing the legacy and logic of caste. Pushing back against the caste system's implicit use of hierarchy via forms of ethnicization if not patent racialization, Du Bois's novel illustrates the cracks in the veneer of decolonial cosmopolitanism in its characterization of the anti-imperialist group to which the princess presents Matthew, since the group members, hailing from various nations in Asia and the Middle East, offer numerous objections to his forming an intimate relationship with the princess—those which reverberate throughout the novel ([1928] 1995, 28–29, 299). As Goyal emphasizes, the phenomenon of caste need not be limited to its supposed origins in South Asia, for, as Du Bois noted, in South Asia as elsewhere, "caste-based social divisions" are imbricated with "race-mixing" (2019, 57). Goyal concludes: "In mapping race onto caste, Du Bois is not making a conceptual mistake, nor is he projecting from the American case, but instead is inviting us to unravel the deep historical entanglement between race and caste" (57).

Moreover, as Madhusudan Subedi details in a review of the histories and theories of caste, there have been and are cognate forms of caste practiced throughout Asia, Europe, and Africa (2013, 54). And in fact, despite Du Bois's choice of an Indian princess for a heroine, signaling his interest in drawing out the analogy between anti-Black racism in the United States and caste discrimination in India, his invocation of caste is not limited either to a South Asian or a US historical context. Indeed, when Matthew returns to his hotel room after the party, he finds that his efforts to join forces with the princess—and thus to demonstrate the centrality of African Americans to global programs of resistance—are immediately threatened, both by the princess's Indian compatriots and by the Japanese member of the group, who calls upon his high-caste, "Samurai" origins to undermine Matthew's presumption of equality and fitness to participate in the global decolonial fight: "We Samurai have been lords a thousand years and more; the ancestors of her Royal Highness have ruled for twenty centuries—how can you think to place yourselves beside us as equals? No—no—restrain your natural anger and distaste for such truth" ([1928] 1995, 30).[7] Vowing to seize any missives that Matthew would send to the princess, and even threatening Matthew with bodily harm if he would not submit, the "Samurai" representative is stopped in his tracks by the princess, who reasserts her authority and marshals her righteous sense of indignation, beginning a pattern of rescuing Matthew from harm's way (including those dangerous scenarios in part effected by his own ethical lapses) that continues throughout the novel. As Homi Bhabha concludes, summarizing the views of the diverse conservatives among the group, Matthew is presumed a "bête noire," one whose "blood, [. . .] low caste, and [. . .] African American origin are all anathema to [the] foundational belief in the 'natural aristocracy' of blood and talent" (Bhabha 2004, 143). Nevertheless, the princess is determined to step down from her pedestal, ironically, by asserting her royal authority if not her upper-caste status outright. Arguably, Princess Kautilya, like Matthew (and perhaps even like Du Bois himself), crosses the boundaries of given caste systems in ways that do not always nullify casteism as an overarching principle. (This is a point to which I will return.)

From Political Assimilation to a Politics of Resistance

In Matthew's first official report to the princess, he mentions the "caste and discrimination" still afflicting African Americans—largely as enforced by white Americans ([1928] 1995, 57). But he quickly adds the caveat that "the Negro has advanced so rapidly and is still advancing at such a rate that he is more satisfied than complaining" (57). He repeats the term *caste*, noting the "color-caste" that he deems to be especially resented by the educated class of Black Americans (57). It is important to note that Matthew crosses caste by moving across a range of professions: from doctor and wandering exile to Pullman porter and secret activist. Although, as Du Bois noted in his 1898 commencement address at Fisk University, "Careers Open to College-Bred Negroes," Black Pullman porters were crucial in helping to facilitate the "uplift" of the African American community and in anchoring the emerging Black middle class ([1898] 1989, 830), they were also the victims of lamentable and retrograde forms of cross-caste discrimination. In depicting the tragedy of Matthew's friend and fellow porter Jimmie, who is lynched after being falsely accused of making advances to a white female passenger on the train, *Dark Princess* highlights not only the hierarchies of professions endemic to caste systems but also the risks of cross-caste intimacy, which within such hierarchical structures of affective labor, in particular, prove unavoidable (79). Overall, Du Bois establishes the way the hierarchical, racial politics that dictate which individuals have access to certain professions and how such professions are either deemed meritorious or menial exemplify and uphold the caste system. Such political practices were, for Du Bois, as corrupt as they were endemic to American political life.

While some of Du Bois's literary works show how the exigencies of assimilation are brokered through attempts at intimacy to promote conciliation between Black and white persons, in this novel, Du Bois again illustrates the drawbacks, even of successful assimilation, through his portrait of a racially indeterminate and social climbing Black woman: Sara Andrews. Andrews represents both the tragically "mulatta" figure whose loyalties to her Black brethren are considerably strained and the modern "new woman," committed to working, having her own money, and maintaining her own structures of power while beating back the leviathan of racism by winning at the game of capitalism. "Cold," "hard," and uninterested in romance, even in the wake of her marriage to Matthew, Sara relies upon Matthew, not as a love interest but simply as a business partner who might lend her respectability as well as power ([1928] 1995, 145, 157). As Sara belongs to the procapitalist and proassimilationist camps of modern Black folk, her marriage to Matthew is also one forged across culture and caste lines. She is as foreign to him as any white woman could be, and his relationship with her requires him to cede his personal power and abandon his more authentic self by becoming a corrupt politician and giving up all thoughts of anti-imperialist revolution (147, 151). Overall, Matthew's marriage to Sara suggests that the greatest risk posed by assimilation is not primarily the Black subject's submission to Eurocentric mores and rules but rather their internalization of Eurocentric values. Recalling Du Bois's trope of cross-cultural romance as a means of assimilation in the first chapter of *Souls,* I contend that Sara is another of Du Bois's literary substitutions for the figure of the young white girl from the visiting card tale of his youth, and thus she symbolizes Du Bois's modernist and increasingly postcolonial critique of his former commitment (no matter how ambivalent) to the assimilation of African Americans into a Eurocentric and Euro-dominated body politic.

Ultimately concluding that Sara was only a "failed artist" whom he would always find "unendurable," Matthew resolves to stay with her, not out of love but as "the victim, the sacrifice" ([1928] 1995, 192), enacting a praxis of sacrifice that recalls tenets both of Christianity and Hinduism. Cordoning himself off in his little bachelor apartment adorned with a Chinese rug and a Matisse original hanging on the wall orchestrated to ward off its "dusty, gloomy, and shabby" environs, Matthew determines finally to live a second life there, hiring and then befriending a mason to build him a fireplace and bathroom (one who intermittently serenades him with the violin, mitigating somewhat the intensity of his sacrificial isolation) and then resolving to resign from the legislature, making the run for Congress on his own terms, and letting the chips fall where they may (193–94). Matthew also resolves to clean up the literal and metaphorical dirt he sees everywhere around him that is continuously "accumulate [ing]" (194). Evoking the caste-rooted rhetoric of contamination that he believes to be a "world symptom" of existential malaise, Matthew paradoxically evokes the caste system's interdiction against impurity and contamination even as he resolves to discard the trappings of status that he has gained chiefly by selling his soul in Faustian fashion to the capitalist, Euro-imperialist political machine.

Matthew's ethical resolve is tested on the eve of a grand political party that Sara throws to celebrate the fact that he is set to become "the first Negro congressman since the war" ([1928] 1995, 207). Lured by the promise of wealth and power, along with the veneer of "ideal beauty, fitness, and curve and line" (207) yet troubled by the way in which he must lie and dissemble in order to acquire such, Matthew retreats into his library where he finds a letter written by the leader of the box-maker's union, urging him to promise consistently to vote for the interests of the poor throughout his career in Congress (208). Musing that he is "a son of generations of workers," he is on the verge of recalibrating his political praxis, correcting the error of his corrupt run for Congress, and recommitting himself to the plight of the outcast, when he notices the familiar slope of the letter's handwriting and recognizes the handiwork of the princess. She arrives suddenly "like a soft mist, unveiled and uncloaked before him" (208). Telling Matthew that she has come to save him from ethical devolution—to "save him from hell"—she reminds him of the noble man he had once been. Subsequently, he, with love light in his eyes, returns to the party, refuses his nomination to Congress, and walks out on Sara and off with the princess (210–11).

Reincarnation and the Dialectic of Social Mobility

Unburdened by his marriage of convenience and "uplift" and buoyed by his illicit, interracial romance, based not on conjugal propriety but rather on an eroticized (and aestheticized) commitment to anti-imperial liberation, Matthew now embarks on a path of renunciation in which he must trade his newfound elevated status as a member of the "New Negro" elite for a life of sacrifice, deferral, and downward mobility that in some sense reflects his emulation of the princess, who has already thrown off the trappings of her Brahmin status, first by consorting with and then by falling in love with Matthew. Using the princess as a mouthpiece through which to revisit and recast some key elements of Hindu philosophy, Du Bois suggests that status itself should not be derived from the machinations of modernist industry and imperial capitalism but rather from the traditions of ancient culture and their requisite acts of sacrifice and atonement. The princess deems Matthew "Krishna," alluding to the story of the Hindu God who falls in love with a mere mortal woman, and he responds in turn by likening her to Radha, the peasant girl who becomes Krishna's lover. Interestingly, one cannot help but observe that the princess plays Krishna to Du Bois's Radha, marking a noted inversion of the story's gender roles but maintaining the principle of a divine or elevated figure sacrificing themselves to a supposedly "lesser" being. This trope of elevation by descent, which is animated by the "Radha-Krishna" folktale, is also a key element of the cognate Greco-Roman tale of "Cupid and Psyche," in which a divine figure descends below his station for love and, ultimately, for justice.[8] I submit that Du Bois's adaptation of these folktales enables him to mark a shift in the spirit and behavior of both Matthew and the princess, as they use the occasion of their romance to relinquish the comforts of bourgeois status derived from their parallel initiatives of assimilation into their respective Euro-American and Euro-imperial domains.

To the princess, the value of "lowering" oneself to the position of the masses is best embodied in the example of Matthew's mother, whom she has adopted as if she were her own, during the time of Matthew's imprisonment and thus their forced period of separation. Evoking the Hindu principle of *samsara*, which, according to the ethos of the Hindu religion, refers to the continuous reincarnation of a person's soul in a continuum of past and future lives (Milner 1993, 301), Princess Kautilya identifies Matthew's mother, whom Du Bois pointedly characterizes as a Black southern matriarch and farmer, as the reincarnation of the Hindu leader and founder of Buddhism, Gotama, whose example of humble labor suggests to both the princess and Matthew a path towards salvation:

> I know that out of the soul of Brahma come little separations of his perfect and ineffable self and they appear again and again in higher and higher manifestations, as eternal life flows on. And when I saw that old mother of yours standing in the blue shadows of twilight with flowers, cotton, and corn about her, I knew that I was looking upon one of the ancient prophets of India and that she was to lead me out of the depths in which I found myself and up to the atonement for which I yearned. ([1928] 1995, 221)[9]

Following the example of Matthew's mother, whom, as Madhumita Lahiri notes, is also linked in the text to the Hindu goddess Kali (Lahiri 2010, 187, Du Bois [1928] 1995, 221) and to the West African deity, Shango (221), the princess chooses to express her noble status not by showcasing her ascribed royal persona or even by leading a group of anti-imperialists but rather, by lowering herself in intimate, autoerotic fashion, setting aside her "silken garments," selling her jewelry, and cutting her hair, all to embrace not just an asceticism resembling that of Gandhi but also a praxis of sacrifice by "stepping down" into menial service, just as Matthew has done by becoming a porter at her behest (221).[10] Replicating in figurative fashion the structure of *samsara*, by which Matthew's mother functions as a reincarnated version of an ancient Hindu prophet, the princess is transmogrified by Du Bois's narration into a domestic worker for a white family in Richmond, effectively changing her caste and classed status by nearly becoming *Black*—working the same types of jobs and experiencing the same kind of subjugation forced upon Black subjects throughout the diaspora. This rings especially true when the princess is sexually harassed by her white boss (222).[11] The princess may not be of African descent, but Du Bois effectively renders her an African American woman via the phenomenology of her lived experience and social location. She subsequently becomes a server in a restaurant and, ultimately, a worker in a paper box–making factory, a job that emphatically propels her out of her Brahmin caste status, as it forces her to work with food in a subservient relation to the public and also in "a basement that st [inks] of glue and waste" (223). Arguably, one could read the princess as assuming the position of someone in one of the Shudra, or servant castes—among some of the lowest orders of caste excepting those of the Ati-Shudras, or *avarna* castes, which include those persons who are falsely deemed "Untouchable," "Unseeable," and "Unapproachable," and "whose touch, whose very shadow is considered to be polluting by privileged-caste Hindus," as Arundhati Roy reminds us (2014, loc. 215 of 8199). Thus, Du Bois reincarnates the princess as a member of a caste assumed to be far below her station, effectively deploying reincarnation as a metaphor for an audacious and putatively downwardly oriented class mobility.

As Murray Milner Jr. points out in his essay, "Hindu Eschatology and the Indian Caste System: An Example of Structural Reversal," the principle of reincarnation, whether or not it results in any particular individual's capacity to ascend or descend the rungs of the social hierarchy that governs their life, ineluctably countermands the rigid ascription of identity and status and the attendant social segmentation ordained by the logic of caste. For *samsara*, says Milner, bespeaks a "near endless social mobility" and thus, functions as a "structural reversal of the prohibition against mobility in the caste system" (1993, 301). Implicitly, Milner is pointing out that with the notion of reincarnation comes the possibility of shifting out of one's proscribed social location or caste position, either by ascending or descending the social or caste ladder and being reborn as one of either "higher" or "lower" status. For as Milner explains, "in principle, caste status is inviolable" and thus proves incongruous with the transformative possibilities enabled by reincarnation (303).[12] *Samsara*, then, as broached by Du Bois's novel, could be deemed radical in a number of ways: first, as it might undermine the given, institutionalized power structures of Western imperialism and US racism, elevating those presumed to belong among the lower classes (like Matthew, his mother, and their Black compatriots); second, as it might compel those presumed to belong to the higher classes or caste (like the princess) to descend, falling from an unearned state of grace; and third, as it might mitigate—if only in theory—against the timeless immutability of any set of proscribed social identities (whether, to invoke the phrasing of Adrian Piper, they are rooted in either "honorific" or "derogatory" stereotypes) (Piper 1992–1993, 57–58). This is not just a reversal of the particular structures of caste and class or even of those discourses of anti-Brown and anti-Black racism from which both the princess and Matthew have variously suffered but also a reversal of the very principle of immutable and entrenched forms of ascribed status. This event leads the princess to tell Matthew that she, like him, "recognize[s] democracy as a method of discovering real aristocracy" ([1928] 1995, 225). She adds further that the anti-imperialist group that once rejected Matthew has now adopted the principles of social mobility and deontological subject positions as their chosen means of social elevation.

As Matthew heeds the princess's call to sacrifice his own newly achieved yet tentative position as a member of the middle class, he engages in a series of menial and hard labor jobs, first as a subway digger and then as a worker in a meat factory. In the wake of his professional devolution, he takes on the spare mien of an ascetic, noting to Kautilya that his "muscles have already beg [un] to flow smooth and unconfined," that he has "no stomach, either in flesh or spirit" ([1928] 1995, 265). Du Bois's description of Matthew as having "no stomach, either in flesh or spirit" and a body that "is all life and eagerness, without weight" (265) renders him rather effeminate, as he loses weight and gravity, becoming almost a spirit.[13] After being fired for skipping work to meander in an art gallery, Matthew takes a job even lower on the hierarchical scale of labor—one he had formerly been repulsed by—as a worker in the stockyards. Here, Matthew has descended to the bottom rungs of the caste hierarchy, taking on the occupation relegated to those in the Shudra castes or to enslaved or indentured Black persons. As he muses: "The world stinks about me. I am lifting rotten food. I am helping to murder things that live. The continual bleating of death beats on my ears and heart. I am drugged with weariness and ugliness. I seem to know as never before what pain and poverty mean" (281). Again, it is important to note that although Matthew is not of a high caste or class, he has never experienced this kind of poverty, as he was a member of the "uplifted," nascent Black middle class (although he was stymied in his professional efforts). This bespeaks Du Bois's refutation of a belief held by some late nineteenth- and early twentieth-century scholars of US racism and the South Asian caste system that African Americans under a Jim Crow system were analogous to the Dalit (or "untouchable") caste. Rather, Du Bois puts Matthew in a position more comparable to that of the princess, since he, too, must "lower himself" from a position of relative privilege (however precarious) to embrace the experience and ethos of the proletariat.[14]

At this same moment and in parallel formation to Matthew's path of renunciation, Kautilya, taking refuge from her domestic work, returns to the home of Matthew's mother in the rural landscape of Virginia, surrounding herself with the earth in harvest and, in particular, with cotton fields. Picking cotton, as did the enslaved ancestors of Matthew and his mother before her, the princess finds salvation in her new job, surmising that "everywhere seed that is hidden dark, inert, dead, will one day be alive, and here, here!" ([1928] 1995, 282). The lovers effectively switch places, each crossing the borders of their own identities and histories to take on the lowest status of each other's respective nations: the Indian princess assumes, on some level, the identity position of an enslaved woman, while the "New Negro" doctor becomes symbolically closer to being akin to a member of the Dalit class by working among animals and in the continuous presence of death.[15] Once again, Du Bois proffers the shared cultural ancestry of Matthew and Princess Kautilya as part of the collapse of Indian and African histories and geographies that Du Bois brokers throughout the novel and also as part of the queer reformation of kinship by which Matthew and the princess are paradoxically rendered part of the same family, even before their eventual marriage that produces a child. (I return to unpack this point in the concluding section of this chapter.) Again, Du Bois emphasizes that both the princess and Matthew find, in their parallel descents to the depths, not simply salvation but their very exaltation. As the princess exclaims: " 'My soul doth magnify the Lord!' And now my spirit is rejoicing, and the ineffable Buddha, blood of the blood of my fathers, seems bowing down to his low and doubting handmaiden" (282).

It is in the wake of being exalted through submission and descent that the princess and Matthew begin an epistolary, philosophic debate about the relationship between upper- and lower-caste persons and the virtues of democracy versus those of aristocracy. Matthew acknowledges the "merits" of democracy, yet also finds himself curiously drawn to oligarchy ([1928] 1995, 283). This is in part to address the inevitable "stupidity" and "selfishness" that Matthew ascribes, in Du Boisian fashion, to many among the masses (283). The answer to this puzzle, for Matthew, lies in choosing the "objects" or persons on whose behalf a dictator (or oligarch) might auspiciously work. Matthew declares further that while he believes in democracy, he also believes that it must be supported by "tyrannical dictators" who will ensure that power is sufficiently centralized to be effective (283). With this assertion, Matthew recalls Du Bois's perplexing commendation of Prussian chancellor Otto von Bismarck in his commencement address at Fisk University and his more measured, circumspect admiration of confederate statesman Jefferson Davis, whom he also decried for having taken his penchant of being, in Du Bois's terminology, a "strong man," to the extremes of misanthropy, xenophobia, and the genocidal suppression of subjugated people (Indians and persons of African descent) in the United States.[16] Matthew goes on to insist that "massed and concentrated power is necessary to accomplish anything worthwhile doing in this muddled world, hoping for divine Anarchy in some faraway heaven" (283). The princess counters Matthew's argument in a manner that upholds the overarching logic of casteism while simultaneously undercutting its particular commitment to ascribed rather than earned value and privilege, instructing Matthew that "your oligarchy as you conceive it is not the antithesis of democracy—it is democracy, if only the selection of the oligarchs is just and true" (285). She adds that neither social status nor wealth should be the deciding factors in who is granted the power to lead (as is the case, with few exceptions, within caste systems) but rather "talent," as "served from the great Reservoir of All Men of All Races, of All Classes, of All Ages, of Both Sexes" (285). This is a decidedly anticaste sentiment, in that it advocates for assigning value and determining power, neither by upholding notions of hereditary valor nor by utilizing mechanisms of preferential treatment but rather by championing earned and demonstrated merit—broadly disposed and divined. (Of course, this declaration recalls Du Bois's theory of the "talented tenth," which has been variously adjudicated as elitist but also egalitarian.) Yet the hierarchy of "greater" and "lesser" value and the resultant segmentation of persons into distinct positions with distinct and differential privileges that are inherent to caste systems persist within the princess's rhetoric and worldview (and indeed, such persistent hierarchy haunts Du Bois's novel). Princess Kautilya adds, in contrast to Matthew, that she "believe [s] in the unlovely masses of men" and that civilization must "stand on a broad base, supporting its inevitable apex of fools" (286). She ends her letter by warning Matthew to "choose well the Tyrants" for "there is Eternal Life!" (286). With her invocation of the notion of eternal life and her warning of the cumulative imprint of choosing to submit to the wrong leader, the princess seems to be recurring to a conventional and commonly held interpretation of *karma* as the principle by which an action begets a parallel reaction: or to turn to Christian rhetoric, an instance of "reaping what one sows." This countermands what Murray Milner views as the "endless mobility" suggested by the phenomenon of reincarnation, a mobility (social and celestial) that the princess formerly seemed to endorse. The princess, then, seems to subscribe to a dialectical equation of reincarnation, understood as a continuum of infinite regeneration and reinvention and karma, conceived as a principle by which past experiences or moral acts continue to impose their legacies.[17]

For the princess, whom we are justified in reading as bespeaking Du Bois's ambivalent stance toward oligarchic politics and perhaps even toward casteism itself, posits a rather fatalistic view of being trapped into social roles and political positions that may persist across generations and epochs. Moreover, she seems to uphold the idea of trusteeship that Arundhati Roy ascribes to the caste system, as a practice of seeming to accept giving one's fate to the stewardship of others, if only their judgment is deemed appropriate and judicious. While my analysis of Du Bois's poetics is offered mainly in the service of disclosing the often subtly subversive strains of his politics, I do acknowledge that in his most direct allusion to and treatment of caste (as rendered, at least partly, in the context of South Asian philosophy and history), he comes closest to reanimating some of its tenets, including the segmentation of roles, the privileging of a call for the elite to sacrifice, and, as I will go on to address, the strategic deployment of endogamous kinship.

Given the princess's stubborn investment in the omnipresent pull of *karma* and her related stance as a semiapologist for oligarchy (a position that Matthew tacitly accepts), one might argue that Du Bois simultaneously deploys the principle of reincarnation to proffer the possibility of moving in and out of one's ascribed social position and retains the discourse of karma to check the inclusive reach of metamorphosis. I am thus reminded of what Homi Bhabha describes as Du Bois's "juxtaposition" of such seemingly incommensurate ideals as the "archaic" and the "avant-garde"—those that rest "between the deep inheritance of aristocracy, royal blood, Indian caste hierarchy, and [the] profoundly 'high modernist' tastes for Picasso, Proust, Meyerhold, Kandinsky, Schönberg—even Marx!" that he associates with the princess. How, Bhabha asks, did Du Bois reconcile "world-service" and "inter-national emancipation" with such palpable flirtations with cosmopolitan elitism? (2004, 146).

For Bhabha, the "juxtaposition" of polar opposites in Du Bois's novel (and by implication, in his poetics writ large) has the benefit of undermining and blurring them both (2004, 146). I concur, and I submit further that the potential resolution of the apparent paradox broached by Du Bois's attractions to both elitism and populism—between selective accretions of power and their widespread democratization—lies in the capacity of all persons to cross out of their respective roles and positions and into alternate or opposing ones. By underscoring the possibility for what is seemingly reasonable or ethical at one moment to be reconsidered and either abandoned, reformed, or otherwise transformed, Du Bois offers a dynamic epistemology that courts the paradigm shift, whether forged as a result of moral errors or logical gaps, as the best method of accommodating unexpected truths. With regard to the clash between the "higher" and the "lower" caste levels of a population, the praxis of epistemological crossing would compel those who would rest upon the laurels of their power to descend and those who exist at the lower end of the spectrum to ascend in turn. This praxis of crossing out of one's subjective, sociopolitical location is judiciously expressed in the princess's statement that "Only working thinkers can unite thinking workers" ([1928] 1995, 286). An example of the rhetorical figure chiasmus, her equation means that thinkers of the higher caste must work—and thereby, earn their right to leadership—in order to reach workers who would aspire beyond their caste status—to think, dream, and eventually, perhaps, to beget revolution. It is also a replication of the trope of the elevated who descend while those deemed lower ascend, which recalls notions of Platonic beauty (which I discussed in my earlier reading of "Of the Coming of John") and what Julia Kristeva terms the "theocentric" iteration of love proffered within Judeo-Christian lore (1987, 142). This chiastic structure suggests that Du Bois was committed not only to cross-cultural intimacy across borders (exemplified in the unification of the thinking workers and working thinkers) and to the "juxtaposition" of disparate identity locations and status positions but also to the dialectical imprint of crossing itself, in which persons would not simply learn to coexist with those of their opposing station but in fact to shed some of the contours of their own identities in the process. I thus want to extend Bhabha's concept of "juxtaposition" even further, in order to suggest that it is not simply the *juxtaposition* of but also the *dialectical oscillation* between the opposing viewpoints, ideologies, and rhetorical positions that Du Bois privileges in *Dark Princess*: one representative of an epistemic mobility if not a fully concretized practice of such, as promoted in Murray Milner's reading of *samsara*. For in crossing in and out of their respective caste positions, Matthew and Princess Kautilya neither affirm nor deny the princess's "high-born" Brahmin inclinations—which as Bhabha rightly observes are decidedly aristocratic—but rather proffer the possibility of leaving one's inclinations, traditions, and even the trappings of one's lived identity behind. Moreover, Du Bois's theory of dialectical oscillation is furthered by the very epistolary, Socratic dialogue that he crafts between Matthew and the princess, through which they debate the relative merits of democracy and aristocracy alongside those of love and labor ([1928] 1995, 282–87). In this way, they establish a form of intimacy that surpasses eros and even love itself, culminating in a form of revolutionary romance. But this kind of romance is aimed not at some nationalist assimilation into the power structures of the West, an idea that was animated and contested throughout *Souls*—and in some of the various iterations of Du Bois's literary imagination that I take up here—but instead at a transnational, dialogic, and ongoing overhaul of imperial structures like the nation-state, as well as the stable (and sometimes, stale) cultural genealogies and subject positions encased by them.

The Cross-Caste Romance as a Form of Queer Kinship

As Homi Bhabha notes, the "odd coupling" of Matthew and the princess simultaneously evokes and revokes what he terms the "celebrated two-ness of double consciousness" (2004, 137). For Bhabha, this happens through opening up a third space alternative to the binary structure of double consciousness, which, Bhabha concludes, reflects the "internationalization" of double consciousness and its metamorphosis into a space of "global thirdness" (137). Of course, as my previous analysis of double consciousness as a romance illustrates, double consciousness was always just as international a matter as a national one, as Du Bois's account of a divided Black subjectivity always evoked Africa as a site of an original yet half-remembered consciousness of the Black subject's roots in a storied African past replete with glory and grandeur ([1903] 2007, 9). Insofar as the Black subject is estranged from the American body politic, he or she is also estranged from the legacy of their African past. Thus, to have double consciousness is always already to exist, not in a binary but in a ternary structure, suspended between Africa and America and thus between the putative phenomenological possibilities of Blackness and whiteness that are simultaneously underscored and undermined by the spaces between them.

Extrapolating from Bhabha's interpretation of Matthew and the princess as an "odd" couple, whose union bespeaks the possibility of a "third space" outside the boundaries of their respective racialized, caste-based, and national positions, I want to suggest that Bhabha both registers the presumed normativity of the social structure of "the couple" and implicitly posits that Matthew and the Princess embody a form of coupling that is epistemologically queer. Bhabha's invocation of "oddness," which has been linked historically and etymologically to "queerness," is illuminated by reexamining the queer critique of coupledom as broached by S. Pearl Brilmyer, Filippo Trentin, and Zairong Xiang (and which I discussed in my earlier readings of the complex romances in *Souls* and in the *Horizon* detective stories). Drawing on Brilmyer et al. as they extrapolate from Lee Edelman's contention that the "two-ness" of the couple is always undermined by the haunting presence of a third figure—whether "the queer" or "the child" (2019, 223), I want to suggest that in the birth of Matthew and the princess's child, Madhu Chandragupta Singh, ordained the Maharajah of Bwodpur and Sindrabad and "Messenger and Messiah to All the Darker Worlds," one finds a fitting amalgamation of both figures: both the child who purportedly affirms the heteronormative, patriarchal couple and the "Queer" who disrupts it. With this reading, I diverge somewhat from Herman Beavers's incisive concern about Du Bois's recurrence to patriarchal ideation in his essay "Romancing the Body Politic: Du Bois's Propaganda of the Dark World." There, Beavers critiques the novel's leveraging of Matthew's "sexual potency" as a form of "political capital" and submits therefore that although Du Bois has fashioned a redemptive politics enacting the "rise of the 'darker worlds,'" the plot of his novel "collapses into masculine narcissism" (Beavers 2000, 260). I acknowledge that my reading of the union of Matthew and the princess as an exercise in queer subversion may exceed the realm of Du Bois's writerly intent, and I agree that in forcing the princess to be dependent upon Matthew's body in order to secure an heir to her throne, the novel does harbor vestiges of patriarchy. Still, I maintain that the union of Matthew and the princess is sufficiently illicit and audacious as to constitute an act of hegemonic transgression.

How could the child born of Matthew and Princess Kautilya, a heteronormative couple, queer his parents' union and, moreover, index a queer way of being and knowing? Firstly, his very biracial and transnational body flouts the rules of Indian caste, US antimiscegenation, and global anti-Blackness alike. Second, he is formed from a proliferation of disparate religious traditions: baptized into Christianity by Matthew's mother and blessed by what seems to be a trio of Hindu, Muslim, and Buddhist men ([1928] 1995, 310–11). Moreover, as Bhabha notes, the child Madhu secures the ancestral link between Matthew and the princess, whom Du Bois presents as lost siblings of a formerly divided and Euro-dominated Afro-Asiatic tribe, manifesting a queer family romance that subverts the hegemonic imperatives of Euro-American capitalist imperialism: imperatives, of course, that depend upon a rigid system of hierarchical difference that would separate the Asian from the African (and both from the European) and thus foreclose the possibility of transnational, anti-imperial alliance.[18] By embodying the former ancestral unity of "the darker nations," which not only disrupts imperialist structures but also the essentialist identitarian structures of both Black nationalism and the Hindu caste system, the child exudes the "shadowy presence" of the queer, undermining the normativity and the monolithic scope of his parents' social locations with his emphatic, transgressive production of hybridity.[19] For in his figure, neither "Blackness" nor "Brown-ness"—and neither American nor Indian—can remain as secure hermetic epistemological categories. Thus, the ending of *Dark Princess*, as it collapses into romance and fairytale, proffers a utopian and revisionary Afro-Asian history that serves as recompense for the struggles sustained by Matthew and the princess (and by the communities they represent) and anticipates the audacious and momentous promise of all that the 1952 Bandung Conference, symbolized by the multicultural anti-imperialist group led by the princess, accomplished and foretold.[20]

In reflecting further on the contrapuntal juxtaposition of progressive and failed or deferred political modes in *Dark Princess*, I am reminded of Gayatri Gopinath's analysis in *Impossible Desires: Queer Diasporas and South Asian Public Culture* of the way representations of the diaspora may evince the paradoxical insofar as they may "undercut and reify various forms of ethnic, religious, and state nationalisms simultaneously" (Gopinath 2006, 7). For, as both Gopinath and Yogita Goyal have incisively argued, the dreams of diaspora too often end up reanimating the very desires for lost origins, nationalist boundaries, and heteronormative unions that they would countermand (see Gopinath 2006 and Yogal 2010). However, in their ideal iterations, the projected romances of diaspora are placed in the service of resisting nationalism and imperialism by, in Gopinath's formulation, disrupting the drive to "go back home" to a supposed nation of origin (2006, 3–4). In this way, "Queer diasporic cultural forms suggest alternative forms of collectivity and communal belonging that redefine home outside of a logic of blood, purity, authenticity, and patrilineal descent" (187). To countermand myths of "purity and authenticity," one requires not simply nonheteronormative but also—and perhaps, more importantly—nonhegemonic forms of reproduction. Counterintuitively, this is precisely what Matthew and Kautilya do through their union and through the birth of their child, which is not to be dismissed as heteronormative simply because it is the result of heterosexual procreation. Although Jack Halberstam ascribes the properties of queer time and space to queer bodies in particular, noting that "queer uses of time and space develop, at least in part, in opposition to the institutions of family, heterosexuality, and reproduction," he also acknowledges that queer epistemologies "will encompass subcultural practices," "alternative methods of alliance," and "willfully eccentric modes of being"

(Halberstam 2005, 1). I thus ply the concept of queer time, following Jose Muñoz, to signify beyond the presence of queer in an identitarian sense, embracing Muñoz's conception of queer time as "structuring an educated mode of desiring that allows us to see and feel beyond the quagmire of the present" (2009, 1). With this more flexible conception of queer time and queer epistemology in mind, I dare to read Matthew and Princess Kautilya's creation of an interracial, cross-caste, and transnational family, one only belatedly authorized by matrimony and patrimony yet never by the agents of any state (but rather, by a multicultural crew of religious leaders), as the presentation of a novel family structure that flouts rules of racialism, caste, nationality, and propriety in favor of the liberating and equalizing power of transgression as well as an alternate rendering of social relations ([1928] 1995, 310–11). When heterosexual partnerships are transracial, as Siobhan Somerville, Darieck Scott, and others remind us, they encode the subversive qualities of a queer relation (see Somerville 2000 and Scott 2010). Indeed, as Halberstam declares, and as Gopinath would affirm, queerness opens up "new life narratives and alternative relations to time and space" (2005, 1). As an example of how the paradoxical nexus of queer heterosexual reproduction may suggest novel and alternative trajectories for living, I offer Nicole Waligora-Davis's astute commentary regarding Du Bois's lifelong focus on Black children "as a vehicle for realizing alternative black futures" (2006, 70). Waligora-Davis contends—and I concur—that Du Bois "idealized" the Black child both as a "world-citizen" and as an emblem of the same impulse toward futurity now acknowledged as central to queer epistemologies (73). As Waligora-Davis emphasizes, such a focus on the future and on the possibilities of what *may* be constitutes "a revolutionary political agenda" (73) on Du Bois's part: profound even if chiefly symbolic. Thus, with the union of Princess Kautilya and Matthew, Du Bois both reprises the myth of lost (African and Asian) origins and kinship structures and facilitates a queer disruption of hegemonies tied to the state, to the nuclear family, and to discourses of Euro-Anglo supremacy. Extrapolating from Gopinath, I submit that Du Bois imbued his reinvented Afro-Asiatic diaspora with the nodes of queer of color critique by, in Gopinath's formulation, "recuperating those desires, practices, and subjectivities that are rendered impossible and unimaginable within conventional diasporic and nationalist imaginaries" (2006, 11).

In a manner befitting that of a quintessential romance, Du Bois ends his favorite novel, not just with a triumphant and extraordinary display of cross-cultural intimacy that anticipates the alliance of a Black American proto-

or antinational discourse with an Indian empire considerably loosed from its casteist and colonial moorings but also with a Shakespearean "Envoy" that recalls, as Gayatri Spivak reminds us, the fantasy and societal upheaval of *A Midsummer Night's Dream* (Spivak 2018). In this postscript to *Dark Princess,* the narrator as Du Bois pulls the curtain back and asks that the "sprites" who have helped him write the story "lift with deft delicacy from out of the crevice where it lines my heavy flesh of fact, that rich and colored gossamer of dream which the Queen of Faërie lent to me for a season" ([1928] 1995, 312). The "Envoy" ends with a tribute to the Queen of Faërie and a plea that she might reveal whether the origins of "Truth" lie in "Fact or Fancy? The Dream of the Spirit or the Pain of the Bone?" (312). Pushing truth out of its presumed sphere of reason and proffering the capacity of dreams to displace the precedents of material scarcity and mortal pain, Du Bois further reveals the subversive commitments of his tale of cross-cultural and anti-imperial alliance by positing alongside (and in lockstep with) his queer configurations of intimacy the daring artifice of imagination—truly the stuff of which utopian visions are endlessly made and remade.

Epilogue

Strange Intimacies: On Exogamy and Endogamy in the Cross-Caste Romance

As I reflect upon the way Du Bois's fictions move from proffering interracial assimilation as appropriation to exploring and recommending the pleasures of Black mobility and fugitivity to, finally, idealizing and ordaining a sociopolitical praxis of cross-cultural affiliation that abandons the Eurocentric legacies of racialism, capitalism, and imperialism for the promise of a utopia nourished by the amniotic fluid of "darkwater," I think of two folktales in particular. The first, "Cupid and Psyche," is a staple of Greco-Roman mythology that was featured in the Roman African Apuleius's *The Golden Ass* in the second century AD. The second is "Princess Wata," a largely forgotten tale collected and published in 1933 by Dr. Pauline E. Dinkins, a medical professional and missionary who worked in Liberia and who sought Du Bois's help in publishing her collection of Liberian folktales.[1] The tale of "Cupid and Psyche" is well known and oft-repeated and, as I mentioned in my analysis of *Dark Princess*, a textual source that helped animate Du Bois's poetic figurations of cross-cultural romance. The story of a beautiful young woman, whose beauty purportedly rivals that of the goddess Venus, and is thereby dispatched by an oracle to a crag above the sea to await her marriage to a monster, "Cupid and Psyche" redeems its tragic tale of forbidden beauty, class rivalry, and divine vengeance with a plot twist that ultimately turns on transgressive yet redemptive love. For upon learning the fate of Psyche and, importantly, being transported by her beauty, the god Cupid falls in love with her and determines to rescue her—albeit by covert, coercive, and even violent means barely concealed by literary euphemism (Apuleius [1566] 1962, 111).[2] The caveat, of course, is that he only comes to her at night and forbids her from ever looking upon him or learning his identity (113). As Wendy Steiner generously notes of this story, it ultimately endorses the possibility of crossing barriers of inequality (in this case, between mortal and divine), as it brings together forbidden lovers in what ultimately becomes an egalitarian alliance: one that ensures *caritas* by means of pleasure and joy (Steiner 2001, xxiii).

Yet while Steiner reads this story thusly as "an aesthetic allegory" (2001, xxiii), I interpret it in a more political vein as a pointed allegory for assimilation, one that sanctions the transgression of miscegenation, relishes the pleasure of flouting the laws and taboos of social structures based on ontological distinctions and hierarchies, and accommodates violent and abject forms of intimacy. For in making Psyche his wife, Cupid disobeys the law of caste that would separate mortal from immortal, defies the divine and purportedly immutable decree of his mother (the goddess Venus), and resorts to violent measures in so doing. The violent turn of the story continues when Psyche decides to see her husband's face (against his orders) and accidentally drops a lit candle on him, burning his face. She is promptly punished, both as he flies up and away from her and as Venus beats her for her presumed impudence (Apuleius [1566] 1962, 122, 134). Indeed, even before Venus can find Psyche to beat, humiliate, and assign an impossible slate of tasks to complete, the god Juno admonishes Psyche with a combination of pity and protocol that "propriety will not permit me to run counter to the wishes of Venus [. . .]. Besides, I must not forget the Laws which forbid the entertainment of *fugitive slaves* against the inclination of their owners" (131).[3] Embodying not just the dangers of ignoring the rigid edifice of caste but also the possibility of ascending it by laddered path, Psyche is given a chance to reunite with Cupid and assimilate into his immortal sphere if only she can complete a series of laborious and mostly menial tasks (designed by Venus to ensure Psyche's failure) and thus prove herself "worthy" of meeting the standards set by the dominant class (134–40). By dint of her wit and skill—and a bit of divine assistance from several "donors" including a river reed, the eagle of the god Jove, and finally, Cupid himself—Psyche ultimately proves victorious in her quest to regain Cupid's love and commitment (141).[4] Joined together in matrimony and in parenthood, Cupid and Psyche create another "race" altogether, birthing their daughter Joy who is neither mortal nor divine but something wondrously in-between. While Steiner translates the child's name as "Pleasure" (2001, xxiii), the Apuleuis translation I consulted (by

Jack Lindsay) renders the child's name "Joy" ([1566] 1962, 142). This translation is particularly appropriate in the context of Du Bois's poetics, since the notion of joy plays a key role in his beloved opera, Wagner's *Lohengrin*, which, as I noted in chapter 2, is a central source text for his short story "Of the Coming of John." As many critics have noted, including Christopher Powers and Sieglinde Lemke, when Du Bois translated the wedding march from *Lohengrin* for "Of the Coming of John," he substituted "joy" for "faith" in characterizing the betrothal of the cross-caste and seemingly ill-matched lovers Lohengrin and Elsa (see my chapter 1). In what Sieglinde Lemke has described as the semantic "nexus" of joy and faith (2008, 39), one may locate Du Bois's figuration of cross-caste romance, which may be both spiritually and affectively rewarding if engaged in its most auspicious iteration. The embodiment of cross-caste romance, Joy-as-Pleasure marks the promise and passion of crossing over boundaries of culture and caste.

At the other end of the allegorical spectrum that likewise haunts my thinking about Du Bois's fictional troping on romance lies the forgotten Liberian tale, "Princess Wata," published by Pauline E. Dinkins in 1933 (after being shared with but remaining unpublished by Du Bois in the late 1920s) but likely hearkening back to a much earlier era. I found this tale buried in Du Bois's archives and classified as one of his own invention. But letters in the same archives exist between Dinkins and Du Bois that tell a different story, disproving the notion that Du Bois was the author of the tales. Subsequent research on my part revealed that although Pauline Dinkins shared the tales with Du Bois, she had them published in book form herself under the auspices of the Sunday School Publishing Board in Nashville, Tennessee in 1933—seemingly with no aid, financial or otherwise—from Du Bois.[5] The tale is clearly a cognate text for "Cupid and Psyche," as it tells the story of an uncommonly beautiful young woman who rejects a series of suitors chosen by her parents and drawn from her own kingdom. Rather, she decides to marry a stranger from another land (and likely of another "race" or "caste") and upon doing so, leaves her homeland and follows him to environs unknown. Almost immediately, she regrets her decision. For her husband begins to change so markedly that she hardly recognizes him. In a repeated series of "fort/da" movements, the story describes how her husband enters particular spaces, such as a side road ("by-way") or an inn without her, and upon returning, appears to have lost a body part, seemingly replaced by some corresponding animal analogue. He acquires by turns elephantine ears, a wooden leg, and tusks that supplant his teeth. Each time Princess Wata's husband returns, she fails to recognize him, and each time he reassures her that he *is* her husband by handing her a kola nut, a Pan-African symbol of both hospitality and hostility (Dinkins 1933). Adhering to the tenets of the animal bridegroom tale, the princess essentially finds herself betrothed to an elephantine figure who takes her to an invisible palace surrounded by equally invisible servants and leaves her to pine away most days alone. Finally, she decides to leave him: she incapacitates the cock he has left as a guard by overfeeding it and escapes over the sea by boat, never (the story avers) to leave her father's home again (Dinkins 1933).

Although this story undoubtedly contains numerous culturally specific interpretations (one of which I will shortly go on to discuss), like all folktales, it also contains cues of transnational and transepochal significance. Surely, the story offers a trenchant commentary on the vulnerability of young maidens compelled to marry and be duped, even when choosing mates of their own accord. The Liberian folktale also rebuts the notion inherent in "Cupid and Psyche" that the woman is a "lesser" being whose marriage to a man—whether angelic or monstrous—is the primary means of elevating her. In addition, I hear in "Princess Wata" an intimation of the old adage that "things are not always what they seem." For initial appearances and even senses prove illusory. Moreover, I note that the period of sensory deprivation (chiefly visual) suffered by Princess Wata, who upon arriving at her husband's home, "hear [s] voices, but s [ees] no one," reprises and revises the continuum of sensory deprivation and fulfillment experienced by Psyche, who is only allowed to "see" her husband through the prism of night and whose first visit to her husband's palace includes beautiful vistas and furnishings but no visual proof of the presence of human beings: only a series of "bodiless voices" who address and minister to her until her husband arrives (Apuleius [1566] 1962, 110–11). Considering the refusal or limitation of vision, in particular, for both Psyche and Wata, I also recall the prevalent folkloric interdiction against curiosity—especially in the case of women—that is inherent in so many folktales including "Pandora's Box" and "Lohengrin."

But what strikes me most profoundly about the tale is its allegorical portrait of what is arguably a continuum of exogamy and endogamy. For it is here that "Princess Wata" differs most substantively from "Cupid and Psyche." While the Greco-Roman tale celebrates the productive possibilities of exogamic communion and exchange, with its capacity to realign social and cultural relations, "Princess Wata" cautions against the perils of exogamy, which include sensory deprivation, illusion, monstrosity, and ultimately, self-effacement. There is no evidence that Du Bois ever published or reproduced this tale, which Dinkins sent him in 1929 (past the time period that I cover in this project). Yet even if he did not, the story would surely have resonated with him, for it anticipates the fate of his own princess of "the Hither Isles," who chooses the blessing of death rather than enter into an exogamic exchange with a white king, premised upon her submission to imperialist rule and expropriation, or perhaps even to explore the possibility of a relationship with a Black stranger of her kin group but not of her station (Du Bois [1920] 1999, 43–46).[6]

Moreover, the presence of the sea as a fecund yet fraught passageway in "Princess Wata" and its resemblance to Du Bois's figuration of the sea in "The Princess of the Hither Isles" offer a clue that both stories may be allegories for reversing the Middle Passage. In both stories, Black subjects figured as noblepersons, detached from their homelands (whether figured as paternal or maternal) and correspondingly, estranged from their proper or desired kinfolk, wield the sea as a weapon with which to evade intercultural exchanges that, whatever benefits may be retrospectively ascribed to them, prove palpably disorienting and heartbreaking. Indeed, Princess Wata is likely named after the Pan-African goddess, Mami Wata, a beautiful woman of "fair" skin, dark hair, and large "compelling" eyes, who, as Misty L. Bastian observes, is often rendered as a powerful water spirit both protective and perilous in her dealings with mortals, whom she reserves the right to punish if they "transgress one of her many prohibitions" (Bastian 1997, 123–24).

As Bastian further explains, Mami Wata tales often prove examples of "undeniable but alien kinship" (1997, 124). One the one hand, Mami Wata may caution her offspring, often rendered as a "Mammy water daughter," not to enter into sexual or affective exchanges but rather "to tease her human family [. . .] with her refusal to enter into marriage and motherhood" (124–25). Yet on the other hand, Mami Wata and her offspring may entice others into marriage, only to make a series of demands upon them that sustain, as Bastian details, an "asymmetrical" relation, mandating such hierarchical stipulations as "ownership, enclosure, and a requirement for deference from the subordinate spouse" (126). Extrapolating from Bastian's analysis of Mami Wata folklore, I submit that Dinkins's embattled Princess Wata may symbolize either Mami Wata herself, poised to resist and ultimately to disavow marriage, or alternately, a victim of Mami Wata, whose subjection to trickery, dispossession, and unchecked authority signals the destructive capabilities, both of divinity and of exogamous kinship.

In essence, I submit that Du Bois forged myriad literary portraits of cross-cultural union and affiliation falling upon a polarized continuum of exogamy and endogamy—bespeaking by turns failed assimilation, fraught interracial union, and frustrated yet ultimately fruitful collaboration among the different communities of color constituted by non-Western nations. In the main, his literary creations seem to instruct that the assimilation of Black persons into white-dominated worlds is a pragmatic but lamentable practice and that, whenever possible, persons of African descent should forge new unions, alliances, and communities among themselves and other subalterns of color.

Yet, even in his most idealized portraits of romance, Du Bois reveals how frequently the quixotic nodes of intimacy engender not simply ambivalent yearning but also estrangement. Analyzing the characterization of romance in Western philosophy and romanticist literature, Nancy Yousef observes that relations of intimacy are routinely replete with breaches of knowledge, empathy, and equity (Yousef 2013, 2). Yousef explains further that "insofar as intimacy, like sympathy, designates feelings for and with another, it also admits and discloses affective expectations and disappointments—from aversion to self-basing admiration, from gratitude to resentment, from frustration to fascination—that involve neither mutuality nor reciprocity" (2). Indeed, when the intimate relation in question is broached in the context of distinct and seemingly incommensurate cultures, especially those for whom unification is both undergirded and undermined by violence, the propensity for estrangement, misunderstanding, and inequality increases tenfold.

The ineluctable link among intimacy, estrangement, disappointment, and inequality is poignantly rendered by Saidiya Hartman in her blend of memoir, history, and cultural theory *Lose Your Mother: A Journey Along the Atlantic Slave Route*. There, reflecting upon the legacy of the Middle Passage for African American and Afro-Caribbean persons in particular, she instructs that the etymological roots of the Akan word for "slave," *odonkor*, are found in the words for love: *odo* and "don't go": *nti nka* (Hartman 2006, 86–87). Hartman continues, theorizing the phenomenon by which "Love makes a place for the stranger; [. . .] domesticates persons from 'outside of the house' and not 'of the blood'; [. . .] [and] assuages the slave's loss of family." She concludes that "Love extends the corner of belonging and shrouds the slave's origins, which lie in acts of violence and exchange, but it doesn't remedy the isolation of being severed from your kin and denied ancestors" (87). In Hartman's lyrical declamation and in her historical reminder that "love cannot be separated from dispossession or property in persons" (87), I find all of the complex registers of Du Bois's treatment of cross-caste romance as a form of intimacy steeped in despair and dispossession yet aspirational in its arching toward remediation and reclamation. Enacting yet perhaps also suturing what Fred Moten and Nathaniel Mackey have variously expounded upon as the condition of "wounded kinship" endemic to Black life, initiated by the Middle Passage yet persisting far beyond its temporal frame, Du Bois's works of literature must be acknowledged, not just as proliferating romance but also as pointedly disputing its capabilities.[7] The fruits of Du Bois's creative imagination may privilege romance as a heightened mode of dialogic interplay, but they also query and queer it as a means of fueling transversal forms of fulfillment and justice.

Notes

Notes to the Introduction

1. The visiting card incident, especially when understood as a defining moment, not of Du Bois's childhood, but of his nascent entrance into manhood, also puts one in mind of a later, more mature (and manifest), yet equally unsuccessful interracial romance that Du Bois sustained for a short time with a young German woman with whose family he boarded the summer before beginning his graduate studies in Berlin: Dora Marbach. As Du Bois relates in his 1968 autobiography, an American woman who came to stay with the Marbachs conspired to foreclose any further "entanglement" between Du Bois and his blue-eyed, dark-haired beloved, no doubt informing the Marbach family of Du Bois's lower caste status as a Black American man (1968, 161–62). But even if she had not, Du Bois would likely still have broken off the relationship with Ms. Marbach since, as he acknowledged, "I knew this would be unfair to her and fatal for my work at home, where I had neither property nor social standing for this blue-eyed stranger" (161).

2. See Nico Slate's *Colored Cosmopolitanism: The Shared Struggle for Freedom in the United States and India*, Michelle Alexander's *The New Jim Crow: Mass Incarceration in the Age of Color Blindness*, and Isabel Wilkerson's *Caste: The Origins of Our Discontents*. Moreover, in her introduction to Dalit leader Dr. Bhimrao Ramji Ambedkar's *Annihilation of Caste*, Arundhati Roy writes that "casteism and racism are indeed comparable" insofar as the two "are forms of discrimination that target people because of their descent" (1936, "The Doctor and the Saint"). Yogita Goyal also remarks in her study of the intellectual connections between Du Bois and Indian nationalist writer Rabindranath Tagore that it is useful to "recover a submerged history of a dialogue between India and the USA on whether race and caste can be thought of as analogies" (2019, 55).

3. Victorian in origin, the visiting card was used in late nineteenth-century America primarily as a form of exchange among the bourgeois classes (predominately by women). For a historical sketch of the visiting card, see Blaise Cronin and Yvonne Roger, "From Victorian Visiting Card to VCard: The Evolution

of a Communicative Genre," *Journal of Information Science* 29, no. 1 (2003): 65–68.

4. See Lisa L. Moore, "Acts of Union: Sexuality and Nationalism, Romance and Realism in the Irish National Tale," *Cultural Critique* no. 44 (2000). I, too, conceptualize the "cross-caste romance" as a trope for nationalistic assimilation.

5. I am also influenced by the groundbreaking work of Ann du Cille on the "coupling convention" and Claudia Tate's analysis of "domestic allegories of desire" and of Du Bois's use of the trope of "conjugal symbolism" in a number of Du Bois's literary texts (chiefly, *Dark Princess*) (Tate 1995, xviii). Arguably, Du Bois both deploys and subverts these conventions in his romantic configurations of intimacies of attraction and repulsion.

6. The recovery, reclamation, and celebration of African history, folkways, and politics is a recurrent and defining feature of many of Du Bois's writings (fictional and nonfictional) after the publication of *Souls* including *Darkwater* (1920), *The Gift of Black Folk* (1924), *Black Folk Then and Now* (1939), *The World and Africa* (1946), and *Worlds of Color* (1961), to name but a few examples.

7. Stokes notes that whiteness has "an ambivalent proximity to, and interaction with, heterosexuality" and moreover, that "whiteness works best—in fact, [. . .] it works only—when it attaches itself to other abstractions, becoming yet another invisible strand in a larger web of unseen yet powerful cultural forces" (2001, 13).

8. Emphasis mine.

9. This reviewer was later revealed to be Koritha Mitchell, so I duly credit her here.

10. Indeed, Darieck Scott reflects upon "the doubly queer register that matches, reflects, and helps constitute the well-known double consciousness of blackness" (2010, 7).

11. Of course, as Nahum Chandler makes clear, Du Bois's honorific valuation of Blackness and allusions to Black blood were ineluctably tinged with irony, as they were undertaken precisely in order to debunk Enlightenment-era notions of ontological purity, such as those evinced by figures including Immanuel Kant and Thomas Jefferson. Rather, as Chandler insists, Du Bois compels his readers to "rethink the premises of all concepts of historicity and sociality by which such entities [like race, ethnicity, nationality, or caste category] are demarcated" (2013, 59).

12. See Kathryn Bond Stockton's *Beautiful Bottom, Beautiful Shame: Where Black Meets Queer* regarding the currency of "bottom states" and "bottom values for [queer] women and men" (2006, 107).

13. Two such examples, to which I earlier alluded, are Hazel Carby's work in *Race Men* (also in the volume *Next to the Color Line*), and Claudia Tate's analysis of Du Bois's poetics in the introduction to his novel *Dark Princess*, which were key in shaping my thinking about how the trope of romance functions in Du Bois's literature. Another is the generative essay by Michele Elam and Paul C. Taylor, "Du Bois's Erotics," in which they provocatively link Du Bois's aesthetic and philosophic investments in Nietzschean aesthetics, eroticism, and hedonism to his presumed

"priapism" (2007, 209–33). While I acknowledge the insights of such critics into Du Bois's repeated deployment of tropes of eroticism, sentiment, and heterosexual (although not always conjugal or successful) romance, I join a growing cohort of scholars and cultural critics who also see in Du Bois's rhetoric and poetics the presence of queer epistemologies and antiheteronormative ideation.

Notes to Chapter 1

1. Wolfram von Eschenbach (1961, 429–30) popularized this twelfth-century medieval folktale by including the story of Parzival's son, Loherangrin (Lohengrin), in his epic poem *Parzival.*

2. I have extrapolated here from summaries by Russell Berman (1997), Robert Gooding-Williams (2009), and Sieglinde Lemke (2008).

3. See, for example, Carl Dalhaus (1979, 35–41). Key critical analyses that reflect upon Du Bois's adaptation of Wagner note that textual reanimations of *Lohengrin* complicate its treatment of love, reflecting its complex political and poetic legacy. Russell Berman (1997, 127) observes that the opera represents a fraught love that surmounts the seeming obstacle of difference and highlights subsequently the "theme of justice and judgment" to which, as he submits, Du Bois would have been particularly attracted. By contrast, Lawrence Kramer (2002, 203) observes how Du Bois's retelling of *Lohengrin* marks a "reversal" of its Wagnerian ethos, which privileges Christianity and German nationalism even as it traffics in egalitarian ideals. Because "Of the Coming of John" proffers "the necessity of freeing desire from ideology," Kramer concludes that Wagner would not "have smiled" at its homage to *Lohengrin*.

4. Christopher Powers (2015, 63–64) makes this point, saying the two works share a "field of philosophical inquiry" that queries "the incommensurability of ideals and history." A number of insightful works of criticism analyze the significance of Du Bois's deployment of *Lohengrin* in the service of an overarching project to theorize the African American experience of double consciousness. Robert Gooding-Williams (2009, 219) comments on Du Bois's use of the opera to symbolize the "impossible" marriage between a Black man and an ungenerous white world. Eric Sundquist (1993, 521–52, 578) submits that Du Bois's retelling is a "perfect incarnation" of double consciousness and implicitly connects this to what he supposes to be Du Bois's "ironic" reprise of the opera's trope of "mystic transfiguration." And R. A. Judy (2015, 219) remarks upon the clash of "incommensurable grammars" connoted by the "neo-slavery" context in "Of the Coming of John," on the idealism *Lohengrin* evokes, and on John's enjoyment of that idealism.

5. Here I am expanding on Elaine Scarry's characterization of beauty as offering a "pressure towards the distributional" and, thus, as evoking a love with universal currency (1999, 67; 81–82).

6. Martha Nussbaum (2013, 15) submits that a pluralistic democracy requires not just reason or "respect" but the emotional charge of love, which she defines

as an "intense attachment to things outside the control of our will," deployed to promote care across differing interests.

7. See for example Paul Guyer's *Kant and the Claims of Taste* (1997, 319).

8. R. A. Judy (2015, 215–16) incisively acknowledges Du Bois's invocation of the legend, which, as it is accompanied by his rhetorical use of a frame tale, places his story firmly in the generic tradition of folklore.

9. In his analysis of folkloric conventions, Vladimir Propp (1986, 26–27) remarks upon the prevalence of the prohibition, or as he calls it, the "interdiction," which is both imposed and violated in folklore. *Lohengrin*, too, is centered by the thematic tension of a prohibition against gaining knowledge about Lohengrin's national and cultural origins.

10. Here I diverge from Charles Nero's analysis (2005, 263).

11. See, for example, Terry Eagleton's (1990) critical history of aesthetics.

12. In my analysis of Du Bois's Neoplatonic commitments, I am emboldened by the work of Eric King Watts (2001) and Monica Miller (2003), who offer a positive view both of Du Bois's belief in the political potential of aesthetic experience and of his overall engagement with Neoplatonic ideas. Robert Gooding-Williams (2009), on the other hand, problematizes Du Bois's Platonism, which he fears bespeaks a regrettable recourse to a notion of elite leadership. Although I concur with Watts and Miller in reading Du Bois's Platonism as not ineluctably elitist, I concern myself with how Du Bois's literature proffers an aesthetic idealism that he believed promoted ethical practice as a prerequisite for, if not a guarantor of, political justice.

13. Such a possibility reflects what Eric King Watts (2001, 193) describes as Plato's "sense of the panoply of universal values that compose the transcendent realm" and affirms Monica Miller's (2003, 743) view that Du Bois was committed to "a universal right to access the beautiful as a category."

14. In the Bible (Esther 4:16) Esther, who had been passing as a gentile, confesses to her husband and king her previously hidden Jewish identity in order to save her people from the dispossession and annihilation that anti-Semitic law prescribed.

15. In *Symposium* (1989, 55–56), Diotima relates the noble gesture of King Kodros of Athens, who gave his life to fulfill a prophecy that Athens would be victorious only if the enemy killed him. This story bears an eerie resemblance both to the plot of *Lohengrin* and to John's tragic fate.

16. Here I differ somewhat from Robert Gooding-Williams (2009, 122), who avers that the expulsion recalls the theme of "impossible" marriage in *Lohengrin* since it marks John's separation from the material confines of a Euro-American world that has "drawn away from and repudiated him."

17. Du Bois here echoes his declaration in an earlier chapter of *The Souls of Black Folk* ([1903] 2007, 76): "I sit with Shakespeare and he winces not."

18. Emmanuel Levinas (1961, 4) speaks eloquently of "the face" of the other, which "is present in its refusal to be contained." He also submits that "infinity is

produced in the relationship of the same with the other," a notion that corresponds both to Plato's account of the transcendence furnished by love's distribution and to Du Bois's sense of the broad reach of a putatively Afro-centered affection.

19. Griffin (1995, 8) notes the opposition inherent in many African American "migration narratives," as she terms them, between a familiar, nurturing ancestor and an alienating, challenging stranger. Moreover, she submits that in more complex iterations of this genre (of which Du Bois's story is certainly exemplary) the stranger and the ancestor "seem to exist in the same figure."

20. See Priscilla Wald (1995, 175–76) and R. A. Judy (2015, 218–19).

21. In his analysis of John's dilemma, Robert Gooding-Williams (2009, 145) suggests that John's community, endowed with a folk ethos based in Black history, cannot respond favorably to him because he does not "express" their culture to them. For, having crossed out of his caste position by receiving a Euro-inflected, Western education and coming thusly to appreciate an eclectic range of interests beyond what is rooted in the traditions of his birth culture, John has elected not to base his program of leadership on a set of assumptions and habits shared among his people.

22. It is worth acknowledging, as R. A. Judy (2015, 218) does, the limitations of such cultural practices that are practical and even attentive to the human need for pleasure but are also somewhat parochial in nature—more oriented to the barest nodes of "cultural survival" than aspiring toward cultural evolution or revolution. See also Taylor (1994, 52).

23. Julia Kristeva (1987, 73) insists that all love requires "objects" by which it might be recognized.

24. Although Du Bois deploys this paradigm in his modernist novels, *Quest of the Silver Fleece* (1911) and *Dark Princess* (1928), he declines to do so here, which arguably indicates some measure of ambivalence about the viability of erotic love on his part and moreover suggests that he, along with other critics of *Lohengrin*—for example Berman (1997)—see the Grail knight's exercise of patriarchal authority as an error on his part, since it relies upon devotion in the guise of subordination.

25. Lemke analyzes the seemingly paradoxical relation of joy and trust in both Wagner and Du Bois by allowing that "Linking joy to trust, [Du Bois] implicitly refers back to the "Treue/Freude nexus," underscored by Du Bois's "elision" of the difference between the two in his citation of Lohengrin's bride-song. Lemke further imputes to Du Bois's story a central question: "Do trust, loyalty, and faithfulness necessarily lead to joy?" (2008, 39).

26. There is a debate in Plato's *Phaedrus* (1995, 8–10) about whether erotic love, though ultimately a pathway to universal beneficence, might do as much harm as good to the particular beloved chosen as its instrument. In Plato's *Symposium* (1989, 156), Diotima implicitly idealizes hetero-normative, biological procreation, whereby beauty, desire, and love are purported to produce immortality and a legacy at least symbolic of solicitude. Yet she also alludes to the possibility of being "pregnant in soul" and looking, therefore, for another or others with whom one

might reproduce: not other humans, but the humanistic products of artistic practice, philosophic ideation, and even social welfare.

27. The narrator (Du Bois [1903] 2007, 157) tells us that John is touring with his college quartet when he discovers the opera being performed in a New York City theater. With this detail, Du Bois subtly evokes the tradition of the Fisk Jubilee singers, whose musical tours were part of an international, anti-racist movement. See Paul Gilroy (1993, 88–90).

28. Although John mentions the French Revolution specifically, I believe that Du Bois is also alluding here to the Haitian Revolution, whose leaders co-opted the Enlightenment discourse ironically proffered by their colonizers and whose successes informed the American abolition movement in turn. See Eric Sundquist (1993, 144–46).

29. See Plato's *Symposium* (1989, 56–57).

30. It is worth remarking that with the tragic ending of John's story, Du Bois taxes the idealistic possibilities of cross-cultural love as he has heretofore presented them, since John Henderson's sexual assault upon John Jones's sister is the very antithesis of a beneficent cross-cultural relation. John Jones's defensive response, while arguably justified (and even heroic) is, as Du Bois notes, driven by latent "hatred" ([1903] 2007, 165) that threatens to displace the universal love he has nurtured throughout the story. Yet the reprise of the bridal song from *Lohengrin,* which arises spontaneously from the sea and which Du Bois describes as being directionally opposed to the "dark shadows where lay the noise" of the lynch mob (166) arguably suggests love's perseverance in the face of palpable attempts to undermine it.

31. Hearing the lynch mob approach, John wonders what "the boys at Johnstown" would say about his fate, and in turn, he wonders about theirs. "The night deepened. He thought of the boys at Johnstown. He wondered how Brown had turned out, and Carey? And Jones,—Jones? Why, *he* was Jones, and he wondered what they would say when they all knew, in that great long dining-room with its hundreds of merry eyes" (Du Bois [1903] 2007, 166).

32. Arguably, John's sacrifice of himself to a world movement toward justice marks Du Bois's evocation both of Afro-pessimistic and Afro-futurist thought, since it registers the vulnerability of Black lives subjected to principles of scarcity even while projecting the legacy of Black suffering into a future that might one day honor them. See Lisa Yaszek (2010).

Notes to Chapter 2

1. Scott cites Sharon Holland's observation that the first "sexual revolution" in the United States, read as a form of transgressive or queerly "liberated" sexuality, "occurred under the auspices of slavery" (quoted in Scott 2010, 8). In offering my queer reading of Du Bois, I am informed by the work of a number of scholars of

queer theory and practitioners of "queer of color" critique, including Scott, Sharon P. Holland, whose book *The Erotic Life of Racism*, explores the way racialized subjects are eroticized even outside the explicit context of sexual relations, and Siobhan Somerville, whose book *Queering the Color Line: Race and the Invention of Homosexuality in American Culture* examines the way interracial relationships were persistently and paradoxically eroticized in nineteenth-century American sexology and literature.

2. Although "The Case" appears in a collection of Du Bois's works edited by David Levering Lewis, it is not widely known, and there are scant allusions to Du Bois having written detective fiction in the compendium of academic criticism on Du Bois. One notable exception is Britt Rusert's allusion to Du Bois's poetics of the "weird," as applied to a number of distinct generic conventions that Du Bois plied to produce his works of short fiction. See Rusert's "W.E.B. Du Bois, Aesthetics, and the Weird," Online Forum, AAIHS, February 20, 2018.

3. Hortense Spillers, "Mama's Baby, Papa's Maybe," *Diacritics* 17, no. 2 (1987): 64–81. Spillers explains that the Black slave's status was determined by the status of the mother whose condition he "followed," by decree of US law. I submit further that the feminization of the Black male is not just a historical fact of Black culture but also, in Du Bois's estimation, an epistemological practice.

4. The "femme fatale" is a stock figure within detective fiction, especially "noir" novels of the 1920s and 1940s. As Veronika Pitukovà explains, "Hard-boiled novels present the femme fatale as a dame with a past, a spider woman, and the detective as a hero with no future, caught in her web of intrigues." See Pitukovà, "Clash of Desires: Detective versus Femme Fatale," *Journal of Arts and Humanities* 7, no. 1 (2012): 26.

5. Note that the porters are not explicitly named detectives in these stories. However, in Du Bois's short story "Murder on Ninth Avenue," *Crisis* 19, no. 3 (1920), the porter explicitly refers to himself as an "amateur detective," lamenting that a racist America has precluded his becoming a professional one.

6. For Asa Philip Randolph's recognition of Du Bois's support of Pullman porters, see "Letter from Brotherhood of Sleeping Car Porters to W. E. B. Du Bois, December 28, 1927," W.E. B. Du Bois Papers (MS 312), Special Collections and University Archives, University of Massachusetts Amherst Libraries.

7. Du Bois, "Careers Open to College-Bred Negroes," 1898, *W.E.B. Du Bois: Writings*, ed. Nathan Huggins (New York: Library of America, 1986), 841.

8. David Perata, *Those Pullman Blues: An Oral History of the African American Railway Attendant* (Lanham, MD: Madison, 1996). Perata adds, "Of all the employees on the train, [the porter's] skills were perhaps the most highly developed, owing to the extreme intimacy of the Pullman car" (xxiv).

9. Mikhail Bakhtin describes the chronotope as a phenomenon by which "spatial and temporal indicators are fused into one carefully thought-out, concrete whole. Time, as it were, thickens, takes on flesh, becomes artistically visible; likewise,

space becomes charged and responsive to the movements of time, plot and history." See Bakhtin, *The Dialogic Imagination,* trans. Caryl Emerson and Michael Holquist (Austin: University of Texas Press, 1983), 84.

10. All quotations are taken from the version of "The Case" published in *W.E.B. Du Bois: A Reader,* ed. David Levering Lewis, published by Henry, Holt, and Co., 1995 (109–13). For the original version of the story, as published in *Horizon,* see also the W.E.B. Du Bois Papers (MS 312), Special Collections and University Archives, University of Massachusetts Amherst Libraries.

11. Soitos elaborates further on the centrality of narration to detective fiction: "narration is [. . .] from the viewpoint of a close associate or friend told in the first person or from the viewpoint of the detective told in the first person" (1996, 23).

12. See also Du Bois 1907a, W.E.B. Du Bois Papers (MS 312), Special Collections and University Archives, University of Massachusetts Amherst Libraries.

13. Du Bois, whose daughter's marriage failed due to her husband's homosexuality and whose assistant Augustus Dill was arrested for homosexual "activity," claimed to be ignorant of any but heterosexual desires: "In the midst of my career there burst on me a new and undreamed of aspect of sex. [. . .] I had never understood the tragedy of Oscar Wilde." See Mason Stokes, "Father of the Bride: Du Bois and the Making of Black Heterosexuality," in *Next to the Color Line: Gender, Sexuality, and W.E.B. Du Bois,* eds. Susan Gillman and Alys Eve Weinbaum (Minneapolis: University of Minnesota Press, 2007), 309–10. Stokes characterizes Du Bois's confession as implausible, a reading that the homoerotic subtext of his detective fiction affirms.

14. Aliyyah Abdur-Rahman, "'The Strangest Freaks of Despotism': Queer Sexuality in Antebellum African American Slave Narratives," *African American Review* 40, no. 2 (2006): 225.

15. For more on the link between heterosexuality and whiteness, see Mason Stokes, *The Color of Sex: Whiteness, Heterosexuality, and the Fiction of White Supremacy* (Durham, NC: Duke University Press, 2001). See also Gayle Rubin, "The Traffic in Women," *Toward an Anthropology of Women,* ed. Rayna R. Reiter (New York: Monthly Review, 1975), 157–210.

16. Recall that, in "Of Our Spiritual Strivings" Du Bois describes a "veil" separating Black persons from the white American mainstream ([1903] 2007, 8).

17. Du Bois, "The Souls of White Folk," in *Darkwater* (Mineola: Dover Thrift Editions, [1920] 1999), 17.

18. I do not claim, of necessity, any direct reference here, but rather, point out a similar philosophic and poetic approach to the detective story that is discernible in both "The Man of the Crowd" and Du Bois's *Horizon* mysteries. However, as Poe's story was published in the mid-nineteenth century, and as I have already underscored Du Bois's commitment to various forms of literary romanticism, I do believe it quite plausible that Du Bois was acquainted with and perhaps even influenced by this story of Poe's and its subtle approach to the detective genre.

To see another generative link drawn between Du Bois's fiction and "The Man of the Crowd." See R. A. Judy's *Sentient Flesh: Thinking in Disorder Poesis in Black* (Durham, NC: Duke University Press, 2020), 124–25.

19. The trope of the detective as both hero and potential suspect is a stock trope of 1940s-era hardboiled detective fiction and film noir. But the presence of moral ambiguity in the detective genre can be traced as far back as Edgar Allan Poe. As Stephen Soitos reminds us, Poe pioneered "the complicated detective persona," in which the detective was possessed of "a double nature" needed for solving crimes—and thus, of an equal propensity for "good" and "evil" (1996, 17–18).

20. See, for example, Wright's novel *Native Son* (1940) and his short story "The Man Who Lived Underground"—published in the short story collection *Eight Men* (1961).

Notes to Chapter 3

1. Alys Weinbaum also notes that "The Hands of Ethiopia" is linked to "The Princess of the Hither Isles," as does Hee-Jung Serenity Joo (See Weinbaum 2007, 102; Joo 2019, 109). Despite their attention to the placement of Du Bois's story in *Darkwater,* neither critic plumbs this fact to arrive at my interpretation of its significance: that the princess is a white-passing or white-appearing Black or mixed-race woman.

2. For more on the Native Land Act of 1913, see Iris Berger's "South Africa in World History" in *The New Oxford World History* (Oxford: Oxford University Press, 2009).

3. Sitting upon a throne amidst a damp and unfertile landscape with her soul veiled, the princess may also mark Du Bois's subtle allusion to the Egyptian goddess Isis, who was said to have been born in a region that is "moist" (see Markus Carabas 2018, 16). Specifically, the dampness of the Hither Isles, which Du Bois renders a "swamp," recalls the geographic space of the Nile, which, as Du Bois reminds us in his 1939 ethnographic history "Black Folk Then and Now," connects Egypt and Ethiopia to the Mediterranean (see Du Bois [1939] 2009). And, as Henry Ridgley Evans relates, the Greek philosopher Proclus recorded the following proclamation etched on a statue of Isis: "I am that which is, has been, and shall be. My veil no one has lifted" (Evans 1903, 498).

4. The "Empire of the Sun" may also be an allusion to China, a country whose anti-imperial struggle was of great interest to Du Bois. Yet it may also be an allusion to the North African empire of Egypt, a country whose worldview marked the veneration of the sun, and in particular, to the pantheon of Ra, the sun deity, and his descendants: Isis, the goddess of light, and Osiris, who was characterized variously as the god of sun, light, agriculture, and the underworld (Carabas 2018, 18–20).

5. The ethnic slur "dago" has historically been leveled against persons of South American, Italian, Spanish, and South Asian descent and not primarily against those of African descent.

6. I hasten to add that I had long been working on this chapter and had already arrived at my original interpretation of "The Princess of the Hither Isles" before the publication of Logan Alexander's book, which I was excited to acquire, since it seems a felicitous affirmation of my own thinking.

7. One could see a paradox in the fact that the king could hate "niggers and dagoes" while still be courting the princess. I earlier suggested that the princess could be white-passing. Yet it is also the case that she may simply exist at a higher point on the spectrum of color and class (caste) classification. As Du Bois allowed, race mixture was volubly decried yet materially practiced throughout *Darkwater*, in "Criteria of Negro Art," in his stories of "tragically mulatta" women in love or sexual relationships with white men that end in tragedy (e.g., *The Quest of the Silver Fleece*), and in his novel *Dark Princess*, in which a South Asian princess must fend off the advances of a white British man who wishes to marry her only for imperial gain. As Juliet Hooker notes, Du Bois also drew on a Latin American version of whiteness, not as starkly purist as presented in the United States, but as a result of inevitable miscegenation (see Hooker 2017).

8. Alys Weinbaum and Amy Kaplan make similar arguments about how Du Bois connects American racism to European imperialism. See Joo (2019, 122).

9. The king's act of dismemberment also recalls the Belgian King Leopold's violent practice of cutting off the hands of Congolese colonial subjects, as Lawrence J. Oliver points out in "Apocalyptic and Slow Violence: The Environmental Vision of W. E. B. Du Bois's *Darkwater*" in *Interdisciplinary Studies in Literature and Environment* 22, no. 3 (Summer 2015): 473.

10. See Doris Sommer's *Foundational Fictions: The National Romances of Latin America* (1991) and Lisa Moore's "Acts of Union: Sexuality and Nationalism, Romance and Realism in the Irish National Tale" (2000).

11. Moten grounds his notion of fugitivity in the story of an enslaved woman who chose to return to Tennessee with her owners rather than consent to having her "freedom" be premised upon the state's dominion over her person (2018, 246).

Notes to Chapter 4

1. Romila Thapar explains in her article "The Theory of Aryan Race and India: History and Politics" that nineteenth-century racialist discourse invented the "Aryan" as a group of Indo-European descent. The theory was amplified by the sociologist Max Müller, who argued that a group of Aryans, "fair-complexioned Indo-European speakers," conquered the darker-skinned *dasas* who were indigenous to India. Thapar elaborates further: "The *arya-varna* and the *dasa-varna* of the *Rigveda*

were understood as two conflicting groups differentiated particularly by skin color, but also by language and religious practice, which doubtless underlined the racial interpretation of the terms" (1996, 5–6).

2. Rai's progressive commitments have been critiqued by some scholars as being diluted by a liberal humanism that fell short of being radically egalitarian. For example, Sunita Pathania asserts that although Rai fought to abolish the practice of mistreating and rendering abject those members of the "depressed classes," he nevertheless maintained an investment in the overall structure of caste. As Pathania further explains: "Lala Lajpat Rai's conception of Indian society contains in principle all the salient features of an ideal civil society, but paradoxically he insists on seeing these attributes in a collectivity which is premodern and is characterized by divisions along lines of caste and religious groupings" (2000–2001, 966). The limitations of any mode of reformism that is more attuned to anti-imperialism than to anticasteism is an issue I will revisit.

3. See Yogita Goyal (2010, 9, 94) and (2019).

4. In fact, Du Bois did not base Princess Kautilya on any royal figure (the importance of her royalty has chiefly symbolic import, as I will show). Rather, she is likely a composite of South Asian historical figures—both men and women. While Madhumita Lahiri speculates that the princess was based partly upon the pro-Indian nationalist leader Annie Besant (Lahiri 2010, 541), Homi Bhabha suggests that she may have been modeled after Madame Bhikaji Kama, a Parsi woman from Bombay who exiled herself in Europe in 1902 and eventually settled in Paris (Bhabha 2004, 142). Indeed, critics have speculated about numerous possible sources for the princess, including Annie Besant (Lahiri), Gandhi (Lahiri), and the Indian male philosopher Kautilya, who advised King Chandragupta circa 317–293 BCE and who published an influential work of political statecraft, *Arthashastra* (see Boesche 2003 and Allston 2019).

5. For a useful overview of the central concepts of caste, which involve "mutual repulsion between social groups, division into opposed fragments, isolation at the group level, and mechanisms to prevent alliances and relations across the group boundary, like endogamy, pollution concepts, and food taboos," see Madhusudan Subedi's "Some Theoretical Considerations on Caste" (Subedi 2013, 57).

6. Note that Du Bois had connections to Raj, Gandhi, and Dalit leader Bhimrao Ramji Ambedkar (Goyal 2019, 265). Like Gandhi, Du Bois was not wholly resistant to some aspects of caste logic, as I go on to detail. For more on Gandhi's anti-Black racism and initially reformist rather than abolitionist stance toward casteism, see Arundhati Roy's introduction to Bhimrao Ramji Ambedkar's *Annihilation of Caste*, in which she notes that when Gandhi was working as a legal advisor in South Africa in the late nineteenth century, he was "not offended by racial segregation" but only that Indian merchants were treated as being on the same level as "native Black Africans" (Roy 2014, loc. 902 of 8199). Roy notes that by 1928, Gandhi had shifted his views, allying himself more with the Zulu people than the

British working to defeat them (loc. 991 of 8199). With the 1932 passage of the Poona Pact, a governmental agreement by which those classified as "Untouchables" were allotted seats in the legislature rather than being granted a separate electoral voting bloc, Gandhi dedicated himself to trying to "eradicate" Untouchability—if only partially affixed to the praxis of eradicating caste, producing what Roy characterizes as simply a placebo approach to healing caste hierarchy ([1896] 1940). For Goyal, Rabindranath Tagore serves as a more appropriate Indian nationalist model for Du Bois than does Gandhi, as he was a vociferous critic of caste-based forms of oppression who shared Du Bois's somewhat mystical belief in the "soul" value of non-Western people that might mitigate the effects of "(Western) mechanization and militarism" (Goyal 2019, 57).

7. The Samurai were a high warrior caste from the medieval era to the early modern period (1185–1868) in Japan, which was disbanded with the onset of modernity. It is interesting to note that members of the Samurai caste could legally murder those of lower castes who had "disrespected" them, a historical fact that Du Bois uses to dramatize the hypocrisy and moral lapses within some factions of the princess's anti-imperialist and purportedly revolutionary group (see "Samurai," Asia for Educators, afe.easia.columbia.edu).

8. Madhumita Lahiri calls Du Bois's adaptation of the Hindu story of Radha-Krishna to figure Matthew and the princess's affair "a problematic conversion" (2010, 187). Clearly, Du Bois's allusion to the Hindu tale reflects his desire, noted by Lahiri, to idealize the Black body and also to redeem "illegitimate," subversive love (187). But I contend that Du Bois was also drawn to the story for its privileging of cross-caste love, also reflected in the Greco-Roman tale "Cupid and Psyche" and in the medieval tale of Lohengrin, which Du Bois adapts in "Of the Coming of John," as I earlier detailed.

9. Here, with the princess's fusion of Gotama, "the soul of Brahma," and Matthew's mother, Du Bois draws a link between Hinduism, Buddhism, and Christianity—all noble and ancient religious traditions, under the broad strokes of his brush. It is also important to note that Dalit leader and co-creator of the Indian Constitution, B. R. Ambedkar, converted to Buddhism and advocated for many Dalit persons to do the same. The princess's invocation of the Buddha thus indicates her partial abdication of a narrowly understood Brahmin and Hindu identity and Du Bois's subtle allusion to an anti-Brahmin and anticaste ideation. See Yengde's *Caste Matters* (2019) and B. R. Ambedkar's *Annihilation of Caste* (2014).

10. Note that Yogita Goyal also observes how Du Bois invokes Kali and Shango, both grand deities of Asian and African lore, to reflect "history, not merely as destiny but as a recovery of a time past" (2010, 94). Du Bois's revision of history is a point I revisit in my epilogue.

11. This plot point mitigates somewhat the claim of critics like Alys Weinbaum and Hazel Carby that Du Bois abandoned the representation of Black women in his literary discourses. See both their essays in *Next to the Color Line: Gender, Sexuality, and W.E.B. Du Bois* (2007).

12. As Milner acknowledges, there is an extant scholarly debate about to what extent reincarnation is governed by the degree of one's conformity to one's ascribed caste status. A key question arises: does conformity to caste norms influence the trajectory that one's path of reincarnation might take?

13. Madhumita Lahiri sees Matthew's body as hypermasculine and akin to that of a Greek athlete and thus in "stark contrast to the emaciated figure of Gandhi" (2010, 213). Yet I see Matthew's body as more like that of an emaciated (fasting and sexually abstinent) figure and thus more akin to Gandhi than Lahiri allows, in part because his "hard" limbs are also juxtaposed with what I ascertain as loose muscles and the absence of a stomach. In this description of Matthew's physical transformation as a hard laborer, I also hear echoes of Hortense Spillers on the desire to get out of the abjected black body and back to or even beyond the "flesh" (Spillers 1987).

14. As I note in my introduction, historian Nico Slate offers evidence of the way race scholars and civil rights leaders like Booker T. Washington and, of course, Du Bois engaged in comparative analyses of (anti-Black) racism and casteism (See Slate 2012, chap. 1: "Race, Caste and Nation"). And in her study of caste, Isabel Wilkerson notes the astonishment of Martin Luther King Jr., when, during a 1959 trip to India, he was lauded as an honorary member of the Dalit people (Wilkerson 2020, 416). Moreover, while Gandhi tended to differentiate the Dalit struggle from that of people of African descent (at least until much later in his career), Dalit leader and legal scholar B. R. Ambedkar also believed that the struggle of the Dalit people was akin to that of African Americans in the United States. In an illuminating exchange of letters between Du Bois and Ambedkar in 1946, several years after the publication of *Dark Princess*, Ambedkar declared, "There is so much similarity between the position of the Untouchables of India and of the position of the Negroes in America," see (W. E. B.) (William Edward Burghardt) Du Bois, 1868–1963. Letter from B. R. Ambedkar to W. E. B. Du Bois, July 1946. Letter from W. E. B. Du Bois to B. R. Ambedkar, July 31, 1946, W. E. B. Du Bois Papers, MS312, Special Collections and University Archives, University of Massachusetts Amherst Libraries). Du Bois's response, while congenial, was decidedly less impassioned, as he replied that the NAACP would shortly release a statement of support for the Dalit people of India yet asserted only that he had "every sympathy" for the cause of Dalit liberation. Unlike Ambedkar, Du Bois fell short of acknowledging a shared struggle or common cause between Black Americans and Dalit people. Nevertheless, Du Bois's relegation of Matthew to a member of an itinerant, low-wage working class still reflects the common struggle of those members of the Shudra castes (and perhaps also, if only by inference, those classified as belonging to the Ati-Shudra castes) and the African American working classes.

15. I do not wish to overstate or to interpret as literal Matthew's invocation of Dalit experience, especially since I believe that the novel's allusion to Dalit experience may have been incidental and perhaps forged outside the range of Du Bois's conscious intentions. Moreover, Matthew's approximation of Dalit experience

occurs only on the level of his job. He is still privileged in being able to retreat to his bachelor pad and enjoy palpable measures of social mobility, both within and without the mixed-class Black communities with whom he freely associates. Still, Matthew's movement along extreme lines of class (and caste) status underscores Du Bois's decision to place the arbitrary and rigid concatenations of casteist structures under a microscope.

16. See Du Bois's 1888 Fisk valedictorian address, "Bismarck," in the W. E. B. Du Bois Papers (MS 312), Special Collections and University Archives, University of Massachusetts Amherst Libraries and "Jefferson Davis as a Representative of Civilization" in *W. E. B. Du Bois: Writings*, Library of America, 1986.

17. Note that Milner says that some scholars disagree about whether *karma* really colludes with systems of caste hierarchy (300). Also see Subedi (2013, 327).

18. In *Domestic Allegories of Political Desire: The Black Heroine's Text at the Turn of the Century*, Claudia Tate identifies the novelistic representation of the "ideal conjugal relation" as "resemble [ing] one between a loving brother and sister" as a literary strategy that "fosters an approximate egalitarian relationship between the spouses" (1992, 169). With Tate's theory in mind, I submit that Du Bois's subtle figuration of Matthew and the princess as romantic siblings fosters gender parity alongside ethnic pluralism.

19. Brilmyer, Trentin, and Xiang refer to the "one-tological," which is contrasted with the "abiogenic three," which marks the possibility of becoming three or more (Brilmyer et al. 2019, 226).

20. In his essay "Du Bois, *Dark Princess* and the Afro-Asian International," Mullen credits *Dark Princess* with having "anticipated" the Bandung conference, in which a number of newly decolonized African and Asian countries met to collaborate on the shared continuance of their revolutions and to condemn ongoing imperialism in Asia (Mullen 2003, 235).

Notes to the Epilogue

1. See *African Folk Tales As Told to Pauline E. Dinkins* (Sunday School Publishing Board, Nashville, Tennessee, 1933). For the letters that passed between Pauline Dinkins and Du Bois, see "Letter from Pauline Dinkins to W. E. B. Du Bois," April 3, 1929, and "Letter from W. E. B. Du Bois to Pauline E. Dinkins," September 11, 1929. W. E. B. Du Bois Papers (MS 312). Special Collections and University Archives, University of Massachusetts Amherst Libraries.

2. Apuleius writes that Cupid, the anonymous "bridegroom" who appears in her bed at night "made Psyche his bride" and that his maidservants then "tended" to her "ruptured virginity" (Apuleius [1566] 1962, 111). As many of my students quickly point out, this amounts to a forced sexual act to which Psyche did not likely

consent. Although the narrative attempts to suture the rupture of sexual violence by avowing Psyche's eventual love for Cupid, the reality of intimacy as an instrument of violation is never stricken from the story's record.

3. Emphasis mine.

4. The character who assists the embattled hero is described by Vladimir Propp as the "donor" or "magical helpmate." See Propp (1986, 39–43).

5. See W. E. B. Du Bois Papers (MS 312), Special Collections and University Archives, University of Massachusetts Amherst Libraries and "Vintage Points," News from Special Collections, Williams College Archives and Chapin Library, October 17, 2016.

6. As I detail in my analysis of this story in chapter 3, Du Bois plies the ambiguous semantics of the folktale, which lend themselves to multiple and even conflicting interpretations (see Menninghaus 1995) to allow for two different readings: either the princess *falls* to her death in the process of trying to join the black beggar or the princess *jumps* to her death rather than enter into any economy of exchange—romantic or otherwise.

7. See Fred Moten's *In the Break: The Aesthetics of the Black Radical Tradition*, in which he describes Nathaniel Mackey's theorization of the "broken claim [. . .] to connection between Africa and African America that seek[s] to suture corollary, asymptomatically divergent ruptures—maternal estrangement and the thwarted romance of the sexes," which he names the condition of "wounded kinship" (quoted in Moten 2003, "Resistance of the Object: Aunt Hester's Scream").

Works Cited

Abdur-Rahman, Aliyyah. 2006. "'The Strangest Freaks of Despotism': Queer Sexuality in Antebellum African American Slave Narratives." *African American Review* 40, no. 2 (January): 223–37.
Alexander, Adele Logan. 2019. *Princess of the Hither Isles: A Black Suffragist's Story from the Jim Crow South.* New Haven, CT: Yale University Press.
Alexander Michelle. 2010. *The New Jim Crow: Mass Incarceration in the Age of Colorblindness.* New York: The New Press.
Allston, Vermonja. 2011. "Cosmopolitan Fantasies, Aesthetics, and Bodily Value in W.E.B. Du Bois's *Dark Princess* and the Trans/Gendering of Kautilya." *Journal of Transnational American Studies* 3, no. 1 (March).
Appiah, K. Anthony. 2014. *Lines of Descent: W. E. B. Du Bois and the Emergence of Identity.* Cambridge, MA: Harvard University Press.
Aptheker, Herbert. 1937. "American Negro Slave Revolts." *Science and Society* 1, no. 4 (Summer): 512–35.
Apuleius. (1566) 1962. *The Golden Ass.* Translated by Jack Lindsay. Bloomington: Indiana University Press.
Bakhtin, Mikhail. 1983. *The Dialogic Imagination.* Austin: University of Texas Press.
Bastian, Misty. 1997. "Married in the Water: Spirit Kin and Other Afflictions of Modernity in Southeastern Nigeria." *Journal of Religions in Africa* 27, no. 2 (May): 116–34.
Beavers, Herman. 2000. "Du Bois's Propaganda of the Dark World." *Annals of the American Academy of Political and Social Science* 568 (March): 250–64.
Berlant, Lauren. 1998. "Intimacy: A Special Issue." *Critical Inquiry* 24, no. 2 (Winter): 281–88.
Berman, Russell. 1997. "Du Bois and Wagner: Race, Nation, and Culture Between the United States and Germany." *German Quarterly* 70, no. 2 (Spring): 123–35.
Bhabha, Homi K. 2004. "The Black Savant and *Dark Princess.*" *ESQ: A Journal of the American Renaissance* 50, nos. 1–3: 137–55.

Boesche, Roger. 2003. "Kautilya's Arthashastra: On War and Diplomacy in Ancient India." *The Journal of Military History* 67, no. 1 (January): 9–37.

Brilmyer, S. Pearl, Filippo Trentin, and Zairon Xiang. 2019. "The Ontology of the Couple, or What Queer Theory Knows about Numbers." *GLQ* 25, no. 2 (April): 223–55.

Bruce, Dickson, Jr. 1999. 'W.E.B. Du Bois and the Idea of Double Consciousness." In *The Souls of Black Folk*, edited by Henry Louis Gates Jr. and Terri Hume Oliver, 236–44. New York and London: W.W. Norton and Co.

Butler, Judith. 1995. "Melancholy Gender-Refused Identification." *Psychoanalytic Dialogues* 5, no. 2: 165–80.

Carabas, Markus. *Ra: The History and Legacy of the Ancient Egyptian God of the Sun*. Ann Arbor, MI: Charles River Editors, 2018. Kindle.

Carby, Hazel. 1998. *Race Men*. Cambridge, MA: Harvard University Press. Kindle.

———. 2007. "The Souls of Black Men." In *Next to the Color Line: Gender, Sexuality, and W.E.B. Du Bois,* edited by Susan Gillman and Alys Weinbaum, 234–68. Minneapolis: University of Minnesota Press.

Chandler, Nahum. 2013. *The Problem of the Negro as A Problem for Thought*. New York: Fordham University Press.

Cronin, Blaise, and Yvonne Roger. 2003. "From Victorian Visiting Card to VCard: The Evolution of a Communicative Genre." *Journal of Information Science* 29, no. 1 (February): 65–68.

Dalhaus, Carl. 1979. "Lohengrin." In *Richard Wagner's Music Dramas*. Cambridge: Cambridge University Press.

Dinkins, Pauline E. 1933. "Princess Wata." *African Folk Tales as Told to Pauline E. Dinkins*. Sunday School Publishing Board.

Diouf, Sylviane A. 2009. *Slavery's Exiles: The Story of the American Maroons*. New York: New York University Press, 2014. Kindle.

Du Bois, W. E. B. (1896) 2009. *The Gift of Black Folk*. New York: Square One.

———. (1897) 1996. "Jefferson Davis." In *The Oxford W.E.B. Du Bois Reader*, edited by Eric J. Sundquist, 243–45. Oxford: Oxford University Press.

———. (1898) 1989. "The Conservation of Races." In *Writings*, edited by Nathan Huggins, 815–26. New York: Library of America.

———. (1898) 1989. "Careers Open to College Bred Negroes." In *W.E.B. Du Bois: Writings*, edited by Nathan Huggins, 827–41. New York: Library of America.

———. (1903) 2007. "Of Our Spiritual Strivings." In *The Souls of Black Folk*, edited by Brent Hayes Edwards, 7–14. Oxford: Oxford University Press.

———. (1903) 2007. "Of the Training of Black Men." In *The Souls of Black Folk*, edited by Brent Hayes Edwards, 63–76. Oxford: Oxford University Press.

———. (1903) 2007. "Of the Coming of John." In *The Souls of Black Folk*, edited by Brent Hayes Edwards, 153–66. Oxford: Oxford University Press.

———. (1907a) 1995. "The Case." In *W.E.B. Du Bois: A Reader*, edited by David Levering Lewis, 109–13. New York: Henry Holt and Co.

———. 1907b. "The Shaven Lady." W. E. B. Du Bois Papers (MS 312), Special Collections and University Archives, University of Massachusetts Amherst Libraries.

———. 1920. "Murder on Ninth Avenue." *The Crisis* 19, no. 3 (January).

———. (1920) 1999. *Darkwater: Voices from Within the Veil*. Mineola: Dover.

———. (1926) 2000. "Criteria of Negro Art." In *African American Literary Theory: A Reader*, edited by Winston Napier. New York: New York University Press.

———. (1928) 1995. *Dark Princess: A Romance*. Jackson: University Press of Mississippi.

———. 1936. "Opera and the Negro Problem." *Pittsburgh Courier*, October 31.

———. 1968. *The Autobiography of W.E.B. Du Bois: A Soliloquy on Viewing My Life from the Last Decade of Its First Century*. New York: International Publishers.

Du Cille, Ann. 1993. *The Coupling Convention: Sex, Text, and Tradition in Black Women's Fiction*. Oxford: Oxford University Press.

Eagleton, Terry. 1990. *The Ideology of the Aesthetic*. Oxford: Basil Blackwell.

Elam, Michele, and Paul C. Taylor. 2007. "Du Bois's Erotics." In *Next to the Color Line: Gender, Sexuality, and W.E.B. Du Bois*, edited by Susan Gillman and Alys Eve Weinbaum, 209–33. Minneapolis: University of Minnesota Press.

Eschenbach, Wolfram Von. 1961. *Parzival: A Romance of the Middle Ages*. Translated and edited by Helen Mustard and Charles E. Passage. New York: Vintage.

Evans, Henry Ridgley. 1903. "The Mysteries of Isis and Osiris." *Open Court*, May.

Ferguson, Roderick A. 2004. *Aberrations in Black: Toward a Queer of Color Critique*. Minneapolis: University of Minnesota Press. Kindle.

Gillman, Susan. 2003. *Blood Work: American Race Melodrama and the Culture of the Occult*. Chicago: University of Chicago Press.

———. 2007. "Introduction: W.E.B. Du Bois and the Politics of Juxtaposition." In *Next to the Color Line: Gender, Sexuality, and W.E.B. Du Bois*, edited by Susan Gillman and Alys Weinbaum, 1–34. Minneapolis: Univerity of Minnesota.

Gilroy, Paul. 1993. *The Black Atlantic: Modernity and Double Consciousness*. Cambridge, MA: Harvard University Press.

Gooding-Williams, Robert. 2009. *In the Shadow of Du Bois: Afro-Modern Political Thought in America*. Cambridge, MA: Harvard University Press.

Gopinath, Gayatri. 2006. *Queer Diasporas and South Asian Public Cultures*. Durham, NC: Duke University Press.

Goyal, Yogita. 2019. *Romance, Diaspora, and Black Atlantic Literature*. Cambridge UP, 2010.

———. "On Transnational Analogy: Thinking Race and Caste with W.E.B. Du Bois and Rabindranath Tagore." *Atlantic Studies* 16, no. 1 (January): 54–71.

Griffin, Farah Jasmine. 1995. *"Who Set You Flowin'?": The African American Migration Narrative*. Oxford: Oxford University Press.

Guyer, Paul. 1997. *Kant and the Claims of Taste*. Cambridge: Cambridge University Press.

Halberstam, (Judith) Jack. 2005. *In a Queer Time and Place: Transgender Bodies, Subcultural Lives*. New York: New York University Press. Kindle.

Hartman, Saidiya V. 2006. *Lose Your Mother: A Journey Along the Atlantic Slave Route*. New York: Farrar, Straus, and Giroux.

Henry, Paget. 2006. *Journeys in Caribbean Thought: The Paget Henry Reader*, edited by Jane Gordon, Lewis R. Gordon, Aaron Kamugisha, and Neil Roberts. Lanham, MD: Rowman and Littlefield.

Hohr, Hansjörg. 2010. "Does Beauty Matter in Education? Friedrich Schiller's Neo-Humanistic Approach." *Journal of Curriculum Studies* 34, no. 1 (November): 59–75.

Holland, Sharon P. 2012. *The Erotic Life of Racism*. Durham, NC: Duke University Press. Kindle.

Holy Bible. 1989. New Revised Standard Version. Oxford: Oxford University Press.

Hooker, Juliet. 2017. *Theorizing Race in the Americas: Douglass, Sarmiento, Du Bois, and Vasconcelos*. Oxford: Oxford University Press. Kindle.

Joo, Hee-Jung Serenity. 2019. "Racial Impossibility and Critical Failure in W.E.B. Du Bois's *Darkwater*." *Science Fiction Studies* 46, no. 1 (March): 106–26.

Judy, R. A. 2015. "Lohengrin's Swan and the Style of Interiority in 'Of the Coming of John.'" *New Centennial Review* 15, no. 2 (Fall): 211–57.

———. 2020. *Sentient Flesh: Thinking in Disorder, Poiesis in Black*. Durham, NC: Duke University Press.

King-Watts, Eric. 2001. "Cultivating a Black Public Voice: W. E. B. Du Bois and 'The Criteria of Negro Art.'" *Rhetoric and Public Affairs* 4, no. 2 (Summer): 181–201.

Kramer, Lawrence. 2001–2002. "Contesting Wagner: The *Lohengrin* Prelude and Anti-anti-Semitism." *Nineteenth-Century Music* 25, nos. 2–3 (Fall-Spring): 190–211.

Kristeva, Julia. 1987. *Tales of Love*. Translated by Leon S. Roudiez. New York: Columbia University Press.

Lahiri, Madhumita. 2010. "World Romance: Genre, Internationalism, and W.E.B. Du Bois." *Callaloo* 33, no. 2 (Spring): 537–52.

Lemke, Sieglinde. 2008. "Of the Coming of John." In *The Cambridge Companion to W. E. B. Du Bois*, edited by Shamoon Zamir, 37–47. Cambridge: Cambridge University Press.

Lenz, Günther H. 2009. "Radical Cosmopolitanism: W. E. B. Du Bois, Germany and African American Pragmatist Visions for Twenty-First Century Europe." In *Representation and Decoration in a Postmodern Age*, edited by Alfred Hornung and Rüdiger Kunow, 65–96. Göttingen: Universitätsverlag Presse.

Levinas, Emmanuel. 1991. *Totality and Infinity: An Essay on Exteriority*. Translated by Alphonso Lingis. Amsterdam: Kluwer Academic Publishers.

Lewis, David Levering. 2000. *W.E.B. Du Bois: The Fight for Equality and The American Century, 1919–1963*. New York: Henry Holt.

Menninghaus, Winfried. 1995. *In Praise of Nonsense: Kant and Bluebeard*. Stanford, CA: Stanford University Press. Kindle.

Miller, Monica L. 2003. "W. E. B. Du Bois and the Dandy as Diasporic Race Man." *Callaloo* 26, no. 3 (Summer): 738–65.

———. 2009. *Slaves to Fashion: Black Dandyism and the Styling of Black Diasporic Identity*. Durham, NC: Duke University Press. Kindle.

Milner, Murray Jr. 1993. "Hindu Eschatology and the Indian Caste System: An Example of Structural Reversal." *Journal of Asian Studies* 52, no. 2 (May): 298–319.

Moore, Lisa L. 2000. "Acts of Union: Sexuality and Nationalism, Romance, and Realism in the Irish National Tale." *Cultural Critique* 44 (Winter): 113–44.

Morrison, Toni. 1992. *Playing in the Dark: Whiteness and the Literary Imagination*. New York: Vintage.

Moten, Fred. 2003. *In the Break: The Aesthetics of the Black Radical Tradition*. Minneapolis: University of Minnesota Press. Kindle.

———. 2007. "Uplift and Criminality." In *Next to the Color Line: Gender, Sexuality, and W.E.B. Du Bois*, edited by Susan Gillman and Alys Eve Weinbaum, 317–49. Minneapolis: University of Minnesota Press.

———. 2018. *Stolen Life: Consent Not to Be a Single Being*. Durham, NC: Duke University Press.

Mullen, Bill V. 2003. "Du Bois, Dark Princess, and the Afro-Asian International." *Positions: East Asia Cultures Critique* 11, no. 1 (Spring): 217–39.

———. 2004. *Afro-Orientalism*. Minneapolis: University of Minnesota Press.

Mullen, Bill, and Cathryn Watson, eds. 2005. *W.E.B. Du Bois On Asia: Crossing the World Color Line*. Jackson: University Press of Mississippi. Kindle.

Muñoz, Jose. 2009. *Cruising Utopia: The Then and There of Queer Futurity*. New York: New York University Press. Kindle.

Nehamas, Alexander. 2000. "Review: The Return of the Beautiful: Morality, Pleasure, and the Value of Uncertainty." *Journal of Aesthetics and Art Criticism* 58, no. 4 (Autumn): 393–403.

———. 2007. "'Only in the Contemplation of Beauty Is Human Life Worth Living,' Plato, *Symposium* 211d." *European Journal of Philosophy* 15, no. 1 (March): 1–18.

Nero, Charles. 2005. "Queering the Souls of Black Folk." *Public Culture* 17, no. 2 (Spring): 255–76.

Nussbaum, Martha C. 2013. *Political Emotions: Why Love Matters for Justice*. Cambridge, MA: Harvard University Press.

Oliver, Lawrence J. 2015. "Apocalyptic and Slow Violence: The Environmental Vision of W.E.B. Du Bois's *Darkwater*." *Interdisciplinary Studies in Literature and Environment* 22, no. 3 (Summer): 466–84.

Pathania, Sunita. "Lala Lajpat Rai's Vision of Social Change: A Study of the Depressed Classes in India." *Proceedings of the Indian History Congress* 61, Part 1, Millennium, 2000–2001, 961–75.

Perata, David. 1996. *Those Pullman Blues: An Oral History of the African American Railway Attendant.* Lanham, MD: Madison Books.

Piper, Adrian. 1997. "Xenophobia and Kantian Rationalism." In *Feminist Interpretations of Immanuel Kant,* edited by Robin May Schott. University Park: Pennsylvania State University Press.

Pitukovà, Veronica. 2012. "Clash of Desires: Detective versus Femme Fatale." *Journal of Arts and Humanities* 7, no. 1 (August).

Plato. 1989. *Symposium.* Translated by Alexander Nehamas and Paul Woodruff. Indianapolis: Hackett.

———. 1995. *Phaedrus.* Translated by Alexander Nehamas and Paul Woodruff. Indianapolis: Hackett.

Poe, Edgar Allan. (1840) 1993. "The Man of the Crowd." In *Tales of Mystery and Imagination.* London: Wordsworth Editions.

Powers, Christopher. 2015. "Figurations of Passage through 'Of the Coming of John.'" *CR: The New Centennial Review* 15, no. 2 (Fall): 59–82.

Propp, Vladimir. *Morphology of the Folktale.* Translated by Laurence Scott. Austin: University of Texas Press, 1986.

Rankine, Claudia. *Citizen: An American Lyric.* Minneapolis: Graywolf, 2014.

Roy, Arundhati. 2014. "The Doctor and the Saint" (Introduction). In *Annihilation of Caste: The Annotated Critical Edition.* B. R. Ambedkar, edited and annotated by S. Anand. London and New York: Verso. Kindle.

Rubin, Gayle. 1975. "The Traffic in Women." In *Toward an Anthropology of Women,* edited by Rayna R. Reiter, 157–210. Monthly Review, 1975.

Sayers, Daniel O. 2014. *A Desolate Place for a Defiant People: The Archeology of Maroons, Indigenous Americans, and Enslaved Laborers in the Great Dismal Swamp.* Gainesville: University Press of Florida.

Scarry, Elaine. 1999. *On Beauty and Being Just.* Princeton, NJ: Princeton University Press.

Schiller, Friedrich. (1795) 1959. *Letters on the Aesthetic Education of Man.* Translated by Reginald Snell. New Haven, CT: Yale University Press. Kindle.

Scott, Darieck. 2010. *Extravagant Abjection: Blackness, Power, and Sexuality in the African American Imagination.* New York and London: New York University Press, 2010. Kindle.

Sedgwick, Eve. 1985. *Between Men: English Literature and Male Homosexual Desire.* New York: Columbia University Press. Kindle.

Slate, Nico. 2012. *Colored Cosmopolitanism: The Shared Struggle for Freedom in the United States and India.* Cambridge, MA: Harvard University Press, 2012. Kindle.

Smith, Shawn Michelle. 2007. "Second Sight: Du Bois and the Black Masculine Gaze." In *Next to the Color Line: Gender, Sexuality, and W.E.B. Du Bois,* edited by Susan Gillman and Alys Weinbaum, 350–77. Minneapolis: University of Minnesota Press.

Snorton, C. Riley. 2017. *Black on Both Sides: A Racial History of Trans Identity.* Minneapolis and London: University of Minnesota Press. Kindle.
Soitos, Stephen F. 1996. *The Blues Detective: A Study of African American Detective Fiction.* Boston: University of Massachusetts Press.
Somerville, Siobhan B. 2000. *Queering the Color Line: Race and the Invention of Homosexuality in American Culture.* Durham, NC: Duke University Press. Kindle.
Sommer, Doris. 1991. *Foundational Fictions: The National Romances of Latin America.* Berkeley: University of California Press. Kindle.
Spillers, Hortense. 1987. "Mama's Baby, Papa's Maybe." *Diacritics* 17, no. 2 (Summer): 64–81.
Spivak, Gayatri C. 2018. "Du Bois in the World: Pan Africanism and Decolonization." *Boundary 2.0*, Boundary Editorial Collective, online edition.
Steiner, Wendy. 2001. *Venus in Exile: The Rejection of Beauty in Twentieth-Century Art.* Chicago: University of Chicago Press.
Stockton, Kathryn Bond. 2006. *Beautiful Bottom, Beautiful Shame: Where Black Meets Queer.* Durham, NC: Duke University Press. Kindle.
Stokes, Mason. 2001. *The Color of Sex: Whiteness, Heterosexuality, and the Fictions of White Supremacy.* Durham, NC: Duke University Press. Kindle.
———. 2007. "Father of the Bride: Du Bois and the Making of Black Heterosexuality." In *Next to the Color Line: Gender, Sexuality, and W.E.B. Du Bois*, edited by Susan Gillman and Alys Eve Weinbaum, 289–316. Minneapolis: University of Minnesota Press.
Subedi, Madhusudan. 2013. "Some Theoretical Considerations on Caste." *Dhaulagiri Journal of Sociology and Anthropology* 7, no. 7 (January): 51–86.
Sundquist, Eric J. 1993. *To Wake the Nations: Race in the Making of American Literature.* Cambridge, MA: Harvard University Press.
Tate, Claudia. 1995. Introduction to *Dark Princess* by W. E. B. Du Bois. Jackson: University Press of Mississippi.
———. 1992. *Domestic Allegories of Political Desire.* Oxford: Oxford University Press.
Taylor, Charles. 1994. "The Politics of Recognition." In *Multiculturalism: The Politics of Recognition*, edited by Amy Gutmann, 25–73. Princeton, NJ: Princeton University Press.
Taylor, Paul C. 2010. "Race, Rehabilitated—Redux." *Critical Sociology* 36, no. 1 (February): 175–90.
Thapar, Romila. 1996. "The Theory of Aryan Race and India: History and Politics." *Social Scientist* 24, nos. 1–3 (January-March): 3–29.
Triplette, Stacey. 2010. "Chivalry and Empire: The Colonial Argument of the Princess Micomicona Episode in *Don Quijote* Part I." *Cervantes: Bulletin of the Cervantes Society of America* 30, no. 1 (Spring): 163–86.
Wald, Priscilla. 1995. *Constituting Americans: Cultural Anxiety and Narrative Form.* Durham, NC: Duke University Press.

Waligora-Davis, Nicole. 2006. "W. E. B. Du Bois and the Fourth Dimension." *New Centennial Review* 6, no. 3 (Winter): 57–90.

Watts, Eric King. 2001. "Cultivating a Black Public Voice: W.E.B. Du Bois and 'The Criteria of Negro Art.'" *Rhetoric and Public Affairs* 4, no. 2 (Summer): 181–201.

Weinbaum, Alys E. 2007. "Interracial Romance and Black Internationalism." In *Next to the Color Line: Gender, Sexuality, and W.E.B. Du Bois,* edited by Susan Gillman and Alys Weinbaum, 96–123. Minneapolis: University of Minnesota Press.

Whitman, Walt. (1900) 1998. "To a Stranger." *Leaves of Grass.* Gutenberg Ebook. Accessed October 10, 2021.

Wilkerson, Isabel. 2020. *Caste: The Origins of Our Discontents.* New York: Random House. Kindle.

Woodard, Vincent. 2014. *The Delectable Negro: Human Consumption and Homoeroticism Within US Slave Culture,* edited by Justin A. Joyce and Dwight A. McBride. New York: New York University Press. Kindle.

Yancy, George. 2017. *Black Bodies, White Gazes: The Continuing Significance of Race in America.* Lanham, MD: Rowman and Littlefield.

Yaszek, Lisa. 2006. "Afro Futurism, Science Fiction, and the History of the Future." *Socialism and Democracy* 20, no. 3 (November): 41–60.

Yengde, Suraj. 2019. *Caste Matters.* New Delhi: Penguin Random House India.

———. 2021. "From India to the United States, Societies that Hang on to Caste Lie to Themselves." *Wire,* April 7.

Yousef, Nancy. 2013. *Romantic Intimacy.* Stanford, CA: Stanford University Press. Kindle.

Zamir, Shamoon. 1995. *Dark Voices: W. E. B. Du Bois and American Thought, 1888–1903.* Chicago: University of Chicago Press.

Index

Abdur-Rahman, Aliyyah, 62
abjection, 9, 15, 24, 54, 122, 139n2, 141n13. *See also* Blackness; double consciousness; enslavement
aesthetic education, 35–36, 39, 42, 48–49. *See also* beauty; justice
aesthetic experience, 36–37; as collective, 48–49; and desire, 40–41; and social justice, 37–39, 41–45. *See also* beauty; justice
affect, 6–8, 10, 37, 39–40, 126; as affective labor, 24, 105. *See also* desire; intimacy; romantic nationalism
affiliation, 6, 15, 25, 45, 98, 121. *See also* alliance; intimacy
Africa (in Black thought), 16–21, 24. *See also* W. E. B. Du Bois, and the recovery of Africa in Black thought; Pan-Africanism
Afro-futurism, 134n32
Afro-pessimism, 134n32
agency, 54, 57, 71–72
Alexander, Adele Logan, 85, 138n6
Alexander, Michelle, 5
alienation, 3, 31, 44–46; and double consciousness, 7, 12–14, 16, 18, 31–32; and failure, 3; and race, 6–7, 31–32; resolving rather than redeeming, 22–23. *See also* ancestor; double consciousness; stranger

allegory, 7–8, 21, 75–77, 79–80, 84–88, 122–25, 130n5, 142n18. *See also* fairytale; folktale; romance
alliance: Afro-Asian, 29, 116–19, 142n20; among Black people, 126; between Black and White peoples, 57, 64–65, 67–68, 72–73; failures of, 68, 76. *See also* affiliation; intimacy
Amadis de Gaula, 93
Ambedkar, Bhimrao Ramji, 129n2, 139n6, 140n9, 141n14
ambivalence, 6, 11, 16, 54, 56, 85, 87, 113, 126, 130n7
America. *See* United States
American Negro Slave Revolts (Aptheker), 83
ancestor, 44, 89, 111, 126, 133n19. *See also* stranger
anti-imperialism, 76–77, 86, 98–99, 102–103, 107–10, 116–17, 119, 137n4, 139n2, 140n7. *See also* W. E. B. Du Bois, *Dark Princess*
anticapitalism, 74, 77, 87–88. *See also* capitalism; enslavement
Appiah, K. Anthony, 8, 37, 89
appropriation, 22, 54, 87, 93–94, 99, 121. *See also* assimilation; caste, analogy between Indian system and American racial apartheid; *Don*

153

appropriation *(continued)*
    Quixote; W. E. B. Du Bois, "Criteria of Negro Art"; romance
Aptheker, Herbert, 83–84
Apuleius, 121–22, 142n2. *See also* "Cupid and Psyche"; *The Golden Ass*
Arthashastra (Kautilya), 139n4
Arya Samaj (Hindu reform movement), 98. *See also* Hinduism
Aryans, 97, 138n1
assimilation, 22–23, 41, 53, 90, 121–22, 125–26; conciliatory forms of, 76, 99; drawbacks of, 105; and feminization, 62; queer mode of, 55; refusal and failures of, 91–93. *See also* appropriation; romance
attraction, 6, 130n5. *See also* desire; repulsion
Austen, Jane, 88
autogenesis, 19
aversion, 7, 9, 126

Bakhtin, Mikhail, 135n9
Bandung Conference, 117, 142n20. *See also* alliance, Afro-Asian
Bastian, Misty L., 125
beauty, 31–32, 131n5, 132n13; and community, 39, 41–45; and justice, 37–39, 41–45; Neoplatonism of, 33, 37–38, 42–45, 114. *See also* aesthetic education; justice; music; opera
Beavers, Herman, 99, 116
beggar (type), 29, 76, 80–81, 83–84, 87–95, 143n6. *See also* W. E. B. Du Bois, "The Princess of the Hither Isles"
Belgium, 138n9
belonging, 8–9, 11, 82, 117. *See also* nation and nationalism
Berlant, Lauren, 4, 11, 64. *See also* intimacy

Besant, Annie, 139n4
betrothal, 22, 123
Bhabha, Homi, 98–100, 104, 113–15, 139n4
biopower, 5
Bismarck, Otto von, 111
Blackness: and abjection, 9; and binarism, 16; and criminality, 73; and effeminacy, 56; and forced intimacy with whiteness, 13–15; and gender, 17–18, 71–72; and kinship, 16; and legibility, 20; and the maternal, 17–18; and subjectivity, 18–19; and trans experience, 71–72. *See also* alienation; caste; desire; double consciousness; enslavement; fugitivity; subjectivity; whiteness and white supremacy
blood, 24–25, 130n11. *See also* purity
bottom position, 25–26, 130n12. *See also* queerness; submission
Brilmyer, S. Pearl, 23, 115–16, 142n19
Brotherhood of Sleeping Car Porters, 59
Brown, John, 73
Bruce, Dickson, 13–14
Bruce, J. E., 58
Bud Weisob (pseudonym). *See* W. E. B. Du Bois
Buddhism, 140n9
Butler, Judith, 14, 18

Campbell, T. E., 84
capitalism, 15, 23, 30, 53, 56, 73–74, 77, 80, 83–84, 87, 98–99, 105–107, 116, 121. *See also* anticapitalism; imperialism; race and racialization; whiteness and white supremacy
Carby, Hazel, 3, 12, 130n13, 140n11
caritas, 33, 37–38, 43, 48, 122. *See also* love

Index

caste: and alienation, 44; analogy between Indian system and American racial apartheid, 98–99, 100, 110–11, 129n2, 141n14–15; and anti-Black racism in the United States, 5–6, 101–103; boundaries of, 33–34; and citizenship, 6; and class, 5–6, 70, 108–10, 113; and colonialism, 80–81; crossing, 20; defining, 5, 139n5; and difference, 6; and discrimination among groups of subaltern people, 102–104, 140n7; in Europe, 101; and hierarchy, 104–105, 112–13, 138n7; immutability of, 109–10; and mobility, 113–14; and rhetoric of purity, 26, 106. *See also* cross-caste romance; Hinduism; intimacy; nation and nationalism; race and racialization

Cervantes, Miguel de, 93

Chandler, Nahum, 19, 130n11

Chesnutt, Charles, 58

chiasmus, 113–14. *See also* caste, and mobility

child (figure), 4–5, 98, 116–18, 122–23

China, 137n4

Christianity, 106, 112, 114, 116, 131n3

Citizen: An American Lyric (Rankine), 1–2

citizenship, 6, 10, 15, 20–21. *See also under* caste; white supremacy

class, 5–6. *See also* caste

closure, 65–68

collectivity, 21–23, 41–46, 49

colonialism, 75–76, 82–83, 90–91, 93. *See also* anti-imperialism; decolonialism; imperialism

communism, 73. *See also* anticapitalism

community, 39–40, 44–48

compulsion, 12–16, 37. *See also under* heteronormativity; whiteness and white supremacy

conciliation, 92–93

concubinage, 24

Congo, 138n9

conquest, 76

contamination, 106. *See also* caste, and rhetoric of purity; purity

cosmopolitanism, 33–34, 103. *See also* internationalism; transnationalism

coupledom, 115–16, 130n5, 142n19. *See also* queerness

Craft, Ellen, and William, 71–72

criminality, 73–74. *See also* Blackness, and criminality; fugitivity

Crisis, The (journal), 58–59, 81–82, 85

cross-caste romance: and autoerotic resistance, 90–91; as cross-cultural, 105–106, 121–22, 134n30; and decolonialism, 99; and double consciousness, 7; failures and limits of, 27, 53, 76; and global solidarity among people of color, 98, 118–19; in Irish novel, 9; as homoerotic and homosocial exchange, 55–56, 58, 60; as literary tradition, 7; and nationalism, 10, 99, 130n4; and queer intimacy, 21; racial and sexual difference and, 7; as revolutionary, 114–15; violence and expropriation, 93

cross-cultural exchange, 24–25, 35–37

cross-cultural romance. *See under* cross-caste romance

cross-dressing (trope), 69–73. *See also* queerness

crossing (trope), 26. *See also* cross-caste romance; *and under* caste

cultural reclamation, 12

"Cupid and Psyche" (myth), 107, 121–24, 140n8, 142n2

Davis, Jefferson, 111–12
death, 41, 50–51, 90, 95, 143n6; and women, 68. *See also* suicide
decolonialism, 98–100, 103–104. *See also* anti-imperialism; colonialism; imperialism
Delaney, Martin, 83
democracy, 17, 33, 42, 111–12, 114; and pluralism, 45, 49, 131n6. *See also* oligarchy; pluralism
denationalism, 26
desire, 6–7; and aesthetic pleasure, 40–41; aversive, 9; and Blackness, 14–15, 57, 61–64, 69; frustration of, 68; and gaze, 60–61; and gender, 14; and vulnerability, 68. *See also* affect; intimacy; *and under* aesthetic experience; gender
detective fiction, 55–58, 60–74, 135n4–5, 136n18, 137n19; and criminalization of Black men, 68; and folktale, 59–60; narration and plot, 65–66, 136n11; and Pullman porters, 58–59. *See also* W. E. B. Du Bois, "The Case" and "The Shaven Lady"; "The Man of the Crowd" (Poe)
dialectical oscillation, 112–14
diaspora, 86, 88, 90, 100; and queer collectivity, 117–18; and shared political histories of Africa and Asia, 97. *See also* alliance
difference, 6, 45. *See also* pluralism; *and under* caste
Dill, Augustus, 136n13
Dinkins, Pauline E., 121–23
Diotima. *See Symposium* (Plato)
Diouf, Sylviane A., 83
disidentification, 23. *See also* José Muñoz
dispossession, 78–80, 90, 126–27. *See also* expropriation

Don Quixote (Cervantes), 93–94
double consciousness, 2, 6–8, 11, 16, 19, 53, 79–80; as ante-knowledge, 89; and critique of white, heteropatriarchal practice, 58, 67; and cross-cultural romance, 54–55; as international and global, 115; mitigating, 20; psychoanalytic approaches to, 13–14; queerness of, 130n10; resolving rather than redeeming, 22. *See also* alienation; Blackness; subjectivity
doubleness, 74
dowry, 22
Du Bois, W. E. B., works by: *Autobiography of W. E. B. Du Bois* (1968), 4–5, 11–12, 129n1; "Bismarck" (1888), 142n16; "Careers Open to College-Bred Negroes" (1898), 105; "The Case" (1907), 8, 54–69, 135n2, 136n10; "The Conservation of Races" (1898), 25, 81–82; "The Countess's Sables," 73; "The Criteria of Negro Art" (1926), 43, 48, 138n7; *Dark Princess: A Romance* (1928), 8, 98–119, 133n24, 138n7, 139n4, 141nn13–15, 142n18, 142n20; *Darkwater: Voices from Within the Veil* (1920), 8, 66, 75, 80, 92, 137n1, 138n7; *The Gift of Black Folk* (1896), 87; "The Hands of Ethiopia" (1920), 77–80, 93, 137n1; "India" (1935), 97; "Jefferson Davis" (1896), 87, 142n16; "Murder on Ninth Avenue" (1920), 58, 135n5; "Of Our Spiritual Strivings" (1903), 36, 55, 136n16; "Of the Coming of John" (1903), 8, 31, 33–51, 76, 90, 114, 123, 131nn3–4, 132n15, 133n21, 133n25, 134nn27–28, 134nn30–32, 140n8; "Opera and

the Negro Problem" (1936), 31; *The Philadelphia Negro* (1899), 74; "The Princess of the Hither Isles" (1920), 8, 75–95, 125, 137n1, 137n3, 138n7, 143n6; *Quest of the Silver Fleece* (1911), 133n24, 138n7; "The Shaven Lady" (1907), 8, 54–56, 68–74; "The Sorrow Songs" (1903), 24; *The Souls of Black Folk* (1903), 1–8, 16–17, 21–24, 31, 36, 53–54, 56–57, 62, 66, 70–71, 76, 80, 86, 92, 99, 101, 106, 115, 132n17, 138n7; "The Souls of White Folk" (1920), 66–67, 80, 92; "The Tale of the Visiting Card" (1903), 1–7, 19, 22, 57–58, 62–63, 86, 92, 106, 129n1

Du Bois, W. E. B.: Afrocentrism and recovery of Africa in Black thought, 15–20, 89, 130n6, 132n18; alleged misconduct with young women, 27, 129n1; anti-imperialism and transnational politics of, 33–34, 77–79, 86, 91–92, 97–100, 137n4, 138n8, 141n14; and autogenesis, 19; on Blackness, 12–13, 15, 89, 118, 140n11; childhood and youth, 2–5, 53, 129n1; on class and support for workers, 59, 73, 135n6; and detective fiction, 136n18; and eroticism, 130n13; on India and Hinduism, 97, 103, 107, 139n6, 140nn8–9; and melancholy, 16, 18; on nationalism and the US, 8, 10–12; neglected writing of, 54–55, 75–75; and Neoplatonism, 43–45, 47–48, 132nn12–13; and Pauline Dinkins, 123; photography, 82; privileging of the masculine and patriarchalism of, 17, 18, 111–13, 116; queerness of and relationship to sexual and gender minorities, 10–11, 18–19, 26–27, 71–72, 130n13, 136n13; and respectability politics, 74; romanticism and historical revision, 8–9, 84–85, 89, 140n10; and Wagner, 131nn3–4; on whiteness, 12–13, 92

duCille, Ann, 130n5
Dunbar, Paul Laurence, 73

Eagleton, Terry, 132n11
Edelman, Lee, 116
Edgeworth, Maria, 9
Edwards, Brent, 8, 99
effeminacy, 56, 110. *See also* gender; submission
Egypt, 137nn3–4
Eight Men (Wright), 137n20
Elam, Michele, 99–100, 130n13
elitism, 111–14, 132n12. *See also* caste, and hierarchy; oligarchy; talent
Ellis, Havelock, 71
endogamy, 124–26. *See also* exogamy
enslavement: and dispossession, 126–27; and mother's status, 17–18, 135n3; and normativity, 24; pain and suffering of, 90; and sexual abuse, 62; and sexuality, 134n1; and spiritual tradition, 102. *See also* alienation; Blackness; caste; fugitivity; race and racialization
epistemology: and authority, 61; limits of, 65–66, 88–89; and mobility, 113–14; queer forms of, 117–18. *See also* queerness
erklären. *See* explanation
erotics and eroticism: cross-caste exchange and intersubjective relations, 7, 24–25, 48, 133n26; and politics, 7–8; and racism, 7. *See also* desire; homoeroticism; intimacy; romance and romanticism
erotomania, 100

Eschenbach, Wolfram von, 131n1
Esther (Bible), 41, 132n14
Ethiopia, 92, 93
eugenics, 71
Eurocentrism (Europhilia), 11, 13, 15
Europhilia. *See* Eurocentrism
exile, 98, 100–102, 139n4
exogamy, 124–26. *See also* endogamy
explanation (*erklären*), 37
expropriation, 78–80, 83, 88, 93. *See also* dispossession; imperialism

failure, 94. *See also* queerness
fairytale, 75–76, 79, 84–85
femme fatale, 57, 62–64, 67–68, 135n4. *See also* detective fiction
Ferguson, Rod, 23
Fisk Jubilee singers, 134n27
folktale (genre), 34–35, 84, 107, 121, 132n9, 143n6. *See also* allegory
fragmentation, 10, 13–4. *See also* double consciousness
frame: as frame tale, 34–35, 50–51, 57, 132n8; as frame story, 59–60. *See also* W. E. B. Du Bois, "The Case" and "Of the Coming of John"
French Revolution, 49–50, 134n28
Freudianism, 2–3
fugitivity, 12, 55–56, 73–74, 83, 94–95, 121, 138n11

Gandhi, Mahatma, 103, 108, 139n4, 139n6, 141nn13–14
Gates, Henry Louis, Jr., 74
gaze, 60–63, 68
gender, 14, 71; and Blackness, 16–19, 24, 61–62; fungibility of, 70–72; and homosexual desire, 14. *See also* crossdressing; heteronormativity; misogyny; queerness; race and racialization

geopolitics, 82–83
ghost (figure), 50–51
Golden Ass, The (Apuleius), 121–22
Gooding-Williams, Robert, 8, 131n4, 132n12, 132n16, 133n22
Gopinath, Gayatri, 117–18
Gotama. *See under* Hinduism
Goyal, Yogita, 5, 97, 100, 103, 117, 129n2, 139n6, 140n10
Great Dismal Swamp, 83
Griffin, Farah, 44

Haitian Revolution, 134n28
Halberstam, Jack, 117–18
Harlem Renaissance, 8, 99–100
Hartman, Saidiya, 126
Henry, Paget, 20
heteronormativity, 10, 23–24, 26; as compulsory, 14–16; and heterophily, 14; and heterosexuality, 118, 130n7, 136n15; and reproduction, 19, 21; and transracial partnerships, 118; and whiteness, 130n7, 136n15. *See also* gender; queerness
heterosexuality. *See under* heteronormativity
Hinduism, 106–15; Dalit caste, 103, 110–11, 129n2, 141nn14–15; Gotama, 108; Kali, 108; karma, 112–13, 142n17; Radha-Krishna folktale, 107; reform movements, 98; samsara, 108–10, 114, 141n12; Shudra (servant) caste, 109–10, 141n14. *See also* W. E. B. Du Bois, *Dark Princess*
Holland, Sharon P., 7, 134n1
homocentrism, 63–64
homoeroticism, 55–57, 60–64, 67, 69, 71–73. *See also* erotics and eroticism; intimacy; queerness
homophobia, 63–64, 71–72. *See also* heteronormativity

homosociality, 23, 55, 61–63, 67, 71, 73. *See also* heteronormativity; homoeroticism
Hooker, Juliet, 138n7
Hopkins, Pauline, 58
Horizon (magazine), 8, 54, 58, 68, 76, 115–16, 136n10, 136n18

identity, 20–21
imperialism, 78–80, 83, 88, 93. *See also* anti-imperialism; colonialism; dispossession; expropriation
Indian Home Rule, 98
internationalism, 99–100, 115. *See also* caste, analogy between Indian system and American racial apartheid; transnationalism
intimacy: and caste, 26, 105; disappointment and foreclosure of, 26, 92–94, 126; and entanglement, 20; intercultural, 3; and knowledge, 88–89; minor form of, 4; queer nodes of, 54–55; as reinforcing logics of racialism and racism, 94; and reciprocity, 20–21; self-enclosure and refusal of, 20, 57–58; sociopolitical implications of, 6–7, 100; as violent and abject, 122, 142n2. *See also* caste; cross-caste romance; desire; romance and romanticism
inversion, 71–72
Ireland, 9

Jacobs, Harriet, 83
Japan, 140n7
Jim Crow, 24, 39–40, 45–46, 49, 62, 103, 110
Joo, Hee-Jung Serenity, 90–91, 137n1
joy, 122–23, 133n25
judgment, 62–63, 66
Judy, R. A., 99, 131n4, 132n8, 133n22

justice, 37–39, 41–45, 94. *See also* aesthetic experience; beauty
juxtaposition, 114

Kali. *See under* Hinduism
Kama, Bhikaji, 139n4
Kant, Immanuel, 34, 37–39
Kaplan, Amy, 138n8
karma. *See under* Hinduism
Kautilya, 139n4
King, Martin Luther, Jr., 141n14
kinship, 46–47, 88–89, 99, 125; Black, 16; global, 98–99; and melancholy, 18; wounded, 19, 127, 143n7. *See also* intimacy; queerness
Krafft-Ebing, Richard von, 71
Krishna. *See under* Hinduism
Kristeva, Julia, 114, 133n23. *See also* theocentric

labor, 24–25
Lady Liberty, 19
Lahiri, Madhumita, 98, 100, 103, 108, 139n4, 140n8, 141n13
Lemke, Sieglinde, 123, 133n25
Leopold II, King (Belgium), 138n9
Letters on the Aesthetic Education of Man (Schiller), 39
Levinas, Emmanuel, 44, 132n18
Lewis, David Levering, 27
liberalism, 1–2, 139n2
Lindsay, Jack, 122
Logan, Adella Hunt, 85
Lohengrin (Wagner), 31–34, 36–43, 47–48, 50, 123–24, 131n1, 131nn3–4, 132n9, 132nn15–16, 133nn24–25, 134n30, 140n8. *See also* aesthetic experience; W. E. B. Du Bois, "Of the Coming of John"; music; opera
Longfellow, Henry Wadsworth, 83

Lose Your Mother: A Journey Along the Atlantic Slave Route (Hartman), 126
love: and community, 46–47; and inclusion, 44–45; as Neoplatonic ideal, 33, 42–45; impossibility of, 32–34. See also *caritas*; romance
loyalty, 11, 13–15, 47. See also joy; solidarity

Mackey, Nathaniel, 19, 127, 143n7
"Man of the Crowd, The" (Poe), 66–67, 136n18
"Man Who Lived Underground, The" (Wright), 137n20
Marbach, Dora, 129n1
marginalization, 11, 25–26
maroon communities, 82–84
marriage, 46–47
masculinity, 12, 16–17, 141n13; and authority, 60–61, 67; and Blackness, 26, 55, 58, 62–64, 67; as heteropatriarchal, 60; and perversion, 62; queer accounts of and recuperating, 56, 58, 63–64. See also gender; heteronormativity; patriarchalism
masquerade. See minstrelsy
melancholy, 14–19
#MeToo, 27
microaggressions, 1–2
Middle Passage, 16–17, 88, 90–91, 125–27. See also diaspora; enslavement; sea
Miller, Monica, 132nn12–13
Milner, Murray, Jr., 109, 112, 114, 141n12, 142n17
minor and minorness, 4, 11, 57, 64–65
minstrelsy, 72–73
miscegenation, 5, 11, 25, 54, 68, 100, 122, 138n7. See also caste; cross-caste romance; race and racialization

misogyny, 26, 72–73. See also gender; minstrelsy
mobility, 107–15, 121
Moore, Lisa L., 7, 9–10, 93, 138n10
Morrison, Toni, 8–9
Moten, Fred, 12, 16, 18–19, 55, 73–74, 94, 127, 138n11, 143n7. See also fugitivity
motherland, 19
Mullen, Bill, 97, 99–100
Müller, Max, 138n1
Muñoz, José, 23, 94, 118
music, 36–41, 43, 89–90, 102; as collective experience, 48–49. See also W. E. B. Du Bois, "Of the Coming of John"; opera
mutuality, 22–23, 126
mystery. See detective fiction

nation and nationalism, 20–22; and conciliation and failures of conciliation, 10, 22, 25–26, 76, 78, 114–15; and exclusion, 7–8; in India, 98, 103, 117, 129n2, 139n4, 139n6; and queerness, 15–16, 23, 53–55; and race, 55, 98, 115; and romance, 7–10, 130n4. See also anti-imperialism; caste; citizenship; cross-caste romance; exile; romance and romanticism; romantic nationalism
Native Land Act of 1913 (South Africa), 78, 137n2
Native Son (Wright), 137n20
negativity, 12–13, 46, 93–95
Nehamas, Alexander, 43
neo-Kantianism, 37–39, 43
neo-romanticism, 8, 89
Neoplatonism, 33, 37–38, 41, 43–45, 132n12
Nero, Charles, 132n10
New Negro, 8, 31, 106–107, 111
New Woman, 105–106

Nietzsche, Friedrich, 100. *See also* perfectionism
noir (genre), 135n4. *See also* detective fiction; femme fatale
normativity, 24. *See also* heteronormativity
Nussbaum, Martha, 45, 131n6

oligarchy, 111–13. *See also* democracy; talent
Oliver, Lawrence J., 138n9
opera, 36–42, 90, 131n4, 134n27; and everyday struggles of African Americans, 31, 39–40. *See also* aesthetic experience; W. E. B. Du Bois, "Of the Coming of John"; *Lohengrin* (Wagner); music
Owenson, Sydney, 9

Pan-Africanism, 16–17, 77–78, 83–84. *See also* Africa; W. E. B. Du Bois, Afrocentrism and recovery of Africa in Black thought
paranationalism, 22–23. *See also* nation and nationalism
Paris Exposition, 82. *See also* W. E. B. Du Bois, photography
Parzival (Eschenbach), 131n1
passing, 9, 29, 76, 79, 84–85, 91, 137n1, 138n7
Pathania, Sunita, 139n2
patriarchalism, 26–29, 40, 47, 60, 62, 63, 79, 116, 133n24. *See also* heteronormativity
pedagogy, 48–49
pederasty, 49
perception, 60, 66. *See also* aesthetic experience; gaze
perfectionism, 100. *See also* Friedrich Nietzsche
perlocutionary violence, 1. *See also* microaggressions

Phaedrus (Plato), 38, 49, 133n26
Piper, Adrian, 109
Pitukovà, Veronika, 135n4
Plato, 33–34, 37–39, 41–45, 48–49, 132nn12–13, 132n18, 133n26
Playing in the Dark (Morrison), 8–9
pluralism, 7, 9, 11, 21, 45, 49, 99, 131n6, 142n18. *See also* democracy
Poe, Edgar Allen, 66, 136n18, 137n19
pollution (trope), 25, 102, 109, 139n5. *See also* caste, and rhetoric of purity; contamination; purity
Poona Pact, 139n6
populism, 111–14. *See also* caste, and hierarchy; democracy
porter. *See* Pullman porter
power, 6, 26, 70–71
Powers, Christopher, 123, 131n4
projection, 1–2, 45, 53, 55, 62, 103, 134n32
"Princess Wata" (tale), 121–25
Propp, Vladimir, 132n9, 143n4
psychoanalysis, 13–14
Pullman porter, 58–74, 105, 135nn5–6. *See also under* detective fiction
purity (trope), 106, 117, 130n11, 138n7. *See also* contamination; pollution; *and under* caste

queerness, 15, 26–27; and agency, 54; as deontological in quality, 23; and double consciousness, 130n10; and enslavement, 134n1; and the figure of the child, 116–17; and kinship, 99, 111, 115–19; and intimacy, 21, 53–55, 58; and melancholy, 14, 18; queer of color critique, 23, 134n1; relation to hegemonic formulations, 16–17, 19, 23; and revolution, 99; and submission, 25–26, 56; and time, 117–18; and transracial partnerships, 118. *See also*

queerness *(continued)*
  assimilation; compulsion; cross-caste romance; desire; erotics and eroticism; heteronormativity; intimacy; subjectivity

race and racialization, 7: and caste, 3–6, 17–18, 24–25; and eroticism, 7; and legibility, 81–82; and location, 81, 97–98, 100; and passing, 85; and racism among liberal whites, 1–2; as unifying ideal, 21. *See also* abjection; alienation; Blackness; caste; double consciousness; enslavement; miscegenation; purity; subjectivity; whiteness and white supremacy
racial caste system. *See* race and racialization, and caste
Radha. *See under* Hinduism
Rai, Lala Lajpat, 98, 139n2
railroad. *See* trains and railroad
Randolph, Asa Philip, 59, 135n6
Rankine, Claudia, 1–2
reciprocity, 23–24, 126. *See also* mutuality
recognition, 50–51
reconciliation, 11
red herring (trope), 70
reincarnation. *See* Hinduism, samsara
remediation, 24
repossession, 12
reproductive messianism, 98
repulsion, 6, 130n5. *See also* attraction
respectability politics, 74
revolution, 99
romance and romanticism: in the United States, 9; ambivalence of, 126; and assimilation, 21–22; and Blackness, 8–9, 12; and caste, 6, 87–88; frustration and failure of, 4–5, 91; as global and collective, 21; and heteronormativity, 10–11, 53; history of, 8, 93–94; interracial, 3, 56, 75–76; as queer, 53–54; as social relation, 3–4, 6–7; and transfiguration, 35. *See also* allegory; cross-caste romance; detective fiction; intimacy; nation and nationalism; queerness; romantic nationalism
romantic nationalism, 7–12, 21–22, 53–54, 56, 93, 138n10. *See also* allegory; cross-caste romance; nation and nationalism; romance and romanticism
Rousseau, Jacques, 88
Roy, Arundhati, 5, 109, 113, 129n2, 139n6
Rubin, Gayle, 63
Rusert, Britt, 135n2

sacrifice, 106
samsara. *See under* Hinduism
Scarry, Elaine, 37–38, 131n5
Schiller, Friedrich, 34, 39, 48–49. *See also* aesthetic education
Scott, Darieck, 118, 134n1
sea (figure), 39–40, 125. *See also* Middle Passage; waters
Sedgwick, Eve Kosofsky, 6, 62
segregation, 34–35
self-regard, 12
sexology, 71
sexual violence, 86–87, 91–92, 108, 142n2
Shango (West African deity), 108
Slate, Nico, 141n14
"Slave in the Dismal Swamp, The" (Longfellow), 83
Smith, Shawn Michelle, 82
Snorton, C. Riley, 71
social death. *See* death
social exclusion, 3
social justice. *See* justice

socialism, 73
Soitos, Stephen, 59, 65, 136n11, 137n20
solidarity, 25, 98–100
Somerville, Siobhan, 71, 118, 134n1
Sommer, Doris, 7–8, 93, 138n10
soul-beauty, 89. *See also* W. E. B. Du Bois
South Africa, 78, 137n2, 139n6
sovereignty, 82–83. *See also* imperialism
Spillers, Hortense, 17–18, 56, 135n3, 141n13
spirit, 24. *See also* spirituals
spirituals, 24, 89, 102
Spivak, Gayatri, 119
Steiner, Wendy, 122
Stockton, Kathryn Bond, 25–26, 71
Stokes, Mason, 15–16, 71, 136n13
Stowe, Harriet Beecher, 83
stranger (figure), 44, 47, 65, 88–89, 123, 125–27, 133n19. *See also* ancestors
Subedi, Madhusudan, 103
subjectivity: and agency, 54; and alienation, 31; and cross-caste romance, 3–4; and fugitivity, 55; and power, 70–71; as precolonial and modern, 100; queer location of, 24. *See also* alienation; Blackness; double consciousness; fugitivity; queerness
submission, 25–26, 47, 56. *See also* bottom position
suicide, 90, 92, 95. *See also* death
Sundquist, Eric, 131n4
sympathy, 88–89
Symposium (Plato), 38, 41, 44, 49, 132n15, 133n26

taboo, 7, 11, 61, 64, 100
Tagore, Rabindranath, 129n2, 139n6
tale (genre), 8–10, 21–22, 32. *See also* allegory; folktale; fairytale

talent, 112
Tate, Claudia, 8, 92, 99, 130n5, 130n13, 142n18
Taylor, Paul C., 99–100, 130n13
Thapar, Romila, 138n1
theocentric, 114
trains and railroad, 58–60, 64–65. *See also* Pullman porter
transnationalism, 7, 26, 35, 78–79, 93, 98–100, 115, 116–18, 124. *See also* nation and nationalism
transness, 71–72
transvestism, 72–73. *See also* minstrelsy
Trentin, Filippo, 23, 115–16, 142n19
Triplette, Stacey, 93
Tuskegee, 85
two race theory, 97

understanding (*verstehen*), 37, 89
United States: and nationalism, 22; racial caste system of, 2, 4–5, 11; violence of traditions of thought and practice, 8–9. *See also* caste; enslavement; nation and nationalism; whiteness and white supremacy
uplift, 105, 107, 110
utopianism, 117, 118–19, 121

veil (trope), 1–2, 6, 12, 20, 65, 69–71, 79–80, 86, 101, 106–107, 136n16, 137n3
verstehen. *See* understanding
violence, 68
visiting cards, 129n3. *See also* W. E. B. Du Bois, "The Tale of the Visiting Card"
Vlastos, Gregory, 43
voluntarism, 25

Wagner, Richard, 31, 90, 131n3
Wald, Priscilla, 40
Waligora-Davis, Nicole, 118

Washington, Booker T., 46, 85, 141n14
waters (motif), 39–40. *See also* Middle Passage; sea
Watts, Eric King, 43, 132nn12–13
Weinbaum, Alys, 8, 88, 99, 137n1, 138n8, 140n11
Wesley, Charles H., 85
whiteness and white supremacy, 25, 81; and citizenship, 15; as compulsory, 15–16; and destruction, 68; and heteronormativity and heterosexuality, 15–16, 130n7, 136n15; and minstrelsy, 72–73; negation of, 67; overvaluation of, 11–12; and ownership, 92; patriarchal economy of, 40; and power, 72–73; and purity, 138n7; and racial hierarchy, 82; and remediation, 22–24; and threat of death, 50; in US, 11. *See also* Blackness; caste; heteronormativity; nation and nationalism; race and racialization
Whitman, Walt, 88–89
Wilkerson, Isabel, 5, 141n14
Wolfenstein, Eugene, 2–3
Wordsworth, William, 88
Wright, Richard, 70, 137n20

Xiang, Zairong, 23, 115–16, 142n19

Yancy, George, 3
Yengde, Suraj, 5, 26
Yousef, Nancy, 20–21, 88, 126